UNDER THE RADAR 537-555

- TRUMPENCE -

by Boyd Anderson

Copyright © 2017 Boyd Anderson

All rights reserved.

ISBN-13: 978-1973923473
ISBN-10: 1973923475

Copyright © 2017 by Boyd Anderson
All rights reserved.

All rights reserved. No part of this book may be reproduced in any form or by any means – electronic, mechanical, photocopying, scanning or otherwise – without permission in writing from the publisher, except by a reviewer who may quote brief passages in a review. For information on licensing or special sales, please contact the author directly at: trumpence.book@gmail.com

ISBN-13: 978-1973923473   ISBN-10: 1973923475

No part of this publication may be reproduced, stored in a retrieval system, or transmitted in any form or by any means, electronic, mechanical, photocopying, recording, scanning or otherwise, except as permitted under Section 107 or 108 of the 1976 United States Copyright Act, without the prior written permission of the Publisher.

Limit of Liability/Disclaimer of Warranty: While the publisher and author have used their best efforts in preparing this book, they make no representations or warranties with respect to the accuracy or completeness of the contents of this book and specifically disclaim any implied warranties of merchantability or fitness for a particular purpose. No warranty may be created or extended by sales representatives or written sales materials. The advice and strategies contained herein may not be suitable for your situation. You should consult with a professional where appropriate. Neither the publisher nor author shall be liable for any loss of profit or any other commercial damages, including, but not limited to, special, incidental, consequential, or other damages.

Before commencing any of the tactics and strategies contained herein , check with the appropriate authorities to ensure compliance with all laws and regulations in your region.

Printed in the United States of America

R 01.16.18.4

CONTENTS

	Acknowledgments	iv
	Definition	vi
1	"You did it!"	Pg 1
2	'5307' -- A Death-Defying Effort, a Life-Defining Number	Pg 25
3	From Hockey Star to Bio-Feedback Czar	Pg 39
4	"Thomas will chew you up and spit you out"	Pg 93
5	Flicking on the prison lights	Pg 111
6	Will the REAL Thomas Lilly please stand up?	Pg 129
7	Project Prophecy by the numbers: *The murderous timeline fulfilled*	Pg 145
8	"Now that we have the gold, we need to sell it"	Pg 177
9	The Dominoes are Falling	Pg 189
10	The Tale of the Numbers: 5, 555 & 17	Pg 235

CONTENTS
(continued)

11	What do the Vikings, the Roman Empire, the CIA, and CERN have in common? *(Hint: it's not a joke)*	Pg 253
12	Russian deals, Middle East atrocities, and Bitcoin today	Pg 275
13	The first Jesuit pope & the Dead Pools	Pg 347
14	Fake News & Feast of Trumpets (Trumpence)	Pg 409
15	Release the Kraken, Donald of Dubai, the Aga Khan, Canada, Sharia Law & The Thomas Fire	Pg 449
	About the Author	Pg 497

ACKNOWLEDGMENTS

My dear mother, who has been my supporter and shown unconditional LOVE

Tom Lysiak, who was my good friend and line mate when I scored the '5' goals in 3:07

Definition

TRUMPENCE *(noun)* --

The return on investment of a con, bribe, theft or fraud. This could include the direct financial benefit of a scam or plot, but also can be used to represent the emotional boost a narcissist or sociopath gets from feeling superior to those they have manipulated and tricked.

"You should always make sure the target of your scam isn't overly intelligent, then you can play on their fears to maximize your potential trumpence."

CHAPTER #1 - "You did it"

During the 1972-73 season in Medicine Hat, Alberta, I was 18 years old and playing with the Medicine Hat Tigers. I had completed the best hockey season of my life, setting 3 records in the WHL (major junior league in western Canada), including:

- Most goals in a 20 minute period -- 5 Goals
- Fastest 4 Goals -- 2:35 *(2 minutes & 35 seconds)*
- Fastest 5 Goals -- 3:07 *(3 minutes & 7 seconds)*

Yes, I scored 5 goals in 3:07 minutes... averaging out to 1 goal 37.4 seconds apart. In my mind, 5307 became my favorite number from that day forward!

During that record-setting game, I played alongside Tom Lysiak and Lanny McDonald, who were both a year older than me. Lanny was in the penalty box for 4 of the 5 goals that night.

The 5th goal was the best. I'll never forget it. Lysiak passed the puck to me as I was coming into the slot area. Just then a huge opposing Flin Flon defenseman cross-checked me from behind, hitting me so hard that my neck snapped back and I began falling to my knees. At the same time, as I was beginning to fall forward, I cradled the puck on my stick blade. My feet left the ice and in mid-air, with all my weight on the stick, I was able to snap a wrist shot into the top right corner of the net.

I ended up falling to my knees, sliding with my arms reaching up in celebration. I was on such a natural high that I saw SPARKLES! From that moment on, "5307" became such an influential number in my life.

This record will never be broken:
5 goals in 3:07 equals 5+3+7= 15, 1+5 = 6
1 goal every 37.4 seconds equals 1+3+7+4= 15, 1+5 = 6

Fast forward

On the morning of March 8th, 2014, I was having breakfast at the Willows golf course in Saskatoon, Saskatchewan, Canada. Ironically, this is the same golf course that led to Thomas Lilly's partner, Richard Leibel, getting deported from Canada 15 years earlier.

Still, I was watching the news on TV when CNN announced "Malaysian Airlines flight MH370 has disappeared." I immediately blurted out, "I know who did this," knowing this was the gold heist I'd heard so much about several years earlier. A few people looked at me in surprise.

I remembered back to July 2008, the day before I left Dubai, Thomas Lilly handed me an envelope with about 15 printed pages. It was the Bilderberg's NWO (New World Order) 7-year plan. It also had information about the Vatican and Homeland Security, but I had no idea! I thought it was just another scam.

The 14-year plan (double SHEMITAH) that Thomas handed me back in 2008 described:

- Bitcoin
- Blockchain technology - they have the code
- Release the Kraken
- Monero
- Ethereum

- ETC Classic
- Brexit - this was planned in 2008
- Bit Gold / Gold Money
- USA Election
- Interest Rate Hikes 2017 and 2018

When I'd asked Thomas "Who wrote this?" he answered simply, "Richard".

Just before I left Dubai, Thomas mentioned that Richard had just found a Malaysian Airlines pilot who agreed to go on a simulator, to train for the passenger plane's in-flight destruction. They offered the pilot $10 million and a villa in Bali.

My mother and I are born on the same day March 15th, so while we were celebrating our birthdays at my girlfriend's restaurant, I mentioned to my mother that I believed Thomas was behind the disappearance of MH370. She knew who I was talking about, since she had spoken to him back in 2007-08, and had lent him $4,000 that he'd never returned.

I had long since erased Thomas' phone number from my phone in 2010, but I did have his email address. I was totally positive that Thomas was behind the plane's disappearance, even though I had not communicated with him for 4 years. I had no

idea what had happened with Bitcoin, Block Chain, Release the Kraken, Monero, Ethereum, ETC Classic, BREXIT, etc.
But I was about to find out.

When I began doing research, I started by Googling "Bitcoin" and discovered that, just a few short weeks earlier in January 2014, one Bitcoin was worth $1,100.00 USD ea.

I also read that, in February 2014, Mt. GOX in Japan - the world's largest Bitcoin exchange - and Silk Road in the USA had been robbed. I remembered reading in the NWO 14-year plan (double SHEMITAH) how Thomas and the Swiss Jews have the code for the blockchain.

Mt. Gox, known for trading guns, nuclear weapons, and military equipment, immediately collapsed into bankruptcy, reeling from the disappearance of $460 million so soon after another $27.4 million went missing from its bank accounts, in two separate heists. That's almost half a billion dollars stolen! Mt.Gox CEO Mark Karpeles was blamed and sent to prison.

At roughly the same time, Silk Road, a major Bitcoin exchange in the USA, known for doing drug cartel trades, was robbed of $850 million. Founder Ross Ulbricht was sentenced to life in prison.

These were just two of the six biggest Bitcoin heists in the short 3-year history of the blockchain technology's use as a currency at the time. Hundreds of millions of dollars worth of the crypto-currency kept getting taken, apparently through anonymous hacks that were supposed to be impossible. Yet they kept happening... and growing.

From the Pony Botnet's theft of $220,000 in missing crypto-currency in February 2014, to Mt. Gox's loss of half a million dollars' worth in 2011 (supposedly by an unknown user account, which managed to hack into Mt. Gox and make off with about 25,000 Bitcoin), the security of blockchain technology was hugely suspect. Then Silk Road 2, which was cleaned out by a hacker who broke in and swiped over $2.7 million dollars in February 2014, lost its entire balance as the sequel to the deep web's most famous black market.

Rounding out the Top 6, another 96,000 Bitcoins (worth about $56.4 million) disappeared from the Sheep Marketplace in December 2013. But one of the most unusual heists in the top 6 was the original Silk Road marketplace, which was shut down by the FBI in October 2013.

In short, that means that the Feds took over the biggest Bitcoin wallet in the world, valued at roughly $127.4 million at the time.[1]

Bitcoin's Turbulent History

Bitcoin was created by Satoshi Nakamoto, who published the invention on 31 October 2008 as a peer-to-peer electronic cash system. One of the first supporters, and the receiver of the first bitcoin transaction, was programmer Hal Finney, who received 10 bitcoins from Nakamoto on the day it was released. Other early supporters were Wei Dai, creator of Bitcoin predecessor B-money, and Nick Szabo, creator of Bitcoin predecessor Bit Gold.

Eventually, between the years 2012-2013, mainstream websites began accepting Bitcoins, including WordPress and OKCupid. More sites began accepting blockchain currency for payments in 2014, including TigerDirect and Overstock.com, Expedia, Newegg, Dell and even Microsoft in December of that year.

In May 2013, the U.S. Department of Homeland Security seized millions of dollars in assets belonging to the Mt. Gox exchange. The same year, the U.S. Federal Bureau of

Investigation (FBI) shut down the Silk Road 'dark web' website in October 2013.

On 19 November 2013, the value of a Bitcoin on the Mt. Gox exchange soared to a peak of US$900 after the FBI told a United States Senate committee hearing that virtual currencies are a legitimate financial service. Bitcoin actually traded for over RMB¥6780 (US$1,100) in China that same day.

The first Bitcoin ATM was installed in Vancouver, British Columbia, Canada during October 2013. Soon after, in early February 2014, Mt. Gox (one of the world's largest Bitcoin exchanges, in Japan) suspended withdrawals, citing technical issues. By the end of the month, Mt. Gox had filed for bankruptcy protection in Japan, amid reports that 744,000 Bitcoins had been stolen.[2]

$500,000 Bali villa was biggest Bitcoin purchase ever

As I continued digging, I was shocked to discover one of the largest Bitcoin purchases ever completed. "This is where they put the pilot of MH370", I thought.

According to the article, a villa in the Delmango Villa Estate, on the Indonesian island of Bali, was sold on March 12th for more than $500,000 worth of Bitcoin, making it the single largest crypto-currency purchase ever.

Although the exact purchase price and identity of the buyer involved remain unknown, BitPremier founder Alan Silbert described the purchaser of the property in Bali as an early Bitcoin adopter from the US. The sale represented "by far the largest" sale to date on the luxury BitPremier marketplace, which handled the transaction.[3]

Around this time, I was trying to create a web-site for my LED lighting business. I wanted to create a web page about my company, Lofty Technologies, and how it was started. I always thought that if I included my hockey records, it may draw some business in Western Canada, and maybe I could retrofit the hockey rinks that still used the metal halide lights.

I thought back to October 7th, 1972, the night I scored 5 goals in 3:07 minutes, while playing for the Medicine Hat Tigers in Canada's top junior league called the W.H.L. "The 5th goal was the "Best". I'll never forget it. 5 Goals in 3:07, 5307 became my favourite number.

I wanted to use the number "5307" so I purchased the following domain names:

led5307
ledlights5307
ledlightsupply5307
ledlighting5307
ledlightenergy5307
ledlightenergyLLC5307
ledlumens5307

In all, I had about 7 different domains, and for my logo I used the Hemihelix - community of Scholars. But then I Googled 5307, and found a foreboding reference for the number.

According to Strong's Concordance at BibleHub.com, their entry #5307 refers to the Greek/Hebrew definition for naphal:

1) To fall, lie, be cast down, and fail
2) **"to fall (of violent death)"**

This is where I began to uncover more devious connections, after searching for added info regarding Bitcoin. As it turned out, within days of the MH370 plane crash, the CEO of a Bitcoin startup in Singapore had fallen to her death under suspicious circumstances.

On February 28, 2014, Autumn Radtke, the 28-year-old CEO of Singapore-based Bitcoin startup First Meta, died from multiple injuries sustained after **falling from** her 16th floor apartment building.

In a flash of inspiration, I googled "autumn" in the Hebrew – Greek dictionary, where it's known as the **"falling of the leaves"**. At the time of her death, Autumn Radtke must have owned 50,000 -100,000 Bitcoins or more and probably brought in many investors, which were all robbed.

By this time, I knew that all the stolen Bitcoins went to either the Feds or DHS, (Department of Homeland Securities). And who became the Global Regulator?

"Release the Kraken"

Kraken, formed in April 2014 (just after MH370 disappeared), is a Bitcoin exchange located in San Francisco, USA and is now the regulator of Bitcoin and other crypto-currencies.

To this day (May 27th, 2017 as I write this), whenever the Crypto Currencies make a huge correction, it is the Kraken being released automatically to either steal or buy up Bitcoins that are on sell orders, by the

Bitcoin Mines answering difficult equations. This is a self perpetuating
" beast " that will destroy people and the financial systems of countries, as foretold in the NWO 14-year plan (double SHEMITAH) I'd read as "Release the Kraken".

Not only can they steal your Bitcoins, they are also the regulators!

Up until MH 370 went missing, I had no idea this was going on. During the previous 4 years, I had totally lost contact with Thomas. Now I really wanted to find out what was happening, and who was actually involved with the heist.

So, even though I had not communicated with Thomas Lilly since June 2010, I dug up his email address and sent him a short message...

"You did it."

I never got a reply. So I googled "Thomas Lilly Bitcoin Dubai" and sure enough, he had a Forex website online. There was no phone number, but there was a contact form to leave typed comments.

So I typed in this message:

"Have Thomas Lilly Kazansky call Boyd Anderson immediately" and added my phone number. (I later figured out who passed the message along to Thomas, it was Nigel Farage).

Within 5 minutes the phone rang. It was Thomas Lilly, calling me for the first time in over four years. Without hesitating, I said, "I've been reading about Bitcoin and MH370. You've been a busy guy!"

Then I shut up.

After about 5 seconds of silence, Thomas said very calmly, "Yes, we got $200 million for MH370." Then he added, "Boyd, you are smart... very smart.' I think he was telling me that I did the right thing by not getting involved in 2010.

Thomas continued, "I told you, I work for the Swiss Jews, Boyd." Then he said, "Boyd, I don't mind giving you, say, $500,000.00 for helping me back in 2007-08." Without skipping a beat, he joked "Remember the doctor, ha, ha, ha! That was quite a time. I used to see Lutchy once in a while walking down the street, and always would joke with her about you."

"Do you still have your big gut?"

Thomas finished with another one of his wry observations, "So they wanna put a nigger in the Whitehouse, hmm?"

Over the following weeks, we started a series of conversations by phone and email. Below, 3 of the many emails from Thomas:

> #1.
> From: Thomas Liley <usherliley@yahoo.com>
> Date: June 25, 2014 at 10:00:31 PM CST
> To: Boyd Anderson
> <boydanderson.email@gmail.com>
> Subject: Re: $300.00
> Reply-To: Thomas Liley
> <usherliley@yahoo.com>
>
> BOYD I AM NOT TAKING ADVANTAGE OF YOU RICHARD AND I ARE GOING TO MAKE A LOT OF MONEY AND SO WILL YOU I WILL KEEP MY WORD WE ARE THE ONLY ONES WHO ARE ALLOWED TO SELL THIS GOLD IT BELONGS TO THE KING OF THAILAND VENTURES ARE FROM CHICAGO HEIGHT LOOK UP WHO SIGNED THE CONTRACT LOOK AT HIS CREDENTIALS OF T. Paul S. Chawla INDIAN ATTORNEY AND YOU WILL SEE WHO HE IS A CHICAGO ATTORNEY WITH A BIG STAFF. BOYD THEY HAVE PUT $600,000,000 I N STANDARD CHARTER BANK TO BUY GOLD IT

IS NOT A EASY TASK TO FIND BUYERS LIKE THIS AGAIN BOYD THANK YOU FOR YOUR HELP
REGARDS, THOMAS

Mr. Liley:
Thank you for your continued communications and cooperation. From a procedural perspective, kindly direct all communications to both Mr. Srivastava and the undersigned, as we are the ONLY MEMBERS AND MANAGERS OF IVP.

Thank you for your understanding and cooperation.
Please also note our new address:

T. Paul S. Chawla
International Venture Partners, LLC
Member & General Counsel
3908 N. Cass Avenue
Westmont, Illinois 60559
630-325-5557 tel
630-325-6666 fax
630-214-4888 efax
Reply, Rep

BOYD I AM NOT TAKING ADVANTAGE OF YOU RICHARD AND I ARE GOING TO MAKE A LOT OF MONEY AND SO WILL YOU I WILL KEEP MY WORD WE ARE THE ONLY ONES WHO ARE

ALLOWED TO SELL THIS GOLD IT BELONGS TO THE KING OF THAILAND VENTURES ARE FROM CHICAGO HEIGHT SEE ATTACHMENT

#2
From: Thomas Liley <usherliley@yahoo.com>
Date: June 14, 2014 at 9:14:26 AM CST
To: boyd anderson <boydanderson.email@gmail.com>
Subject: Re lighting company
Reply-To: Thomas Liley <usherliley@yahoo.com>

Shalom Dr. Boyd my phone ran out of credit
1- Bulk sale purchase on inventory
2- Right to use the company name and he must change the name of his company
3- Provide list of clients interested in his products
4- Copies of all correspondence between the client and his company
5- Provide all E- Mails, address phone numbers of potential clients
6- Provide all of the above plus list of clients he has already sold along with all paid and un paid balances
7- Assignment of all receivables to new company with right of collection
8- A no compete radius close
9- Boyd we will have our money by the 3rd or 4th of July we should be in Hong Kong by the

2nd of July I have $35,000 USD coming by the 27th of June and in July we will be **Farting In Silk**. I will Buy Round trip business class tickets and make hotel reservation's in Hong Kong

11- My passport was Sent to the States for renewal foe all the new Biometric in new Passport my new passport will be here by the 20th of June if you can send me $250.00 Canadian Today I will be fine until I Receive my money.

12- Please call

Regards,
Dr. Thomas

#3
From: Thomas Liley <usherliley@yahoo.com>
Date: May 15, 2014 at 9:49:22 AM CST
To: Boyd Anderson
<boydanderson.email@gmail.com>
Subject: Re: Brookdale Hospital Lights
Reply-To: Thomas Liley
<usherliley@yahoo.com>

BOYD, I SENT YOU A LIST OF COMPANIES TO TAKE A LOOK AT AND SEE WHICH ONE YOU WANT THAN YOU CAN OPEN BANK ACCOUNT AT STANDARD CHARTER OR CHECK AND SEE WHICH COMPANY MAY HAVE BANK ACCOUNT AT STANDARD CHARTER. BOYD I

WILL DO A PROFORMA INVOICE FOR YOU TO TAKE WITH YOU TO HONG KONG I WILL SEND IT IN THE NEXT HOUR. RAHIM IS OKAY

In one conversation with Thomas, he mistakenly said "We pulled a Wally last night". I made a quick assessment that they used to call "pulling a wally" meaning hacking into someone's Bitcoin 'wallet' and stealing their Bitcoins. Remember, Thomas and the Swiss Jews have the code for the blockchain... which is the platform that Bitcoin runs on.

So they have total control of the blockchain and any transactions that run on it. In other words, they can steal Bitcoins from anyone's wallet whenever they want!

Also, keep in mind that the crypto-currency capital of the world in Zug, Switzerland is home to Ivan G. and the headquarters for Glencore, which has connections to this conspiracy that we'll talk about later.

On one call Thomas mentioned that Ken Copeland was visiting with him in his office. Kenneth Max Copeland (born December 6, 1936) is an American author, musician, public speaker, and televangelist associated with the Charismatic Movement. Copeland has been identified with preaching a prosperity and abundance message, commonly referred to as the prosperity gospel, which has been criticized by various denominations.2013 vaccination controversy: "Some people think I am against immunizations, but that is not true," the statement said. "Vaccinations help cut the mortality rate enormously. I believe it is wrong to be against vaccinations."

Overall, Thomas sent me about a dozen emails from March - July, 2014, mostly pictures and jokes about Obama. He would repeatedly say,

"So, they wanna put a nigger in the Whitehouse, hmmm!"

After another awkward telephone conversation, I told him that I'd gotten into the LED lighting business in 2012. I sent him emails with my quotations for Jamaica Queens Prison in New York City, and Indiana State Prison for Women. I also showed him my quotations for Brookdale University Hospital and Medical Center, and for the Brooklyn Hospital Center.

I think I shocked him, as he called me back immediately to say, "Those are all my main contacts, Boyd."

The warden at Jamaica Queens Prison was Bill Z. In 2013, when I was doing the audit count for their lights, I'd heard that Hollywood had made a movie about his real life experience as a U.S. marshal, telling how he had captured approximately 20 escaped convicts at one time.

Back when we'd hung out together in Dubai in 2007-08, I remembered Thomas always carried two cell phones. He told me the one in his left pocket was connected to the "the Swiss Jews", but at the time I had no idea who the other cell phone was connected to.

As it turns out, Thomas's other phone was connected to the DHS. Jeh Johnson, Secretary of the Department of Homeland Security, was his friend. Thomas knew Jeh's father.

If you ask me, DHS (Homeland Security) created ISIS by constructing a prison in Iraq in 2002, so that all the extremists could get together under one roof and do their planning. And in August 2014, experts were saying that ISIS was using Bitcoins to fund criminal activities.

At this point, I expected Thomas was thinking I must be with the CIA or some group that was involved. He told me he had the co-pilot from MH370 in Dubai. Prior to the call, I'd read about the largest Bitcoin purchase ever, a villa in Bali which sold for $500,000.00 USD on March 12th, 2014.

I thought, "That's where the pilot went with his family."

Soon afterwards, Thomas sent me a contract for $575,000 US to pay me for helping him back in 2007-08. He said, "We use the Standard Chartered Bank in Hong Kong". Then he invited me to Hong Kong at the end of June, 2014 to attend a Bilderberg meeting at the Marriott, as they were giving recognition to 'their fine work.'

I knew he was lying again. He even had the nerve to ask me to send him more money through Western Union. They own Western Union, as well as Brinks and ADT.

On a couple of occasions when I called Thomas in September 2014, I could hear laughing in the background. When I asked him where he was living, he told me "I'm with some guys, we have a house in the suburbs of Dubai."

Thomas and I had probably 10 conversations throughout the first half of 2014, from late March to the end of June.

He even had an investment advisor by the name of 'Nigel' from England call me, to see if I wanted to invest with him. He said he was a FX Forex trader, recommended by Thomas. I still did not trust Thomas, and I never had any money to invest anyway, so I declined.

I believe this 'Nigel' was Nigel Farage, as he spoke with the very same 'whiskey-voiced English accent' as the British politician.

The last conversation I had with Thomas was around mid-September 2014, when he said, "Now that we have the gold we need to sell it." He added, "The people on MH370 are never coming back. You need to know where money originates from, that's the key."

Quickly researching "the origin of money", I discovered it is Turkey and Greece!

Then around the 17th of September, 2014, I got a call from someone I didn't recognize. Speaking with a South African accent, the voice said "Hi Boyd, this is Ivan. I'm Thomas' friend from South Africa."

"Thomas had a stroke last night," Ivan continued, "and it doesn't appear he will recover. He's talking like a baby."

It was as if Thomas was guiding him through the conversation. I could remember Thomas often used that expression "talking like a baby" back in 2008.

I never heard from Thomas again.

FOOTNOTES:

[1] - summarized from http://gizmodo.com/the-6-biggest-bitcoin-heists-in-history-1531881137

[2] - summarized from https://www.worth100.org/bitcoin_history.aspx

[3] - see http://www.ibtimes.co.uk/500000-bali-villa-biggest-bitcoin-purchase-ever-1441101

CHAPTER #2 – '5307': A Death-Defying Effort, a Life-Defining Number

My family's history in Canada, and my belief in the important meaning of numbers, coincidences and fate, began long before the early years of World War II.

Carl Anderson, my father, was born in 1920 in Wynyard, Saskatchewan of Icelandic heritage, and had eight siblings. From 1939, he served four years in England and helped liberate Holland.

Bill Anderson, my uncle, was born in 1919, and died of pneumonia in England 1943. His death was caused by the chemical gas poisoning he was exposed to while training in British Columbia, Canada in 1939, before they went overseas. His respiratory system never recovered.

Their commander was a Rothschild.

My father became an alcoholic which influenced me my whole life. He used to tell me stories of how, in Saskatchewan, the Ukrainian Jewish Immigrants would steal anything they could get their hands on. He said, "A bunch would come, and they'd take the harnesses right off the horses and go through the whole farm looting."

I was born in 1954 on my mother's birthday - 'the Ides of March' - in Carrot River, northeastern Saskatchewan. After World War II, my father decided to join six other war vets to form a co-op farm in a place called Smokey Burn, 25 miles northeast of Carrot River in the wilderness.

Before they arrived in 1947, the area was mainly inhabited by native Indians. The pioneers had to clear all the land, running bulldozers and burning rows of cut down trees, over and over until they were ashes. In return, each vet received ownership of 160 acres of land.

The first schoolteacher in Smokey Burn was my mother, who had to teach in people's homes until they built a one-room schoolhouse. I have pictures of her feeding milk to a moose calf with a baby bottle through the kitchen window. The very first church minister who moved to this frontier recently wrote a book about this era called "The Sin Busters of Smokey Burn".

We moved to Climax, Saskatchewan when I was six years old. I used to ask her, "Mom, what's it all about? What is the world all about?" She'd say, "I guess you'll have to find out…"

Two houses down, my neighbour was Willie Desjardins. Every winter, Willie's father Paul would flood the backyard garden and make a fantastic skating rink. This is where I learned how to skate.

I had previously tried ice-skating when I was four years old, but hated it…mainly due to the fact that the two girls who took me out on the ice had put my skates on the wrong feet!

When Willie was four years old, and I was six, we ice skated together every day for about four months. Since then, I've never seen him in person again. Willie went on to coach in Medicine Hat and the NHL's Vancouver Canucks.

When I was 11 years old, I was becoming a good hockey player. I had just won the MVP in the Pee-Wee league. We lived in a small town 17 miles from Saskatoon, Saskatchewan called Langham.

I was a good kid. It was late June, and I spent most of my time helping build a new ice arena. Up until then, we had always played on outdoor rinks, and we were very excited to play under a covered ice surface for the upcoming hockey season. No more shovelling snow! So that summer, day after day, about five or six of us 11 year olds would climb up to the top rafters pounding nails all day long to build the arena.

My dad, who had an alcohol problem, asked me if I wanted to go duck hunting. When I said "Sure", he got a shot gun and we drove in his new 1964 Dynamic 88 Oldsmobile with a 396 HP engine out into the countryside. We never got out of the car... we just rolled down the windows and shot at ducks in the ponds along the road. After awhile, we ended up in Asquith, another small town about 40 miles away, which had a beer parlour.

It was around 2:00 PM when my father entered the pub, and left me in the car waiting. He came out every couple of hours to hand me some change to play pinball machines, which I really wasn't into. By 8:00 PM, he came out totally drunk and handed me the car keys. Just imagine, at the age of 11 years old, I drove my father home, looking through the steering wheel to peer out over the dash. My mom couldn't believe it.

By the time we moved to Wawota, Saskatchewan, my family had moved 6 times before I was 12 years old. It wasn't easy, being the new kid in town. During the summer of 1966, I spent most of my time hanging out with a couple of local kids, mostly riding our bikes everywhere, raiding gardens at night and playing pool in the daytime.

These guys were cocky. They had heard about me winning the MVP trophy the year before, but couldn't believe a chubby guy like myself could be very good at hockey.

So, when the weather got cold in November, and the ponds froze, we grabbed our skates, sticks and a puck and headed to the nearest frozen pond. While the other kids quickly put on their skates, I took my time, as I wanted to have some fun with these guys. Standing up on my skates, I immediately "fell" down, on purpose.

From there, I got up and proceeded to skate with the 'weakest ankles ever'. I started flip-flopping around as if I had the ankles of a 1 year old. This went on for 5 minutes, with the other kids laughing and pointing their fingers at me.

But when the puck came close to me, I quickly took control of it, and they never touched it again for the rest of the afternoon. They were all shocked. I was 12 years old, and wanted to play as much hockey as possible. I couldn't get enough of it. It made me feel free. I played on 4 teams that season -- Pee-wee, Bantam, Midget and Old-timer.

One night in the small town of Redvers, Saskatchewan, I was playing midget, which were 16 year olds, I was just 12, and even though I was a chubby kid, I could stick handle and skate through the whole opposing team and score. After a few shifts,, I heard some kid from the stands yell out "Way to go, Herbie!" That name stuck with me for the rest of my life... Herbie the love bug, I guess.

In 1970, when I was 16 years old, I was offered a fully-paid, 4-year hockey scholarship from Princeton. Unfortunately, I found out after the hockey season that year that the only stipulation was, if I played one game in the WHL, I would be disqualified. As it turned out, the Estevan Bruins (a WHL team) made sure that I played 8 games so that they would own my rights. I was disqualified from receiving the Princeton Scholarship without even knowing.

During the 1972-73 season in Medicine Hat, Alberta, I was 18 years old and playing with the Medicine Hat Tigers. I had completed the best hockey season of my life, setting 3 records in the WHL (major junior league in western Canada), including:

- Most goals in a 20 minute period -- 5 Goals
- Fastest 4 Goals -- 2:35 (2 minutes & 35 seconds)
- Fastest 5 Goals -- 3:07 (3 minutes & 7 seconds)

Yes, I scored 5 goals in 3:07 minutes... averaging out to only 37.4 seconds apart. In my mind, 5307 became my favorite number from that day forward!

During that record-setting game, I played alongside Tom Lysiak and Lanny McDonald, who were both a year older than me. Lanny was in the penalty box for 4 of the 5 goals that night.

The 5th goal was the best. I'll never forget it.

Lysiak passed the puck to me as I was coming into the slot area. Just then a huge opposing Flin Flon defenseman cross-checked me from behind, hitting me so hard that my neck snapped back and I began falling to my knees. At the same time, as I was beginning to fall forward, I cradled the puck on my stick blade. My feet left the ice and in mid-air, with all my weight on the stick, I was able to snap a wrist shot into the top right corner of the net.

I ended up falling to my knees, sliding with my arms reaching up in celebration. I was on such a natural high that night that I saw sparkles! From that moment on, "5307" became such an influential number in my life.

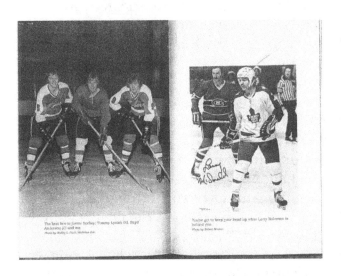

As the season continued, Tommy went #2, and Lanny went #4 in the draft that year. Our team was chosen to represent Canada at Christmas that season. We played the American National team, the Czechs, and the Russians, the same Russian team that played Team Canada in 1972. We lost to the Czechs 6-3, and tied the Americans 4-4 in Colorado Springs... which was respectable, considering we were juniors.

When we played the Russians in Bloomington Minnesota on New Year's Eve, we lost 12-2. I think we were in awe of their skills. We all stayed at the Marriott in Bloomington, across the street from the arena. The Czechs and Americans both resided on the main floor, while the Canadians and the Russians stayed on the 2nd floor.

I had bought a case of Vodka for after the game. My favorite player on the Russian squad was Valari Kharlamov, who wore #17 (the same number as myself). When we arrived at the hotel, I grabbed two bottles of Smirnoff, went down the hall and knocked on his door. When he opened the door, I said simply "You #17 and me #17"(because I knew he could not speak English). Then I handed him a bottle. He unscrewed the cap, threw it away, and took a big guzzle, then ran into his bathroom to gulp down water to chase it.

Within mere moments, he was back for more. We got so loaded that we all ended up in the lobby pool, throwing in all the lawn chairs. The security guards didn't know how to get 30-40 drunken hockey players under control, so they opened the doors to the outside. It was minus-30 degrees outside, and when that cold air hit the warm air in the lobby, it turned to fog that was so thick we could barely see anything a foot in front of our faces.

But we were having such a good time from drinking so much that we started throwing the security guards and police officers in the pool, too. Everyone ended up in the pool with their clothes on.

In July, after we had celebrated the season, I was spending some time at home with my parents. One night, my father went on a binge. He told me I would never amount to anything more than a hockey bum. I left for Medicine Hat the next day.

That year, I was going into my draft year and getting calls from a few agents, One day shortly after I arrived, as I was teaching at a hockey school, I was paged to take a phone call in my coach's office. My coach, Jack Shupe, was sitting there listening to the conversation and when I hung up the phone. He asked, "Who was that?" I said, "It was an agent from Montreal."

At that moment, Jack Shupe threatened me to sign with Richard Sorkin, or he wouldn't play me. Sorkin was a Jewish sportswriter from New York. Tommy and Lanny had signed with Sorkin, and he had gotten them big contracts, but I did not want anything to do with him. I had a very strong feeling that he was dishonest, and it turned out to be true.

Richard Sorkin held a secret meeting with six of the WHL teams, and promised to pay each team $5,000.00 under the table for every player that was directed Sorkin's way. But Sorkin never did pay them. He eventually lost more than $4,000,000.00 of the money he owed to 200 players who he represented. That was a lot of money in 1976. Unfortunately, he was a gambler, betting on all sports games and the race track. He was a liar and a thief.

My father warned me to get rid of him as well, but it was difficult because I had to go to New York to the training camp. There he was, sitting in the stands with Emile Francis, the G.M. for the New York Rangers. We practiced 2 times a day during training camp, and every time I stepped off the ice after a session, he would walk up to me and tell me, that Emile Francis and he were really trying to get me to stay up with the Rangers. Ultimately, he lied, stole, and failed to give me access to my books.

To help me, my father, who had joined AA, never had a drop of alcohol until he flew to New York to ask Sorkin if he could see my account. Sorkin refused. A few months later during the summer, my dad fell off the wagon. When I asked what was wrong the next day, he said simply, "Get rid of Sorkin."

My father called Lysiak's and McDonald's parents, and informed them about Sorkin's refusal to allow his accounts to be viewed. Lanny took the advice and got out early, and escaped with his money as well.

By the time it was all over, Sorkin was charged with 77 counts of fraud & embezzlement, his wife left him and he was sentenced to 7 years in prison. But he was out in 6 months.

So by 1976, at the age of 22, I'd lost approximately $140,000.00, all of my hard earned money, to Sorkin. I'd been threatened by my junior coach, Jack Shupe, to sign over power of attorney to a crook and a liar. After spending 2 good seasons with New York Rangers AHL team in Providence, my hockey career took a serious and abrupt change in direction.

CHAPTER #3 – From Hockey Star to Bio-Feedback Czar

After my burgeoning hockey career was derailed by Sorkin, I actually quit hockey in 1978-80 and went to working on an oil rig as a roughneck. On the 28th day of working what they call the graveyard shift, I was hit in the right hip by a 300 lb. tong. It threw me 25 feet, hitting my head on a steel girder.

I was wearing a hardhat, thank God.

Driving myself home at 6:00AM with tears running down my cheeks, I was in a state of shock. Suddenly, I heard on the radio that Calgary had just purchased the Atlanta Flames. Right then and there, I decided to drive 600 miles to Calgary to sell them houses. And that's exactly what I did.

I remember the first house that I sold, to Bobby Mac. He was my teammate in

Providence, 1976. The house had a 1200 sq. ft front foyer with skylights 30 ft high, marble floors and planters that had fig trees growing up to the ceiling. As we entered, I reached back and pressed the doorbell. It rang "DIXIE". Bobby, coming from Atlanta, said, "I'll take it!".

The next year, interest rates ballooned to over 22% so I went to Sweden to play hockey, planning to stick with it for a 2-year stretch. I ended up playing 3 more years for various teams in Germany, Holland, Austria & in Zug, Switzerland.

My last hockey season started late. I'd played 11 games in Amsterdam before being signed to a 2 game trial in Zug, Switzerland. I was to play left-wing with Ivan Hlinka, one of the world's best players. The season ended early because of the Olympics in 1984, so I came back to Saskatchewan and looked after my sister's farm after their hired man quit. I spent the next 4 months calving 60 head of purebred Simmental cows. What an amazing experience!

The purebred Simmental cows had been bred to a huge bull, so all the calves had to be pulled out of the cows with a puller. I had to chase the wild cows into a barn and attach chains to the calf's hooves, and then crank them out. Sometimes the calf would be too weak to stand up, so I'd have to milk the wild cow, then pour the fresh milk into a pouch with a funnel attached and pour it into the baby calf's mouth. Once they ingested the milk, they were fine

Always on the lookout for a new business I could establish myself in, I started selling Rainbow home purification systems in 1986. My friend, who was a distributor with Rainbow systems that used water as a filter, had just sold 1000 in one month, and invited me to join his team.

Carpet in homes was popular and the Rainbow could not only vacuum, but also purify the air, humidify, sanitize, vaporize and steam clean. I still use one today to clean my house.

Patricia Heaton, who played Ray's wife on the "Everybody Loves Raymond" TV series, had also purchased one in real life. Her six referrals were all cast members from the show. They all bought one too, and were so impressed that they dedicated an episode to the Rainbow which was considered one of the funniest episodes ever.

In 1987, four of us moved to Kitchener/Waterloo in Ontario and started up Rainbow, and within 2 years we had 22 offices and about 400 sales people. I invented the "Ride Along Program", where I would not only get 6 referrals from my customers, but get them to come with me to show their friends. This program took our organization from 200 sales per month to over 1000 sales per month. I wanted to be a supervisor with the head office called Rexair, in Cadillac, Michigan, but my distributor buddy, Mike Russell took all the credit for my program, and he became the supervisor instead. I was so angry and hurt that I chose to move on.

In 1993, I started selling high tech equipment in Kitchener, Ontario. We started out as a broker buying and selling used IBM equipment, and soon became IBM's #2 reseller and business partner for all of Canada. We grew from $1 million to $30 million in sales, over a 10 year period. I led the company with over 8 million in sales in 2002.

During that time, I had invested in four houses in Kitchener/Waterloo, eventually deciding to sell them and buy a penthouse in the old Seagram's barrels warehouses that were converted into condos. My balcony faced the Perimeter Institute, which was a 'think tank' for quantum theoretical physics.

I was in the process of building my penthouse in the old Seagram's Barrels warehouse, planning to move in June 1st, 2000. But construction got delayed, and I had to wait one more year.

Instead, I rented out two bedrooms in my house to two guys who were recommended to me from a friend. One of the guys was Bulan from Turkey, and the other was Reza from Iran. They were both on global scholarships, both had achieved a PhD and were obviously very intelligent.

These guys were very bright young men and very nice. They both worked for Raytheon Canada, a radar and military company that supports the Canadian government and its global missions while strengthening the domestic industrial base.

They rented from me for a year, but we never spoke of their mission in Canada. I thought it was like an exchange program. During that year, I kept to myself. After the year was completed, I never saw or communicated with them again. Before he left, I asked Bulan from Turkey, "Where is your favourite place in your travels so far?" and he replied, "Bodrum," a resort city on the Aegean Sea, in Turkey.

While I was still in Kitchener/Waterloo in 2006, I started selling the EPFX Bio-Feedback Medical Device, a holistic diagnostic & therapeutic device that used electronic frequencies to monitor a person's physical, mental & emotional state. Electrodes would be hooked up to your head, wrists and ankles, and were attached to a little metal box that generated the frequencies.

The software was very large and diversified, showing all organs and the body rotating. At first, the machine wasn't very popular, until the Pentium computer came out that could handle the speed of the brain. Based on the theory that everything is energy, everything has a frequency, even your thoughts have a frequency... positive thoughts are stronger than negative thoughts.

This is part of what is known as the *Law of Attraction*. Most decisions in life are based on our emotions, and our emotions are triggered by our feelings. Effectively, there are only two types of feelings -- 'Good or Bad' and 'Happy or Sad'. As a practitioner, the total focus was based on "positive thoughts".

The EPFX had an uncanny way of revealing things that only you would know about yourself, using quantum mechanics as its interpreter. For example, "When a butterfly flaps its wings in Malaysia, it could cause a hurricane in New York City" is an illustration of the theoretical effects of quantum physics. At the time, the Bio-Feedback industry was not regulated, and with the power of quantum mechanics to support its information, the EPFX machines became widely popular.

In May of 2006, I was approached by Quantum Alliance to become the Regional Director of Sales of the EPFX Quantum Biofeedback Device for the province of Ontario, Canada, which had a population of 12 million people. Quantum Alliance, headquartered in Victoria B.C., Canada, was the Global Distributor of the device, and the company was growing sales worldwide by leaps and bounds. At the time, the DVD *The Secret* had just been released, creating a worldwide phenomenon that boosted our machine's popularity right along with it.

The EPFX was manufactured in Budapest, Hungary, by an American from Ohio named Bill Nelson, who had previously worked for NASA and helped bring down an Apollo mission. Bill set up his home and office in Budapest, after a period in the late 90's living in Toronto where he'd sold approximately 200 EPFXs to the public.

Thanks to him laying the ground foundation for renewed sales, I had approximately 200 practitioners, mostly women, to work with as a sales force.

Since 2003, I had gone through a difficult time in my life, and when I was hooked up to the device in 2006, it helped clear my head and gave me a lot of energy. Dee Brown, the registered nurse who hooked me up to the EPFX the first time, suffered from Parkinson's Disease and had bought it for herself.

I started to pray out loud to the universe many times a day, thanking the creator and letting God Almighty, creator, master of the universe, all-powerful energy, know that I was very happy and grateful for living a healthy, wealthy, happy, long, life. I prayed for my immediate family, and also thanked the creator for allowing me to make millions and millions of dollars.

I purchased a DVD called "The Secret" and watched & listened to it many times a day. If I ever had a negative thought enter my mind, I would pray out loud, identifying myself at the beginning of the prayer. I lived in a penthouse in Waterloo across from the Perimeter Institute, which was built in 2002 for the study and development of quantum theoretical physics. I felt completely immersed in the possibilities and breakthroughs this theory offered.

When I began my Quantum Biofeedback sales career, I hit the MLM (multi-level marketing) meetings in Toronto. I knew from my past sales experience that if I could tap into the Philippine community, it would spread to different ethnic groups, such as the Chinese, Russian, Polish, and on & on. Toronto is the MLM capital of North America, it's amazing. There are at least 10 meetings every night of the week.

It was fun, learning all the new products. I met so many MLM devotees, and some were leaders of thousands of people. I hired an excellent assistant, Katia P., a Bulgarian computer science wiz who helped me organize my meetings in Toronto.

That same year, I met Gilbert Tay, a doctor of Chinese Medicine who worked out of his house in Mississauga. He had a large new home, beautifully decorated, with his clinic downstairs. He was my buddy and he helped me generate sales. When I started in June of 2006, Gilbert held meetings at his house and in his backyard, which was beautifully landscaped with trees and fish-stocked fountains.

I would usually drop in every week for a strategy meeting with Gilbert and his wife, Mai. Mai would always serve tea as we discussed our next group meeting's agenda. Gilbert and Mai were Malaysian, and had been in Canada 10 years.

Another EPFX contact was John S., an ex-cop in Toronto who lived near Aurora, Ontario and worked with his two sons. He opened a bio-feedback clinic on Yonge St. N. The clinic was one of maybe three EPFX training centers in North America, a beautiful office that most North Americans came to for training.

Shortly after I became Regional Director of Ontario in June, 2006, I went on a company cruise out of Los Angeles down to Mexico, making about 4 stops in 7 days. The cruise was fantastic, but John wasn't happy with the situation. He wanted to be Regional Director of Ontario, and he did not like it that Quantum Alliance chose me as Regional Director instead of him.

In reply, I only said one thing after about the 3rd evening at dinner. I promised John that I would fill his classroom every month with a new group of practitioners, and I did. We both made a lot of money from the sales that resulted from my efforts.

Gilbert, the Chinese holistic medicine doctor, was very successful with the EPFX, swearing that he cured many cases of cancer with it. I had a gentleman in Ottawa that actually grew bone with the EPFX. Plus, we had many EPFX practitioners who did distance healing, which blew my mind. I was suffering from gout at one time, and I had a lady work on me from about 200 miles away. I truly could feel the tingling and the pain disappearing while I was on the phone with the practitioner.

The fall of 2006 was very active. I was travelling all over Ontario, from Windsor to Ottawa. My Bulgarian assistant, Katia, entered every name from any event or presentation that we went to, and within a few weeks, with a press of a button, we sent out hundreds and hundreds of invitations. We'd have 50-60 people show up to fill the Hilton Gardens Hotel meeting rooms every Sunday, and sell 2 or 3 units each week. Considering that the EPFX machines sold for $21,000.00 each, the money was pouring in. That went on for a couple of months.

I had a New Year's Eve party ringing in 2007, in my penthouse in Waterloo. With big windows that went from floor to ceiling and a projector for my TV it made for an awesome place to party. Everyone came, all the ethnic groups, many dressed in their beautiful bright coloured dresses. A bunch of beautiful people, all together in one large party room. We danced, ate and drank all night.

In February of that year, I re-connected with John Muckler, my first coach in Providence during the 1974 season, who was the current General Manager for the Ottawa Senators hockey team. Together with Roy Mlakar (Providence's first Public Relations guy, and the Senators' new president and CEO), the two were in charge of the Scotia Centre, where the NHL team played their home games. John always mentioned that I was one of his favourite players that he'd coached. I always respected him, and he was the best coach I ever had.

After I contacted the team, they gave us the green light in February to come into the dressing room and hook up some players to the EPFX. So I contacted Nirvana S., who had a bio-feedback clinic in Los Angeles, and asked her to fly to Ottawa. She was a beautiful brunette, and when we set up the EPFX in the dressing room, the players quickly lined up. The goalie, Dominik H., was infatuated with the EPFX and Nirvana. We left the EPFX with the team for the remaining two months of the season.

The Ottawa Senators ended the regular season in first place (52 wins & 21 losses), destined to go to the Stanley Cup finals that year. Just before the first round of playoffs began, I contacted the trainer and asked him if they wanted to go ahead with the purchase the EPFX. "No," he said, "mainly because the team's medical doctor doesn't want it around."

So I had the machine picked up. They lost their next four games in a row to Buffalo, and their season was over.

With a newly-leased 2000 square foot meeting room in Mississauga, we held meetings every Sunday. On average, we were getting 125-150 people in the meeting room every weekend. I'd do my introductions, then play the 'Body Electric' DVDs featuring Bill Nelson, and finish up with guest speakers talking about the EPFX machine.

We would sell four or five of the $21,000 machines every week. I figured the real cost might have been $1500.00. Quantum Alliance, the company I worked for, was making a lot of money.

One cold & rainy Monday evening, I was sitting all alone in my meeting room, when a very attractive Lebanese girl walked in.

Nancy was a dancer, and behind her was her boyfriend Tarek, a massive, muscular body builder who stood about 5'10". Within an hour after they sat down to talk, Tarek said, "My brother has got to see this thing!" He told me his brother lived in Dubai.

Tarek & Nancy were quite something. They were from Ottawa, as there is a large Lebanese and Syrian community in both Ottawa and Montreal. Over the next few months, while working with the Ottawa Senators, we held lots of presentations at a wellness clinic in the community, and many Lebanese and Syrian people came. Interest in the EPFX was very high all over Ontario.

Around March of 2007, Quantum Alliance staged a seminar in Puerto Vallarta, Mexico, so I made sure Tarek and Nancy came. I had begun drawing up a contract for one thousand EPFX machines to the Saudi sheik. Tarek's brother, Jihad, had set it up in Dubai. The Saudis wanted to start one thousand wellness clinics throughout the Middle East.

Within a couple of days' notice, off we went to Mexico, with about fifty practitioners attending from Ontario. Later that night, Nancy dragged me onto the dance floor and belly danced around me to her Lebanese music. Everyone clapped, I ended up on my knees clapping and smiling.

She was great. She was so excited to meet Bill Nelson, the EPFX's founder.

By the end of April, Tarek and I were growing restless because Quantum Alliance was stalling on writing up the contract, so we decided to travel to Budapest and make it happen.

Around the 15th of May, 2007, when we arrived at Bill Nelson's location in Budapest, we were surprised to see that their offices were in an apartment building. I had this pre-conceived vision that I would be going to a large facility where they were manufacturing EPFX's. Bill's manufacturing company was called Maitreya kft, and Richard Lloyd was the General Manager.

Bill Nelson was an American who moved to Budapest back in the late 90's. He was a math teacher from Ohio who had done work with NASA. During that time, Bill was undergoing sexual reassignment surgery, to transform into a woman. In 2007, he was now referred to as Desire Dubonet, and he owned a huge drag queen bar in the old Nazi WWII office building in Budapest.

The nightclub was located in the building's lower level, and the place was done up well. With a capacity to hold 1500 people, there were drag queen shows every Wednesday, Thursday, Friday, and Saturday. Bill liked to brag about his movie productions. Tarek offered his services, if Desi ever wanted to do a porno, letting Desi know that he had a nine inch penis.

We stayed in Budapest for seven days, and went to the nightclub every chance we could. We got to know Desi and I found her quite interesting but at other times, very hard to take... she could be very outspoken and obnoxious. Desire Dubonnet truly believed that the EPFX was the "language of the universe" and that she was an "angel" sent from God.

Ken W. and his girlfriend Gage from Quantum Alliance knew we were in Budapest, so they quickly flew over to finalize the terms of my Saudi agreement. Now all we had to do is get it signed by everyone involved -- Quantum Alliance, Maitreya kft, my company and Tarek's brother, Jihad.

According to Tarek, Jihad had moved back to Dubai a couple of years earlier after being deported from Canada for assault. While in

Canada, Jihad also sold Rainbow Systems, so we had that in common. Mind you, he had a whole different way of selling them.

Jihad and about five other Lebanese and Syrian guys between the ages of 20-35 would travel into a city in Ontario, and have his team of telemarketers set appointments out of a hotel room. These guys would do four or sometimes five appointments per day, and maybe sell one out of every five appointments. This was no comparison to the "Ride Along Program".

July 16th, 2007 Grace hooked up Jihad to the EPFX

Anyway, one evening in Thunder Bay, Ontario, they went to the local tavern to drink beer and play pool. A brawl broke out between the Lebanese guys and a Canadian hockey team. Jihad got the worst of it and he was beaten to a pulp, hit in the face and over the head with a pool cue. He ended up with a broken nose, ribs and arm, and almost died. It took him years to recover, and he had a serious hatred for North America as a result.

Jihad and Tarek's last name was Charife. Their uncle in Dubai was close to the Bin Laden family, who had the largest construction company in the Middle East.

The bio-feedback business in Toronto was thriving, but I was very excited regarding the Dubai opportunity. I had been audited by the Canadian government and owed them some money, about $90,000. I knew that one of these days I would have to make a decision. Meanwhile, my sales achievements had qualified me to have a year-long lease paid for on a white BMW 320 sports model with beige interior. Loved it!

Boyd and Grace attending wedding in Beijing, July 5th, 2007

Late in June 2007, Grace G., a practitioner from Toronto that I had met through Gilbert's meetings, invited me to a wedding in Beijing, China. In Ottawa, Grace had introduced her cousin to the grandson of a Chinese general. They were both attending Carlton University, on an exchange program that Grace and her husband were involved with. This Chinese general was in charge of Chinese military supplies, and he had just recently retired.

It was a very posh wedding, and I had a great time drinking rice wine and meeting people. We stayed in Beijing for about seven days. Grace's uncle, the mayor of Hibing (a city of approximately 20 million people in northern China) took Grace and I all over Beijing, and we visited the *Great Wall of China*.

Beijing wedding, General in red shirt with his wife

Then we flew to Zenchen, a beautiful city built about 40 years ago in preparation for China's takeover of Hong Kong around 1999. Grace's friend, Lisa, had a health clinic there, and she was to be our distributor of the EPFX System in China. During the five days we were in China, we went to an outside stage show called *52 Denominations of China*. This is the best entertainment I think I've ever seen, with lots of animals.

Zenchen clinic staff, sitting left to right: Distributor Lisa with Grace and Boyd

From Zenchen, we flew up to Shanghai and on to Dubai.

Looking back, I realize I was a very naive guy, when it came to understanding how the world was run. I had no knowledge of any secret societies, Jesuits, Freemasons, religions, or even about the Bible and the Quran. I was a free spirit with a very positive attitude. I was definitely not a member of any group.

I was dedicated in helping people heal by having the EPFX balance their energy. Little did I know that I was about to enter the top of the world's food chain.

When Grace and I arrived in Dubai in mid-July in 2007, I was 53 years old. There was that number again -- "537". Jihad made reservations for us at the Royal Rotana Suites, and Grace and I had our own rooms.

The office where Grace and I were to sign the contract was a block away, near the Marriott in Diera. The temperature outside was 45-50 C, but in the hotel room it was always freezing. The Arabs liked to keep their rooms cold.

When the contract showed up on the day we arrived, Grace commented, "You're the Man!" It was a triumph, since the contract went around the world in order to get signed by all parties involved. It started in Budapest, travelled to Victoria, B.C., and then back over to Dubai.

Jihad picked Grace and I up early in the morning, and we went to the office to do the deal. This was the first time that I met Thomas Lilly, and he was very happy and excited to meet us. As we took some pictures and finalized Jihad's signature, Thomas was very friendly and asked me if we could have lunch the following day.

(L-R) Boyd, Thomas, Obeid and Jihad signing the contract for 1,000 EPFX machines in 2007

The Arab, Obeid, was directly and closely connected to the Saudi sheik who wanted to start 1,000 wellness centers in the Middle East, as he was in charge of all the food supply and wellness (health) for Saudi Arabia.This is the same Saudi group that bought the Canadian Wheat Board in 2015.

For the record, THIS AGREEMENT WAS MADE AT MAITREYA KFT ON JUNE 24th, 2007 IN BUDAPEST, HUNGARY, BETWEEN: MAITREYA KFT - MANUFACTURER, THE QUANTUM ALLIANCE INC - BROKER, QUANTUM POWER CENTER (BOYD) -

AGENT, and AL HAMMOUDI GENERAL TRADING LLC - DISTRIBUTOR.

After signing the contract, Jihad mentioned that the sheik had a cheque for $16MM USD ready to hand over. All he wanted was authenticated proof that the EPFX was a Class II medical device in Canada, as Quantum Alliance had promised.

To celebrate the deal, Jihad took Grace and me out for lunch, a huge tray of fruits, nuts, local meats, pita bread and sauces. This was my first introduction to middle-eastern food... and it was awesome!

Afterwards, Jihad asked Grace if she would hook up his niece, who suffered from spinal meningitis. He explained how she constantly cried and sobbed in bed, and could not sleep. The results of the biofeedback therapy were very impressive, as the little girl became calm and slept peacefully for many months.

Dubai was exciting, with the huge growth and development of real estate in full swing. I absolutely loved the fabulous architecture I saw. For example, the Palm Trump International Hotel & Tower had been announced a couple of years earlier, and construction of the hotel's dramatically-designed towers was already underway on

Palm Island, a man-made island enclave in the Arabian Gulf.

After lunch, I called Richard Lloyd, Bill Nelson's general manager in Budapest. I told him Grace and I were coming to Budapest to get the authenticated proof the sheik needed to finalize our deal.

When Grace and I met Thomas for lunch the next day, he immediately started talking about a huge horde of gold on a US military base in Thailand. I could tell he was infatuated and extremely excited about it, showing us photos of over 55,000 tons of gold plus silver being stored there.

When I asked him "Who's the guy in the photos, standing among all that treasure?" he replied "Oh, that's Richard, my partner in Bangkok."

I could tell from that very first meeting with Thomas that he was completely determined to have me believe him, and I did. I was intrigued, and I got to know Thomas very well during the four days Grace and I stayed in Dubai, before heading back to Toronto by way of Budapest.

Thomas said he worked for "The Swiss Jews", and that he was a banker and an ex-pilot with the CIA. He told me he was a Vietnam veteran, a helicopter pilot who was shot down twice into the Bay of Thailand. He had shrapnel in his right leg and walked with a bit of stiff legged limp.

Noticeably, Thomas carried two cell phones. He said the one in his left pocket was connected to "the Swiss Jews, but he wouldn't tell me who the right pocket was connected to.

On July 20th, we flew to Vienna then took a train to Budapest. The land between Vienna and Hungary is wine country, very flat farm land with the Alps just to the south.

Bill Nelson/Desire Dubonet held first class Drag performances at his Drag Queen Nightclub on Wednesday, Thursday, Friday & Saturday nights. Located in the old WWII - NAZI office building in Budapest, it was quite a night club; the performances were very professional. I drank double scotch with Red Bull, and always stayed till the club closed its doors at 2:00-3:00AM.

Desi (as he wanted to be called) was not a good performer. I believe he had always dreamed of singing and dancing, but unfortunately he did neither very well. Desi usually partied with his Romanian boyfriend

Christian Sirbu, who was also his bodyguard.

Desi lived with his wife in the apartment building where his office was located. He had a following, a group of Hungarian guys who played in his band at night and assembled EPFX's during the day. Desi travelled all over Europe with the entourage, putting on EPFX seminars and playing in Drag Queen nightclubs throughout .

With regards to the "Authenticated Proof" that the EPFX was classified as a Class 2 Medical Device in Canada, we were not successful in acquiring any such document. Both General manager, Richard Lloyd and Desi said they would try to locate it.

Grace and I stayed in Budapest for about 4-5 days, then flew back to Toronto. So we had just flown around the world. Beijing, Zenchen, Shanghai, Dubai, Vienna, Budapest, and Toronto. What a trip!

Szechenyi Thermal Baths in Budapest

While we were in Budapest, some romance began. Grace was unhappy in her marriage. On our second day in Budapest, we decided to take the subway to the Szechenyi Thermal Baths, which is the most beautiful bathing facility that I have ever seen.

Budapest is known for its natural underground hot springs, and the Szechenyi Baths are in a beautiful golden domed building with large outdoor pools. So Grace and I enjoyed the large pool where the water was approximately four to five feet deep, with fountains spraying in all directions.

Szechenyi Thermal Baths in Budapest

Grace put her arms around me and we began slowly striding, relaxing and moving throughout the pool. My thigh was between her legs as we slowly moved through the water, bouncing ever so lightly. She was in ecstasy. The only sound came from the fountains that erupted around us, showering us with water droplets. This went on for more than an hour.

Heading back to our hotel, we took the above-ground subway to the Octagon in Budapest.

She came into my room and we started wrestling on the bed, and the next thing we knew were making love.

Later that night we danced and drank at an outdoor rock concert across the river. The next day, we ended up on an island in the Danube River, where the most beautiful fountain erupts with symphonic classical music. Budapest is one of the most beautiful cities in the world.

Music Fountain on Margaret Island

Back in Ontario, I was being audited by Revenue Canada. I talked to a top accountant, George Voison, a member of Westmount, the same golf club I had joined in Kitchener. Looking at my situation, his advice was to sell my condo for cash and move to Dubai.

By mid-August 2007, I had been constantly pursuing the EPFX's authentication, but still hadn't received any documents confirming the EPFX as a Class 2 medical device in Canada. Quantum Alliance had been promoting this information globally, but would not provide any proof. So, with the advice from the accountant and a 75% chance that the bio-feedback deal would get completed, I proceeded to move to Dubai.

I quickly sold my penthouse in Waterloo for $500,000 cash, leaving me with only $80,000 in equity in mid-September. While my lawyer looked after the transaction, I wanted a certified cheque, but that didn't happen. I also had a meeting scheduled for the following Monday with Revenue Canada, but I left for Dubai on the Friday September 17th, with a cheque from my lawyers trust account.

Unfortunately, by the time I arrived in Dubai, the Canadian government got my

$80,000. So I ended up in Dubai with just $8,000 cash and credit cards. Jihad had made reservations for me at the Rotana Suites, which cost me around $4,500 per month. Living in Dubai in 2007 was going to be expensive.

The two middlemen, Obeid (a smooth talking Arab) and Thomas Lilly Kazinsky, were very happy to see me again. Thomas was about ten years older than me, and he wore a baseball hat over a Kippah (the traditional Jewish head covering). Right away, Thomas and I went for lunch, and again he started talking about the 55,000 tons of gold and silver on a US military base in Thailand.

As he showed me photos of all this gold and silver (mostly gold), I asked again about the guy in the pictures standing with all the treasure. "That's Richard Leibel, my partner in Bangkok," he replied consistently. Years earlier, Richard had been deported from Canada for fraud regarding bringing in Asian money illegally.

Coincidentally, I knew of Richard through my father. Richard, who was from Regina, Saskatchewan, had installed some water slides at Kenossee Lake. Since our family had a cabin there, I had spent my summers at Kenossee throughout the 70's and 80's.

Plus, I remembered that Richard had also developed the Willows Golf Course in Saskatoon, Saskatchewan.

Thomas would not stop talking about this 55,000 tons of gold and silver. When I asked him where it came from, he told me, "The Shah of Iran, back in 1978-79, before the Ayatollah Khomeini took over. The gold sat on this US military base for close to 40 years." The US Military Base was located in Thailand, near the Malaysian border.

Thomas mentioned that because the gold was 'old gold', they had to get it down to Perth, Australia, where the World Gold Mint is located. The gold had to be re-melted to be certified, before it could be put back into the market. Remarkably, the gold was 99.99% pure, so it had to be marked with the 99.99% purity stamp.

He also said that they would probably need to bring the gold out on a passenger plane, otherwise the job would be too risky. Thomas assured me that once the gold was re-melted, nobody could prove who owned it or where it came from.

Meanwhile, the bio-feedback EPFX authentication was not going well.

In October, Grace and I discovered that Brian T. from Quantum Alliance in Calgary, Alberta had paid a guy in England to fraudulently forge a document, attaching the EPFX to an existing Class 2 Medical Device in Canada that had nothing to do with biofeedback. So the Saudis put the deal on hold.

In mid-October, I flew from Dubai to Amsterdam, to meet Grace and attend a biofeedback seminar. On the morning of the flight, I awoke in pain, as my right ankle was attacked by the dreaded gout I'd been experiencing. I was in extreme pain, and needed to get a shot of a strong anti-inflammatory in the Dubai Airport medical clinic before departure.

On my way to the departure gate, I limped onto a shuttle and happened to sit beside the most beautiful girl that I've ever seen. She was from the Ukraine.

Now it was 24 hours later and the pain was back. The first day of the seminar, I could not get out of bed. Grace was with me, and tried to comfort me between seminar sessions throughout the day. Fortunately, Grace mentioned that Desi and his bodyguard/boyfriend were attending the seminar as well. So around 8:00PM, I managed to limp down to Desi's room to relax in the hot tub of her honeymoon suite.

Grace and I told Desi how disappointed we were regarding the authentication problem, and that the $16 million-dollar sale would not be happening. When Desi offered me a sales manager position in Europe, working directly with her, I said I would think about it.

We met many other practitioners at the seminar, and on the very first evening were told about another bio-feedback device that used the same software as the EPFX. It was certified as a Class 2 Medical Device in Germany.

The *Life System* was founded by Chris Kesler, Desi's former sales manager back in the mid-90's. It was being manufactured in Frankfurt, but the head office was in **Syracuse,** New York. Hot on the trail, Grace and I flew to **Syracuse** from Amsterdam the next day. We made a deal with Chris to be the exclusive dealers for the Mid-East and China, with me taking the mid-East region and Grace taking China.

Grace and I made two more trips to Shenzhen, China in the autumn of 2007.

Every time I arrived back in Dubai, I would make sure to visit the duty free and bring a large bottle of Glen Fiddich back to Thomas' office. We'd swap stories for hours, and Thomas would keep me updated on what was happening with the EPFX and let me know if Richard or Fuat or Nick had called.

He mentioned Swajwani was showing interest in buying a lot of Gold, like $600 Million dollars worth. He also mentioned that Marc, his banker from Zurich, would be coming to Dubai in the coming months.

Every once in a while, like 1-3 times a week, Thomas and I would end up in the Bavarian Pub in the Marriott, just a block away from the office. We'd drink a lot of scotch and talk. He told me a lot of things, but I was too naive at the time to comprehend what he was talking about. I think he got frustrated.

He was very intrigued with the EPFX, Bill Nelson/Desire Dubonet, and Budapest. He mentioned that when he got the gold sold, he wanted to buy the old Nazi office building where Desi's nightclub was. It was a massive old vacant, dilapidated building. He also used to talk about Switzerland, saying that he used to live just outside Zurich near a lake.

I mentioned to Thomas that I played hockey in Zug in 1984, but only for a short while. I was at the end of my hockey career in 1984, and began the season late in Amsterdam, Holland.

In mid-November, Zug needed a left winger to play with Ivan Hlinka, one of the best hockey players in the world. The coach, Dominic Dumm, had been in Klagenfort the previous season, and remembered me.

Upon his recommendation, Zug brought me in for a two game trial. I played the first game alongside Hlinka on the road and we lost 1-0. I had an opportunity to score the tying goal with seconds remaining, but hit the goal post.

In Switzerland, if you don't score you don't stay. Hlinka was suspended for fighting during the first game, so I had to take his place for the second game. I asked Hlinka who pays us, and he said "Marc Reich." I had no idea who Marc Reich was, but I heard he was an American who started a new company in Zug. Meanwhile I met Sylvia, a young 19-year-old blonde beauty who now stayed with me most of the time in my hotel room. She was in love, and I really liked her.

Starting the second game without Hlinka. I played my heart out, but I was not in the condition that I was the previous year. When I weighed myself after the game, I'd actually lost 10 lbs. from the workout! But it wasn't good enough for Zug, so I was released from the team and never went back.

Thomas was intrigued with my hockey stories. We traded stories day after day. We spent many evenings in the Bavarian pub in the Marriott, just down the street from his office. We drank a lot of Glen Fiddich, and I always paid. He was cheap, he was Jewish. I thought maybe he didn't have much money. He boasted how he could live on $15.00 per day.

Thomas mentioned that Jihad had called me a "Dump Truck." I wasn't sure what that meant. Then Thomas said, "Boyd, you are here for a reason. I believe in Fate."

Thomas would tell me about Vietnam, and being shot down in the Strait of Malacca in the bay of Thailand. He told me of his mother, a Russian doctor who had emigrated to the USA from St. Petersburg. Thomas said, " I work for the Swiss Jews, Boyd."

He called himself a banker, saying that for many years throughout the 70's and 80's, he helped bankrupt many companies in the USA. He said his family owned a string of motels in America, and had lost them during some tough times. He also mentioned that he lost his son and daughter-in-law in Mexico City, where they were running a nightclub. They were both killed in a shoot-out with the cartel or the CIA.

Basically Thomas was a 'money launderer' for 'the Swiss Jews'. His passport was being held by the UAE authorities, so he was trapped or committed to living in Dubai. I think he'd gotten into some trouble with the mob, and he was on a mission. He never stopped talking about the gold in Thailand.

It seemed Thomas was always talking to Richard Leibel in Bangkok. I overheard many conversations about "getting rid of the damn fiat currency". He used to say bankers were the biggest crooks in the world, as they could simply print money whenever they needed it.

Thomas mentioned how he and Richard were working on a new money system that would eliminate the paper dollar, because the paper dollar wasn't backed by anything -- and because the leaders of the UAE, Saudi Arabia, Iran, Turkey, Israel and Qatar were all brothers. All of them had their ancestry in the Persian Empire.

Thomas mentioned his banker Marc quite often, saying he was going to have Marc set up a Swiss Bank account for me and that we would be very wealthy soon. Thomas often tried to educate me on "spot oil" and "spot gold". He often mentioned the Canadian mining company Barrick Gold, which was the largest gold mining company in the world, owned by another Jewish guy by the name of Peter Munk.

Thomas had about 5 visits from a German banker from Deutche Bank throughout 2007-08.

> **DECEMBER 5th, 2017**
> **Trump-Russia probe: Mueller 'demands Deutsche Bank data'**
> US special counsel Robert Mueller has ordered Germany's Deutsche Bank to provide records of accounts held by Donald Trump, according to reports. [4]

He also mentioned Eric Sprott, a renowned Canadian gold guru. Sprott had set up Sprott University at Carlton University in Ottawa, Canada. Surprisingly (to me, at least),

Thomas knew a lot of people in Saskatchewan, of all places.

I couldn't believe it! Saskatchewan had less than a million people. Yet here I was in Dubai, on the other side of the world, and he's naming people in Saskatoon who grew pot and had big grow operations.

He'd say, 'Do you know Harvey Schmidt in Saskatoon? He used to have a grow operation and trucked all the pot to Vancouver, then he set up in Vancouver in the 70s and 80's and 90's, where he had six or seven houses in neighbourhoods set up as grow operations. He also talked about the Hill family from Regina.

When I was growing up, I never knew any of these people. I had left home when I was fifteen to play hockey, and never spent much time in Regina or Saskatchewan. But Thomas would always say that he had a main contact in Yorkton, Saskatchewan who he still kept in touch with.

Why Yorkton, Saskatchewan??? Thomas mentioned many times, back in 2007-08 that he had a close contact in Yorkton Saskatchewan,, and for two years immediately after MH370 went missing, when Thomas first called me, I had left an old laptop of mine unsecured on·line and found out later, by a technical company that I was being hacked and spied on by someone in North Carolina and YORKTON.

Samuel Bronfman's booze empire began with bootlegging in **Yorkton**, Saskatchewan
His surname means "liquor man" in Yiddish — was a legendary figure in the liquor business.

Once the world's largest distilling firm, Seagram had many links with Saskatchewan. Over the years, the Bronfman family owned businesses in **Yorkton and Regina.**

Al Capone and Chicago relationship with Samuel Bronfman and Saskatchewan has only gotten stronger over the years. This is why the Saskatchewan Potash company Agrium has all executives living in Chicago and why Bitcoin is sold on the Chicago Stock Exchange.

In later years, Bronfman is said to have blended 600 samples of whiskey before creating the prestigious Crown Royal brand in honour of King George VI and Queen Elizabeth's visit to Canada in 1939.
The philanthropist established arts centres and museums in Canada, the U.S. and

Israel. In recognition for Bronfman's community works, he was inducted into the Order of Canada in 1967.

Bronfman served as president of the Canadian Jewish Congress from 1938 to 1962 and was honourary vice-president of the World Jewish Congress at the time of his death in Montreal on July 10, 1971.

According to the Toronto Star and CBC/Radio Canada, the records suggest that the grandson of Samuel Bronfman, **Stephen Bronfman and his family's Montreal-based investment company, Claridge Inc., were linked to an offshore trust in the Cayman Islands that may have used questionable means to avoid paying millions in taxes.**

Bronfman is a close friend of Prime Minister Justin Trudeau, who tapped him in 2013 to fill the role of revenue chair - effectively, the chief fundraiser - for the federal Liberal party.

The offshore trust also involved former chief Liberal fundraiser and senator Leo Kolber and his son, Jonathan Kolber.

Bronfman E.L. Rothschild L.P. Acquires 236 Shares of Boeing Company (The) (BA) - Dispatch Tribunal

Thomas mentioned a guy by the name of Skip Boyce, who was into selling aircraft. He talked about Pakistan and India, Lebanon and Syria. Thomas was a military guy who worked with the CIA and Israeli Mossad but he never told me who was connected to his other cell phone. He would ask me for money whenever he was in need, but I was getting low on funds and he knew it. Still, I kept giving Thomas $500 or so every once in awhile.

I remember one night after both Thomas and I consumed a lot of Scotch, Thomas was staggering a little too much. So I walked him back to his office, where he would crash for the night. Thomas was a big guy, around 6'1"and 250 lbs. When I put my arm around his shoulders to support his weight, he immediately said, "Get your arm off me."

Every two weeks or so, his son Rahim would come by asking Thomas for money. Rahim was the nephew of the President of Kazakhstan, and he lived with his mother in Dubai. Thomas called Rahim his son, and treated him as such. He was a nice 16 year old boy, approximately 5'10' and slim build. The girls liked him, and Thomas was committed to looking after Rahim. I could never understand that relationship.

One day in October, Hussain Sajwani, a wealthy Dubai real estate developer, entered Thomas' office. Thomas had mentioned Sajwani often, as someone who was interested in buying a large amount of the gold. In one conversation after another, Thomas was always trying to convince Sajwani to commit. He told Sajwani that once the gold was re-melted in Perth, nobody could prove whose gold it was.

Between October 2007 and February 2008, both Grace and I had hooked Sajwani up to the EPFX Bio-Feedback device and the Life System for various demo sessions, as I was also trying to find an investor for the devices.

Many religious preachers would come to visit Thomas, I think mostly from the USA. Thomas always kept himself well groomed, walking down the street to the barber every couple of days to get the works (shave, a haircut and hot towel). He also had regular manicures and got his nails polished.

Thomas' partner Richard was working on a new type of currency, and he frequently called Thomas for his opinion while Richard was writing the software for this new money system. At the time, I had no idea that it was Bitcoin he was working on.

On many of his phone conversations, while I was playing backgammon on my laptop in his office, Thomas would mention "flying the first 2-ton tranche out of the military base on a passenger plane. The pilot could take the plane up to 45000 feet and cut off the oxygen to the cabin." He said passengers would die of asphyxiation (lack of oxygen) within 15-20 minutes, then the plane could then make a landing on Diego Garcia, a naval and military base in the Indian Ocean.

From Sept. 2007 till August 2008, I spent every day with Thomas except for my trips to Budapest, Hungary (where Bill Nelson lived) or when Grace and I flew to China or Istanbul to hook up Erdogan. During this time, I did have the use of Obeid the Arab middleman's car, so Thomas and I would go out for dinner (ribs) at Billy Blues/Cactus Cantina.

During October of 2007, Thomas received daily calls from Nick in Greece and Fuat (close friend of Erdogan and had strong ties in Germany) in Turkey, wondering when something new was coming down the pipe. Obviously they had worked together with Thomas for a long time. Thomas kept talking about how they wanted to get rid of the fiat currency, paper money that is not backed by anything.

Thomas said, "People want convenience, in the future, everyone will be using their cell phones to do their banking. Richard and I are working on a new digital currency..." He explained how the International Monetary Fund worked, saying the Fed could just print money.

Thomas' friend Fuat from Turkey was very impatient, and wanted to come to Dubai to see the bio-feedback device he'd described. Grace had come back to Dubai, so one day Fuat came to visit, to get more info on the EPFX. Grace hooked him up to the device, and he was impressed.

Fuat was a nice guy, always asking "You understand?" after anything he said because of his heavy Turkish accent. He was in Dubai for only a couple of days, and then returned back to Istanbul. A couple of days later, after another call from Fuat, Thomas asked if we wanted to go to Istanbul and hook up a politician and a surgeon. Without thinking, off we went.

Jihad had mentioned that the Vice President of Turkey was their good ally. When we arrived, we were picked up by Fuat in a black Mercedes. He had a driver and we were driven directly to Recep Erdogan's office. Erdogan was Vice President of Turkey at the time, but I, being naïve, didn't pay much attention to his rank.

His office was on the second story of an old house that had been renovated. We shook hands, and Grace hooked him up to the device for about an hour while Fuat and I stayed in the lobby. Fuat briefly mentioned that Erdogan was an ex-football player for Istanbul (football in Turkey is huge!!), then he was elected mayor of Istanbul.

So after Grace had finished the bio-feedback session with Erdogan, we shook hands and left for the main hospital in Istanbul, where we hooked up the top surgeon in Turkey for a demo. Because the device is quite subtle, we didn't get much of a reaction from either Erdogan or the surgeon very quickly. After staying only three nights in Istanbul, Grace flew back to Toronto and I flew back to Dubai.

By the time I returned to Dubai, I was broke. Dubai was very expensive to live in, especially since the accommodations I was staying in had a zero vacancy rate. I managed to find a partition in a 3 bedroom apartment on the 6th floor of a low-rise apartment building, across the alley from the Marriott and just a couple of blocks from Thomas' office. (The Bilderbergs, by the way, always meet at Marriotts around the world, which I did not know at the time).

I had first dibs on the outside wall partition of the living room, where I could have a window with the only air conditioner in the place. My partition was approximately 10'x15' with a dividing partition of around 8' high. There were thirty-three Filipinos, and maybe six Sri Lankans, mostly younger men and women between 25-40 years old, living in one 3-bedroom apartment.

I think I slept on the floor the first night, and by the second day I met a beautiful 29-year-old Filipino girl by the name of Lutchy. Lutchy and I went shopping the next day, and I bought a double-sized mattress to put on the floor.

I still can visualize Lutchy and I walking across a huge parking lot with the double mattress on my back. It pretty much took up all the floor space. Lutchy was adorable, and moved in with me in my partition. We were very happy together.

In the partition beside me was a lady, a Filipino nurse who became very jealous and moved out a few weeks later. She kept looking through a peep-hole, spying on us!

Meanwhile, Thomas kept telling me that next week he had a tranche of 10 kilos of gold being sold to some doctor Gupta in India. He insisted that,for sure, it would happen. Thomas said he was selling the gold at a 20% discount, so the deal was irresistible. I'd get excited to hear this news.

False promises and shattered dreams

Day after day, Thomas really had me going on this gold, telling me we were going to be filthy rich. "We'll be farting in silk sheets," he'd say. He played psychological games with my brain. He really had me believing that I'd be a wealthy guy soon, and that I could return to Canada with lots of money. Along the way, he was convincing me to find anyone possible to buy kilos of gold, on speculation that the investor would receive the gold real soon.

Tina was a biofeedback practitioner in Ontario, who had helped me with my Quantum Power Centre in Waterloo, Ontario. She even came to Ottawa with me to work on Dominic Hassek, the Senators goaltender, when he was injured during the winter Olympics in Italy.

Tina really liked working on animals with the EPFX. She had hooked up many dogs, cats and birds, but her favorite was horses. She had even become known as the **'Horse Whisperer'** among some of the horse farms in Ontario. One thoroughbred, Canela, had all the potential in the world to win races, but she'd never seemed to achieve success until Tina did a session.

To start, Tina opened up a large bag and took out her laptop, some related hardware and a series of straps. "This is called quantum bio-feedback," she told the owner, "It will scan the body for 9000 different things, including vitamins, minerals, allergies, nutritional deficiencies, organ and nerve conditions." Canela co-operated fully as Tina wound straps around her ankles, gently placing one on top of the mare's head, under the bridle.

Almost, instantly, the laptop screen came alive with colours and numbers.

"My job is to synthesize all the data the technology provides into simple suggestions to de-stress the horse," said Tina, nodding at the spectacular amount of information on the screen. And in a few minutes, she had a veritable biography of Canela. "Her hydrogen is a tad low. For some reason she's not drinking enough, or else the enzymes in the body that handle the water are not completely functioning."

"Voltage is Adrenal function which is the battery of the body, Tina continued. Tina applied the therapy and confirmed that Canela is at 79. 80-100 is optimum, so that was pretty close.

"She's asking for a remedy. Something for dominating and inflexible and ambition," observed Tina. "I lived with a woman like that once," the owner cracks, but Tina was too absorbed by Canela's feedback to admire his humour.

Tina sent images to Canela, of being at the finish line, of passing the finish line first. "Horses are affected by their riders," continued Tina. "If the rider is anxious, the horse will pick it up easily."

Tina then conducted an interview with the serenely co-operative Canela. "Do you know that you're going to Florida tomorrow?" There was little response. "You're going to be on the road for two days and nights." As Tina spoke in a gentle, almost lilting voice, Canela turned her head towards her for direct eye contact.

"The more calm and relaxed you are, the more fun you'll have with your buddies," Tina said softly. "There's no need to kick and dominate, because you're all going to the same place." To that, Canela let out a playful whinny, and shook her head aggressively up and down. Tina was pleased. "When they start yawning, they're releasing, so the therapy is actually working."

Canela won the next 4 races in a row!

In early October, I received an email from Tina, saying she was traveling to Greece and that she might want to stop in for a visit. So I invited her to Dubai, mentioning that I would set up an appointment at the Dubai Polo Club, where I had taken Lutchy to watch not only Polo on horses, but Polo on Camels.

It was hilarious to watch camels, because they could not turn sharply. To change direction, the camels had to run, lope, in a very large, semi-circular turn which looked quite strange. I also mentioned that my friend Thomas had kilos of gold to sell cheap. I told her she could get 2 kilos for $26,000.00 CDN.

Tina flew in to Dubai, came to Thomas' office and gave him a cheque for the full amount we'd discussed. She never saw any gold, ever.

FOOTNOTES:
[4] - http://www.bbc.com/news/world-us-canada-42240588

CHAPTER #4 – "Thomas will chew you up and spit you out"

Jihad walked into Thomas' office in early November, and was surprised to see that I was still in Dubai. He took me aside and warned me...

"Thomas will chew you up and spit you out."

Now that Grace was back in Toronto, I decided to become a practitioner. As it turned out, Thomas' office was in a very classy building near the Marriott, on the same floor as a doctor's office. I showed all the doctors, and actually hooked them up to the Life System.

The Arab doctors were very impressed with the Life System, but they were unwilling to invest in one. However, they decided to let me move into one of the vacant offices within their clinic. Thomas started putting "Dr." in front of our names – so now we were Dr. Thomas & Dr. Boyd.

And because we were right beside them, the doctors in the clinic would send me all their difficult clients.

One day they sent me an older Arab man, approximately 75 years of age. I immediately went into the emotional section of the diagnostic, and talked about the first item that appeared on my laptop screen. It described a huge marital problem communicating with his wife.

The man was surprised when I told him, and he went from being silent and unsure about this device to opening up and voicing his feelings. He told me the whole story about his arranged marriage, saying that his whole life he was in love with another woman -- which caused him tremendous stress.

Another client came in, a Filipino girl. After the Life System calibrated and diagnosed, it said that her right eyebrow twitched when she was stressed. She was totally shocked, saying "Yes!" as I continued. She had just completed her university studies in Manila, and told me she had been under much stress regarding her final examinations. Her right eye would not stop twitching the whole time.

The Life System could tell you things about yourself that only you would know!

That autumn, I met sheiks from different parts of the Middle East. Sometimes I'd entertain them in the lobbies with the Match trick and the necklace trick, while Thomas had private meetings with the leaders. I had no idea what they discussed, and Thomas was very secretive.

I met a baron from Germany. That was the first time I'd heard of a shadow type government.

James Patterson, an Englishman, was one of Thomas' old cronies, roughly the same age as him. He was a professional con man, a used car salesman who I came to understand had pulled off a huge bank robbery in London. I used to sit and listen to them tell stories of their criminal activity. James had a Russian wife, and he mentioned that in around the year 2016, he would move to Bodrum, Turkey to retire.

It was truly amazing to watch these two in action.

In January 2008, Dubai played host to the World's biggest Health Congress, featuring the world's most comprehensive conference programme at the Dubai International Exhibition Centre. The show was huge, and I set up a booth for people to have 15-minute sessions. During the conference, I talked and hooked up tens of people from all over the Mid-East. Everyone was fascinated with the Life System, but nobody purchased.

One day in 2008, a man I'd never seen before brought a box of Sketcher running shoes to Thomas' office. I went out canvassing in Dubai, but had no success in selling them. It was only during my research for this book that I recognized the man as Robert Greenberg, although at the time I had no idea who he was and was never properly introduced to him.

At the same time, Thomas had a servant from Sri Lanka named Abu. He'd yell "ABUUU!! Get me some tea!" He used to take out his false teeth every day, both upper and lower, sitting behind his desk cleaning them. He prayed a couple times a day, where he'd take off his baseball hat and kneel behind his desk wearing a Kippah. Thomas would sleep in his office a lot, and I never saw his apartment.

Aloub Aloub was a huge 450 lb. Sudanese guy who came into Thomas' office every month or so with a different scam. For example, he mentioned 20 million USD in cash sitting in a locker at the Sierra Lyon airport, diamonds from Africa, or gold bars in wooden cases in Nigeria.

Dimitri was around 35 years old, the son of a Greek ocean salvager. He came in a lot to talk about how they salvaged old freighters and ships. His wife was much younger, a 19-year-old beauty from Egypt. She left for six months to learn Flamenco dancing and live in Seville, Spain.

In June of 2008 I was sitting in Thomas' office when he asked me to leave for a few minutes. He needed to have a private meeting. As I was walking out, Al Baghdadi was entering with three other Arabs (obviously, I did not know who he was at the time). We acknowledged each other with nods, rubbing shoulders as we passed each other.

I later asked Thomas who that was and he shrugged it off. "Just some extremists," he said.

I also saw Bank of Japan's CEO, Haruhiko Kuroda, come to Thomas' office two or three times in 2008. I did not know who he was at the time, but I recognize him on TV now. I thought he was a retired banker looking for some kind of investment. I spoke to his wife while she awaited her husband, and she mentioned that they owned a house in Vancouver. (which is where the first Bitcoin ATM was installed in 2013)

Occasionally Rahim, the nephew of Kazakhstan's president, would come to Thomas' office almost every day, looking for money. Thomas called the boy his son, and treated him that way. Rahim was about 15 years old in 2007, and lived with his mother in Dubai. It was like he was safer in Dubai, I think there were risks of kidnapping if he stayed in Kazakhstan. Thomas had a real soft spot for Rahim and treated him special and always giving him money. When he turned 16 in 2008, he kept asking Thomas for a car.

Hours would go by, and I would watch and listen as I sat in Thomas' office playing backgammon on my laptop. His phones would ring every hour or so. I'd frequently hear Thomas talk about how they could get this gold out on a passenger plane. "Well, the pilot could take it up to 45,000 ft and cut off the oxygen to the cabin, and every one would die within 5 minutes."

After all, it's a chilling fact to realize the brain can survive for up to about 6 minutes after the heart stops.
After 1 minute - brain cells begin to die
After 3 minutes - serious brain damage likely
After 10 minutes - many brain cells have died; the person is unlikely to recover
After 15 minutes - recovery is virtually impossible

Thomas spoke on the phone about landing the plane in Diego Garcia, Banda Aceh, or Butterworth Military base in Malaysia. He also mentioned using the Cosmodrome in Kazakhstan, saying:

- "Maybe we could get the Mossad or the Russians to get involved."
- We can possibly get to Putin through Medvedev.
- "We gotta get that gold to Perth, Australia because it's old gold, and we have to re-melt it to get certified and back onto the market..."
- "We gotta have that 99.99% purity stamped on it."
- "We need a new gold refinery in Dubai so we can do it all here"
- "We need to find a pilot who will agree to go on a simulator."
- We have the use of the Cosmodrome in Kazakhstan, if needed.

Thomas called Richard, and said, "We can offer the pilot a villa in Bali and $10 million dollars." He would go on and on, day after day, trying to put together a plan on getting this gold out of Thailand.

By that point, there were so many scams and unbelievable stories flying around Thomas' office and a lot of sketchy people around, I did not know what to believe.

But it seemed like, while I was in Dubai with Thomas during 2007-08, if there was any kind of International Charitable Funding or Foreign Aid of any kind being given to anyone (like the WHO or any organization who was promoting the betterment of humanity on the planet), Thomas and the Swiss Jews tried to steal it.

The strange thing was, while Thomas always spoke on his cell phones mentioning millions and even billions of dollars that he offered to launder, he was always borrowing money from me. And he loved going to movies, we'd go every week. He seemed to get more out of the movies than me.

He kept calling a Dr. Gupta in India, trying to sell him something like 10 tons of gold. This went on at least 4-5 times a week, he'd be yelling and very blunt.

In the Spring of 2008, I remember he went out to see some 'extremists', and he later told me that he helped bleach a $10,000.00 USD sample from a larger amount of 20 million US dollars. These bills were marked, and these extremists had loads more in their possession. Thomas said he was an alchemist, and explained that he knew the proper chemicals and knew the procedure to clean the money.

In July of 2008, Thomas' banker from Zurich, Marc, came to Dubai to see him. This was after Thomas' meeting with Al Baghdadi (alias Simon Elliot, aka Al-Baghdadi, son of Jewish parents, Mossad agent). Obviously, I had no idea who he was at the time, but recognized him during my recent research for this book.

Again, as Thomas was very secretive and I did not ask any questions, I had no idea what was going on. I had no idea who these people were.

Thomas kept borrowing money from me, which I believe was a joke for him. Looking back, I'd guess he was misleading me, so I wouldn't really know whether to believe him or not. I mean he worked directly with Marc Reich, who was one of the richest men in the world. I was very naive.

You see, when I met Mark Rich, he introduced himself as "Marc Reich", speaking with a German accent. He stayed at the Marriott and seemed rather melancholy, so I sat and listened.

Thomas, Dimitri and I met Marc for a drink in the sports bar in the lower level of the Marriott. Marc lit up a big Cuban cigar and never said much. During the meeting, the only thing I said was "Are you going to get the gold out of Thailand?" His reply was "Yes."

So the next day, Marc Reich set up Swiss bank accounts for both Dimitri and me. That's the only time I ever met Marc Reich, and I had no idea who he was. I thought he was a Swiss banker who had just been demoted in his job.

I mentioned to Marc that I played hockey in Zug, Switzerland, but absolutely did not put it together that he had been the team's owner, because he told me he was from Zurich. It wasn't until after MH370 went missing that I eventually found out who Marc Reich was, long after he died in 2013.

Anyway, back to Dubai, altogether from what my mother, myself & Tina had lent Thomas, he was into us for around $50,000.

So I decided it was time to go back to Canada via Bangkok, to have a chat with this Richard Leibel (his partner).

My flight to Bangkok was around 17th of July, 2008. I'd stay for 5 days, then head back to Saskatoon, Saskatchewan, where my mother lives.

The day before I left Dubai, Thomas handed me an envelope with about 15 printed pages all about Bitcoin, blockchain, Release the Kraken, Monero, Ethereum, ETC Classic, Brexit, Bitgold/Goldmoney, Interest rate hikes, and the 2016 USA Election. It was the Bilderberg's 14-year plan (double SHEMITAH) for the New World Order (NWO).

It also had information about the Vatican, DHS Homeland Security, but I had no idea! I thought it was just another scam. But in surprising detail, the 14-year plan (double SHEMITAH) that Thomas handed me in 2008 described:

- Blockchain technology - they have the code
- Bitcoin
- Release the Kraken
- Monero
- Ethereum

- ETC Classic
- Brexit
- Bit Gold / Gold Money -
- 2016 USA Election
- Interest Rate Hikes 2017 and 2018, when "7" Hikes will occur

I asked Thomas "Who wrote this?"

"Richard", he answered.

Just before I left Dubai, Thomas mentioned that Richard had just found a Malaysian Airlines pilot who accepted to go on simulator. This meant they'd be training him for the gold heist, and to learn the asphyxiation-flight plans and escape routes I'd heard Thomas describe so often. They offered the pilot $10 million and a villa in Bali for his part.

I left two bio-feedback Life Systems and some clothes with Thomas, and the next day I flew to Bangkok to meet with Richard Leibel, who I discovered was suffering from Parkinson's disease.

Richard said he had been working on the 14-year plan (double SHEMITAH) for 7 years, and that they were going to get the gold out one day on a passenger plane. He said I'd definitely hear about it when it happened.

Finally, he confirmed that they'd recruited a Malaysian Airline pilot to go on a simulator, possibly landing the plane in Diego Garcia in the Indian Ocean.

So I headed back to Canada. When I landed in Saskatoon, Saskatchewan, my sister treated me like a dog, worse than a dog because she couldn't understand what I was doing. I was broke, and had borrowed a little money from her. Because of this, along with my mother's repeated urging, I never went back to Dubai.

But I had no idea what I was going to do in Saskatchewan. I was aware of the high crime rate in Saskatoon, so I began selling security systems door-to-door -- because I did not even own a car. In my first month, I sold seventy-seven security systems for Brigadier, and continued to sell between 30 & 50 security systems monthly after that.

Soon I'd met a Vietnamese lady, Rose, and took her back to Vietnam at Christmas in 2009. We stayed for six weeks, and I lost 30 pounds. I felt great.

During our weeks in Vietnam, Rose lived with her four sisters and mother, while I stayed at a quaint, new hotel. The room cost just $15.00 per day, and it was a couple of blocks from a huge city park in Ho Chi Min City. I'd get up at 5:00 AM and go walking in the park.

Pretty soon I was a regular, and had a group of Vietnamese as my following who walked with me every morning. I also went to a Korean doctor who used suction cups on my back. He'd suck out all this jelly-like blood, it was unbelievable and boy, did I feel good!

I called Thomas once in a while trying to get paid back. On one call, he said, "So they wanna put a nigger in the Whitehouse!" Like all of his promised millions while I was in Dubai, he kept putting me off. It was always next week.

Then in June 2010, I received an email from a lady who owned a health store called 'Sparkles', in the Dubai Mall. A 'Marli Thomas' (Bloombergs anchor Caroline Hyde, as I recognized her on TV) emailed that she wanted to buy a Life System, so I let Thomas know I was coming back to Dubai to sell a device. Since I had left some clothes and two bio-feedback devices (1 new & 1 used) with Thomas, I expected they'd still be there when I arrived.

When I got to Dubai, I booked a room downtown. Prostitution is legal in Dubai and there were women everywhere.

Thomas was "Johny-on the spot"... he delivered my gear and the two devices, and asked me if I would have dinner with him later, at Billy Blues. I agreed, then took a cab over to the Dubai Mall, which is 7 stories high at the bottom of the Burj Khalifa, the tallest building in the world.

Fortunately, I sold the new Life System to "Marli Thomas," and received $5,000 cash.

Strangely, while I was selling the device to Marli Thomas, she started showing me pictures of her boyfriend who was living in Ft Lauderdale, Florida. The photos showed her boyfriend standing beside a red Ferrari. I could not understand why she brought him up and showed me these photos at the time, but now I know. (After my recent research, I believe this was a relative of Abdol Moabery)

Later that night, Thomas and I went out for ribs at Billy Blues. While we talked, he started flipping a Bitcoin in the air. Apparently, he'd had some physical Bitcoins made and said "They're worth 30 cents now Boyd, do you want to get involved?"

He confirmed that Hussain Sajwani had agreed to buy $600 Million dollars worth of the gold. At that moment, I felt a huge rush of wealth go through my entire body, a feeling of extreme wealth like I'd never experienced before. (Note: this is the same Hussain Sajwani that attended US President Trump's 2016 New Years Eve party, where Trump boasted to the world that Sajwani was his partner!)

Then a very cold feeling went through my body, as I remembered how Jihad had told me "Thomas will chew you up and spit you out" back in 2007.

Turning to Thomas, I replied, "Listen, you're the money launderer and I'm a salesman. I'm going back to Canada to sell. Pay me back when you can."

Back in Saskatoon, I tried to forget about Thomas and focused on making a living. I deleted his number from my phone, but I still had his email in my records. However, I did not communicate with Thomas for the next 4 years.

And I returned to selling security systems. I bought a house in 2012. During this period, I just happened to knock on the door of Reg Schafer, who was Richard Leibel's former partner in fraud, back in 1999. I mentioned the gold, and found out Reg was still communicating with Richard. He knew about the gold, but thought it is was in Hong Kong.

Apparently, Richard had given him the wrong info. I was so eager to put those memories behind me...

CHAPTER #5 – Flicking on the prison lights

By April of 2011, I was getting tired of knocking on doors, so I called my old associate Bruce M. to see what he was up to. I had met Bruce back in the Rainbow days, 20 years earlier.

After Bruce introduced me to LED lighting and explained the benefits, I flew to Windsor, Ontario and attended Pristine LED's grand opening. Politicians were there along, with over two hundred people to watch the ribbon cutting for this 60,000 square foot assembly plant.

Windsor is located directly on the other side of the Detroit River from Detroit, so we had a desirable location for shipping to the USA. After staying in Windsor a couple of days, I brought back samples to Saskatoon, so I could get started selling. My new sales career was up and running.

An early prospect, Peter F., owned a dairy farm and wanted to try the LED lights in all of his barns and outbuildings. He bought a couple of samples to give them a try, but held back from a complete changeover while he considered selling his farm. When I followed up with him for more sales in November, as my girlfriend Rose was expecting our first child, Peter told me he'd sold the farm for $12MM.

But he also told me he loved the lights, saying "I'd do the whole farm if I hadn't sold it." Looking to help my friend Bruce and his partner get their LED company on solid footing, I told Peter that Pristine was looking for investors. After replying "Let me think about it," he called me in December and gave me a cheque for $345,000.

I did not give the investment to Pristine right away, because I didn't believe in Bruce's partner. Instead, I told Bruce to get rid of his partner, go out and sell a million dollars worth of lights and give me a call. Then I formed my company, Lofty Tech, in December 2011, and decided to spend a few months at home bonding with my new son.

Four months later, Bruce called and told me he was ready to get started with his LED business in a big way.

In July of 2012, I introduced Ron Greschner, my old hockey buddy in New York, to LED lighting. " Gresch," I said, "let's light up New York."

Ron and I started our hockey career together in Estevan, Saskatchewan when we were both 15 years old. We both got drafted to the New York Rangers in 1974, and played in Providence, Rhode Island together. After playing only 5 games in Providence, Ron was brought up to the NY Rangers, where he stayed and played for the next 16 years.

On my first visit to NYC in late June 2012, I had not seen or talked to Ron in 35 years. We drank beer all afternoon and Ron told me how he'd moved to Boca Raton (near the head office of Homeland Security) about 8 years earlier, after his divorce from Carol Alt, and it had just about ruined him financially. He said he did a lot of golfing with the boys.

Ron was the only person that I ever talked to about the gold, and that it was probably bullshit. I also explained the LED Lighting opportunity, since I had become part owner of Pristine LED's assembly plant in Windsor. Ron got excited about LED lighting and was eager to get involved, quickly forming a company called *"4 Beginnings"* with his new partner Kathy P., the sister of Gresch's lawyer and best friend, Kenny.

Kathy P. was CEO of QCCH (Quality Choice Correctional Healthcare), who supplied all the medical staffing to the Department of Homeland Security. DHS controls all the prisons in the US.

Leveraging our new partnership, I began doing "LED Lighting Audits" for Jamaica Queens Prison in New York City, and for the 26 buildings of the Indiana State Prison for Women. While I was doing the audit with Cindy (Kathy's associate from Kentucky), Ron and Kathy were having dinner with Indiana's governor, Mike Pence (before he became Donald Trump's current Vice President in the US).

It was a busy time. They had me flying to Houston, Grand Rapids, New York City, and Indiana, attending prison trade shows and doing lighting audits for pricing quotes. On one flight to Houston, I remember sitting beside CNN reporter Phil Mudd, who whispered to me that the Jewish people who worked at the twin towers stayed home on the morning of 9/11.

I could not believe the Prison business. Each prison is like a factory, with dairies, fish farms, and all types of manufacturing within their walls. Prisoners being paid a dollar a day for their work... what a business! Why would they do this? It takes so many jobs away from the local communities.

And these prisoners were treated with the best of medical care, with both doctors and dentists fully provided. No wonder the US & Canadian prisons are full. I thought it was insanity... the amount of money it costs the tax payers every year for one prisoner, WOW!

I think I was the only guy ever allowed into these prisons to do audit counts on all the lights. I met with Governor of NY, the Mayor of Yonkers, and the retired guy who was in charge of all municipal buildings in Nassau County.

Ron set Bruce and I up with Harry Epstein from Chicago-based McDonalds Quadrant Management Consulting, to meet with us at the Ritz Carlton in Manhattan. It was a strange meeting, as Bruce and I were there to discuss LED lighting for 100

McDonalds locations. Harry said "There's too many people in the world…we will be seeing things in the future that will be very scary and unusual."

Recently doing research, I find out that when Gresch was married to Carol Alt and playing with the Rangers, he was good friends with Donald Trump and would invite Trump to the Rangers games as his guest. Trump owned Miss Universe for two decades and Gresch was a judge for the contest in the '90's,, I'd remembered seeing him on T.V. as a Miss Universe judge in Viet Nam.
Now this brings up another interesting connection with Saskatchewan, as Ron is from Saskatchewan. Recently, in February 2017 , I noticed that Miss Universe Canada is from Moose Jaw, Saskatchewan, the one and only contestant ever from Saskatchewan to make the finals.

I met CNN's Van Jones at a fundraiser for leukaemia, held at a magnificent golf & country club in New York. I also ran into Bobby Nystrom and Clark Gillies there, former New York Islanders hockey players that I'd played against in junior. During our conversations that evening, Ron, Kathy and Van mentioned that we had the lighting contract for the expansion of Rikers Island. This was a $500 million dollar expansion, and the lighting alone would be in the millions.

At that moment, it looked like we were in the big money... but nothing happened. I continued working with Kathy and Ron Greschner throughout 2012-2013, but the sales never seemed to materialize.

For one deal, I even bought $10,000 worth of Pristine LED lights and shipped them to Brookdale Hospital in Brooklyn, to be installed in their lobby. They loved our lights. So after a few months, Ron Greschner called me to ask, "Can we supply 60 lights for $10,000?"

Both Bruce and I said, "No, this was under our cost." Instead, we insisted that Ron either pay me for the demo lights that had already been sent, or return them. Ron did neither.

Two days later, after Bruce and I backed out of the deal, Bruce got a direct call from Brookdale Hospital's third in command, asking, "Why can't we buy your lights?" He had gotten our phone number off the packaging that I had sent.

Bruce replied "Because you only have $10,000 in your budget!" The Brookdale buyer said "No, we have $40,000 in the budget..." So Ron, Kathy, and Gerard (Brookdale's CEO) were personally pocketing $10,000 each!

Needless to say, that was the end of my dealings with Ron Greschner.

The beginning of the end

In October 2012, I decided to focus on Alberta and Saskatchewan to expand my LED lighting sales. I sold some horse arenas near Calgary, then I got a large order to supply Calgary's Canadian Tire's huge warehouse facility with 100 parking lot lights on 50-foot poles.

I called Bruce, Pristine LED's owner, and voiced my concern with the contract."If these lights are not certified and you don't have the confidence in them, don't do the deal." As it turned out, the Pristine lights we installed were not IP67 certified. They all leaked.

A personal triumph for me happened in August 2013, when I installed Pristine LED lighting into the first hockey arena in Maple Creek, Saskatchewan. I'd also managed to make some decent sales to local dairy farms. But heading into December, with a 1-year-old son at home, I decided to focus on making a living in Saskatoon.

In retrospect, that was the beginning of the end for my LED lighting career.

Early in July 2014, I got a call from the mayor of Maple Creek, Saskatchewan, asking me to drive the 4.5 hours to do a LED lighting audit for the Old Armoury. The mayor and town council were impressed with the new Arena lighting, and now they wanted to do the Armoury.

Maple Creek is located in South Western Saskatchewan, situated on the Battle River on the foothills of the Cypress Hills. The area is known for the Cypress Hills Massacre, a mass murder that occurred on June 1, 1873, in the Cypress Hills region of Battle Creek, North-West Territories (now in Saskatchewan). An estimated twenty or more Natives and one American wolf hunter died during the conflict.

As a result, the Cypress Hills Massacre prompted the Canadian government to accelerate recruitment and deployment of the newly formed North-West Mounted Police (today's RCMP, the Royal Canadian Mounted Police) to prevent further conflict.

So after I did a walk-thru and an audit count at the Armoury with the mayor, I had an urge to drive south, up to Fort Walsh. As I was heading upwards into the Cypress Hills, I had an eery feeling of nostalgia... just thinking about the massacre. I stood on top of a hill overlooking the fort, reading the monument and visualizing the slaughter back in 1873.

On my drive back through the rolling hills of the ranch lands to Saskatoon about an hour later, my mind was rolling too. I was thinking about MH370 and Thomas, the Cypress Hills Massacre, the creation of the North West Mounted Police , Bitcoin...

I glanced out my side window and saw a baby calf lying on the grass, on the other side of the barbed wire fence from its mother. I had an urge to stop and try to help this little calf get back with its mother.

So I stopped the car and got out, I walked about 300 meters to where the calf was. I tried, but the calf took off running. So I got back into my car, turned on the ignition key and glanced at the clock.

It read '5:37'. Then I looked at the odometer, it read '53,070' kilometres. I decided to clock the distance to the nearest farm to let the farmer know about the calf. It was '5.37' kilometers to his front door.

Weird or what? It sent shivers down my spine....

Digging deeper

After losing contact with Thomas Lilly again following his apparent 'stroke' in September, I did get in touch with one of his friends, who said he was an architect in Dubai. I called him maybe 4 times during the next 4-5 months.

Around the end of November, this architect told me that Thomas had been escorted by two nurses back to Jackson Hospital in Miami, Florida.

I began to do more research, prompted by my misgivings about Thomas, contacts I remembered from our days in Dubai, and by the details I recalled from the NWO 14-year plan (double SHEMITAH) that still weighed heavily on my mind. To begin, I Googled:

- Marc Reich
- Ivan Glasenberg
- Rothschilds, including Boeing, MH, Freescale semi-conductors
- George Soros - Quantum Fund

- Peter Munk - Barrick Gold
- Bank of Japan
- Eric Sprott - Sprott University
- DHS - Jeh Johnson
- John Baird - Canada's former minister of foreign affairs
- BITCOIN, Blockchain, Ethereum, ETC Classic, Monero
- Release the Kraken
- Interest Rate Hikes 2017-2018

The list goes on, as the rabbit-hole deepened with each web search. But the further I dug, the more I was convinced of the incredible conspiracy that was being revealed right before my eyes.

Let's start with Marc Reich (alias Mark Rich), who fled the U.S. in 1983 after being charged with tax evasion and illegal dealings with Iran. In fact, on his last day in office on January 20, 2001, US President Bill Clinton issued a pardon for the international fugitive, who had used his special relationship with Ayatollah Khomeini to buy oil from Iran -- despite the American embargo at the time.

In what would become perhaps the most condemned official act of Clinton's political career, Marc Rich got a reprieve on a list of charges going back decades. Born Marcell

David Reich on December 18, 1934, he was an international commodities trader, hedge fund manager, financier and businessman who was known for trading illegally with America's enemies, including Ayatollah Khomeini's Iran.

During the notorious Iran hostage crisis at the US Embassy in Tehran, Rich had bought about $200 million worth of oil from Iran while revolutionaries allied with Khomeini were holding 53 Americans hostages in 1979.

Digging further, I also discovered that, after a failed attempt to corner the Zinc market a decade later, Rich sold his interests in the Marc Rich Group (his commodities company in Zug, Switzerland) to some of his executives, who changed its name to Glencore. (Incidentally, Glencore's North American headquarters are located in Regina, Saskatchewan).[5]

One of the new partners in Glencore was **Ivan Glasenberg, who speaks in a clipped South African accent**. Apparently, Ivan constantly interrupts himself, as if his mouth can't keep up with his brain... which sounded exactly like the guy who'd told me about Thomas' stroke during our short phone conversation only weeks earlier!

Glasenberg, who joined Rich's firm in South Africa in 1984, was appointed CEO of commodities behemoth Glencore, with his reputation as the shrewdest, boldest leader in the entire world of copper,coal,oil,aluminum, and wheat. While he's known throughout the commodity mining industry simply as Ivan. Glasenberg's wife is from Toronto, Canada.[6]

More on Marc Rich and Glencore

Rich expanded his investments in the 1980s to additional sectors, purchasing 20th Century Fox studios along with industrialist Marvin Davis in 1981. But in 1984, after Rich fled from the United States, Davis sold his share to Rupert Murdoch for $250 million.

Read more: http://www.haaretz.com/israel-news/business/.premium-1.532365

I believe the 2016 movie, "Assassins Creed", was dedicated to Marc Rich & Thomas Germain Lilly, who were both Mossad agents, regarding MH370, MH17, ISIS projects, and their successful elimination of 125 top scientists, 75 bankers, 4 journalists, and Autumn Radke, the CEO of Bitcoin in S.E. Asia.

Forbes reported Rich had a net worth of US$1.0 billion as of 2010, a few years before he died of a stroke on June 26, 2013, at a Lucerne hospital. He was 78.

On January 20, 2001, hours before leaving office, U.S. President Bill Clinton granted Rich a highly controversial presidential pardon. Several of Clinton's strongest supporters distanced themselves from the decision. Former President Jimmy Carter, a fellow Democrat, said, "I don't think there is any doubt that some of the factors in his pardon were attributable to his large gifts. In my opinion, that was disgraceful." Clinton himself later expressed regret for issuing the pardon, saying that "it wasn't worth the damage to my reputation."

Clinton's critics alleged that Rich's pardon had been bought, as Denise Rich had given more than $1 million to Clinton's political party (the Democratic Party), including more than $100,000 to the Senate campaign of the president's wife, Hillary Rodham Clinton, and $450,000 to the Clinton Library foundation during Clinton's time in office.

In a February 18, 2001 op-ed essay in The New York Times, Clinton (by then out of office) explained why he had pardoned Rich, noting that U.S. tax professors Bernard

Wolfman of the Harvard Law School and Martin Ginsburg of Georgetown University Law Center had concluded that no crime had been committed, and that Rich's companies' tax-reporting position had been reasonable. In the same essay, Clinton listed Lewis "Scooter" Libby as one of three "distinguished Republican lawyers" who supported a pardon for Rich.

Glencore International AG was a corporate successor to "Marc Rich + Co AG." Glencore merged in 2013 with Xstrata to become Glencore Xstrata, headquartered in Baar, ZUG, Switzerland. Today, Ivan Glasenberg and his colleagues are eager to play down the Marc Rich connection. Glencore's website says the company was founded in 1974, but there is no credit given to the actual founder, Marc Rich.[7]

With my cache of information on the people involved growing by the minute, I was beginning to understand how they all seemed to point back to one person... the very same guy I'd heard describing his wicked plan countless times, back in Dubai.

I do remember receiving a phone call from a Swiss Bank around the end of June, 2013 asking if I wanted to keep my bank account open. I answered "NO" because I had not communicated with Thomas for 3 years. Coincidently, from my recent research, Marc Rich died on June 26th, 2013.

Now it was time to figure out just who Thomas Lilly was, and try to decipher his connection to the fateful Malaysian Airlines disappearance that I was certain he was involved in.

FOOTNOTES:
[5] - summarized from https://www.theguardian.com/business/2013/jun/26/marc-rich-commodities-trader-fugitive-dies
and from
http://www.jewage.org/wiki/en/Article:Marc_Rich_-_Biography

[6] - summarized from
https://www.bloomberg.com/features/2016-glencore-ivan-glasenberg/

[7] - summarized from
https://en.wikipedia.org/wiki/Marc_Rich

CHAPTER #6 – Will the REAL Thomas Lilly please stand up?

It took me months to track down Richard Leibel, but in 2015 I finally got in touch with Reg Schafer, his old partner in Saskatoon, and asked him for Richard's email.

As soon as I emailed Richard, he sent a reply denying that he knew anything about anything. We exchanged a few emails, but it was useless trying to get Richard to admit he was "Satoshi Nakamoto" -- the infamous, so-called Japanese programmer who wrote the whole Bitcoin software program.

However, he did say that Thomas' real name was Thomas Germain Lilly, so I searched Google with my new-found information – and just about fell off my chair at what appeared onscreen.

The "Assassin's Creed" web page was full of pictures, and as I scrolled down, there he was. Included in the biography that followed for "Germain Grisez" was a picture of Thomas that was dated July 28th, 2014. I gasped, then clicked on his picture -- he'd lost some weight, but that was him.

Apparently, for thirty years (from 1 July 1979 to June 2009), Germain Grisez was the Most Reverend Harry J. Flynn Professor of Christian ETHICS at Mount Saint Mary's University in Emmitsburg, Maryland. Founded in 1808, the Mount is a unique combination of a seminary that trains men for the Catholic priesthood and a four-year, co-education undergraduate college. The college is the second oldest Catholic college in the United States and the seminary is the second oldest Catholic seminary. It's widely regarded as one of the best.

During his long tenure at Mount Saint Mary's, Grisez's main work had been researching and writing "The Way of the Lord Jesus". When Germain Grisez resigned from the college in Georgetown, Maryland in 1972, he had accepted an invitation to become a professor of philosophy at Campion College, a Catholic college that's also an integral part of the mostly secular university in Regina, Saskatchewan in Canada.

Campion was striving to carry on collegially an apostolate along the lines Grisez had hoped to undertake individually. Grisez was at Campion Catholic College in Regina, Saskatchewan for 7 years - 1972-79.

I'm from Saskatchewan, and so is Richard Leibel, a man my father knew of. He'd actually married my friend's cousin, and Thomas (alias "Germain Grisez") knew lots of drug dealers and powerful people in Saskatchewan. For example, Thomas had mentioned a Harvey Schmidt, living in Saskatoon, saying Harvey had a bunch of houses in Saskatoon and Vancouver neighbourhoods that were grow operations. He told me Harvey's operation grew lots of pot, before transporting it out to British Columbia.

Thomas also talked about the Hill family from Regina, who own half the city and were instrumental in getting Sun Life's headquarters moved from Montreal to Regina. The Hill family is an Air Force family, and was educated at Georgetown. Plus, they started Campion College in Regina, so they have a strong connection with Georgetown (the largest Catholic school in North America), as well as the US Air Force base in Maryland.

Finally, Thomas Lilly used to mention Russia and the Mossad quite often. His mother had emigrated to the US from St. Petersburg, Russia and started a pharmaceutical company.

NOVEMBER 5th, 2017
Paradise papers

These were all part of Thomas' group ,,,,, with trillions of dollars being reported in offshore accounts up until 2007 and have now been invested into BITCOIN and other cryptocurrencies.

'Paradise Papers' Disclosures Of TRUMP-Administration-RUSSIA Ties Warrant Congressional Hearings

Apart from those Russian ties, the Paradise Papers also show that a number of other Trump administration figures, including chief economic adviser Gary D. Cohn and Secretary of State Rex W. Tillerson, have participated in the offshore tax haven network.

U.S. Commerce Secretary Wilbur Ross has kept investments in a shipping firm with significant business ties to Russian President Vladimir Putin's inner circle, U.S.

media reported on Sunday, citing leaked documents from an offshore law firm.

Wilbur Ross and Thomas were old friends. [8]

The Paradise Papers: Massive New Leak Links Russia and Trump Cabinet Member Wilbur Ross

The Paradise Papers: Haaretz Reveals Some of the Israeli Businessmen and Firms Registered in Offshore Tax Havens
The term 'Israel' appears in more than 20,000 documents leaked from the Bermudan law firm Appleby, including Idan Ofer and Jonathan Kolber

Uri Blau Nov 05, 2017 10:53 PM
read more: https://www.haaretz.com/israel-news/1.821229

Jewish investors believed to be buying up Greek Patriarchate land
Purchases by foreign-registered companies have infuriated some in the church amid claims they will change status quo. [9]

OTTAWA - The Canada Revenue Agency says it won't hesitate to investigate new evidence of offshore tax evasion in the wake of a second massive leak of tax haven financial records.

The leak of some 13.4 million records, dubbed the Paradise Papers, lifts another veil on the often murky ways in which the wealthy - including more than 3,000 Canadian individuals and entities - stash their money in offshore accounts to avoid paying taxes.

Among the names that pop up in the records with some connection to offshore accounts are former Canadian prime ministers Brian Mulroney, Paul Martin and Jean Chretien, the Queen, U.S. commerce secretary Wilbur Ross, and the past and current chief fundraisers for the federal Liberal party.

Queen Elizabeth has investments in offshore havens: reports
Stephen Bronfman and his family's Montreal-based investment company, Claridge Inc., were linked to an offshore trust in the Cayman Islands that may have used questionable means to avoid paying millions in taxes.

 Jon Yeomans
6 NOVEMBER 2017 • 3:21PM
Glencore, the FTSE 100 mining giant, is among Appleby's top clients worldwide. The

company has subsidiaries based in Australia, Switzerland, Bermuda and Canada, where it owns Katanga Mining Limited, which operates in Congo but is listed on the TSX. is facing fresh questions about the way it conducts its business following a massive data leak called the 'Paradise Papers'.

More than 120,000 people and companies have been named in 13.4 million files, many of them leaked from offshore law firm Appleby. The documents have been reviewed by the German newspaper Süddeutsche Zeitung and the International Consortium of Investigative Journalists.

Glencore, the mining giant, which employs more than 7,000 Canadians, was one of Appleby's biggest clients: the firm reportedly had a "Glencore Room" in its offices dedicated to handling transactions and management duties for the miner. But what do the leaks reveal?

What is Glencore?
Glencore is the global successor to the trading firm founded by Marc Rich, the financier who spent years as a fugitive on the FBI's most wanted list for sanctions-busting, fraud and tax evasion, before being pardoned by Bill Clinton in the final hours of his presidency.

Glencore, and its forerunner company, have been accused of sanctions-busting in Saddam Hussein's Iraq, apartheid South Africa and Iran. In 2004, Glencore was cited by the CIA as having paid $3.2m in illegal kickbacks in violation of sanctions to Iraq's state-run oil monopoly. It has also been accused of environmental pollution, poisoning rivers, and allowing child labour in its African mines. Glencore denies the allegations.

While hardly a household name, Glencore is one of the biggest miners in the world, with a turnover of $152bn (£116bn). It mines copper, zinc and coal and trades commodities such as oil and wheat all around the globe.

Based in Switzerland, the firm has a reputation for secrecy. But it has had to adapt to greater public scrutiny since listing on the London Stock Exchange in 2011. The float raised $10bn and generated a massive windfall for senior management, including chief executive Ivan Glasenberg, who now owns 8pc of the stock.

Ivan Glasenberg
Glasenberg is feted as a canny deal maker, unafraid to operate in jurisdictions where others fear to tread. For example, Glencore is one of the biggest foreign firms in the

Democratic Republic of Congo, one of the world's poorest countries, where it runs the Katanga copper mine. This mine is at the centre of some of the documents in the Paradise Papers.

What do the Paradise Papers reveal about Glencore in the DRC?

The leaked documents shed more light on Glencore's dependence on Israeli businessman Dan Gertler, who was a minority shareholder in Katanga and is accused of using his closeness to the DRC president and bribes to win mining permits – allegations Gertler has denied.

The documents purportedly show that a number of Glencore subsidiaries in Australia engaged in cross-currency swaps worth up to $25bn. These deals, while legal, have come under scrutiny from the Australian tax office amid concerns they could be used to avoid tax.

Glencore offices
Glencore is based in Switzerland
Other documents purport to show that Glencore kept secret a 47pc stake in a shipping company called SwissMarine, leading to claims it is operating a "ghost fleet" of 167 cargo ships.

In 2013, around the time Glencore was finalising its $46bn merger with Xstrata, its fellow founding shareholder SwissMarine was arrested on charges relating to fraud, which were later dismissed, according to the Australian Financial Review.

Paradise Papers show world's biggest miner lent millions to Israeli billionaire on condition authorities agreed to a deal.

Trump says U.S. now recognizes Jerusalem as capital of Israel
Trump will also direct State Department to move U.S. Embassy from Tel Aviv to Jerusalem
CBC News Posted: Dec 06, 2017

Trump declaration on Jerusalem raises concerns outside Middle East
Let's stop pretending Israel is heading toward a two-state solution: Opinion
What's at stake if Trump moves U.S. Embassy to Jerusalem

Palestinian President Mahmoud Abbas warns U.S. against moving embassy to Jerusalem

Ominous signs that the next war in the Middle East is coming, and it won't be pretty: Opinion
President Donald Trump on Wednesday declared Jerusalem as Israel's capital, hailing it as "very fresh thinking" and a repudiation of "the same failed strategies of the past" employed by his predecessors.

"It is time to officially recognize Jerusalem as the capital of Israel," Trump said from the White House.

Trump also said he would direct the State Department to begin the process of moving the U.S. Embassy from Tel Aviv to Jerusalem. [10]

Former Economy Minister Among 23 On Trial In Kazakhstan
November 07, 2017 11:12 GMT

ASTANA -- Former Kazakh Economy Minister Quandyq Bishimbaev went on trial along with 22 other defendants charged with bribery and embezzlement on November 7. [11]

Meanwhile, as these thoughts and conversations were coming back to me, the list of mysterious and suspicious deaths I was able to discover surrounding scientists, bankers and journalists from 2011 to 2015 was astounding.

For example, the death tolls included:

- 75 High-level bankers, including a Denver banker who supposedly shot himself 8 times in his head and torso with a nail gun
- 125 Scientists, including an infectious disease scientist who was stabbed 196 times
- 3 investigative journalists, who all worked in an explosive area, died within 24 hours of each other. The list goes on and on
- And of course, there was sudden 'falling' death of Autumn Radtke, the American CEO of Bitcoin in southeast Asia, that seemed more suspicious and 'co-incidental' than any Jason Bourne movie ever was.

So in 2015 September, I called Ivan Glasenberg and spoke to his secretary to say, "It's been about a year since Ivan called me to let me know Thomas had a stroke. I'm calling to see how Thomas' health is."

Obviously, I never heard back. Ivan did not want to talk to me.

But that didn't stop my investigations. And finally, in January 2016, I discovered the last piece of the puzzle to MH370's disappearance, the gold heist and a long list of assassinations.

Up until then, I couldn't figure out how they could get 55,500 tons of gold down to Perth, Australia for re-melting and re-certification, until I read about three Boeing Jumbo 747s that had been abandoned at the Kuala Lumpur airport -- the same airport where the fateful MH370 flight originated from.

But after sitting unused for over a year, the three jumbo Boeing 747s were finally auctioned off in December 2015.

Cha Ching!!! BINGO! I had now put 99% of the MH370 gold heist/assassinations together.

Here's how the last key piece played out...

Kuala Lumpur International Airport (KLIA) authorities placed an advertisement in local newspapers, trying to track down the owner of three double-decker passenger aircraft that had been parked and left abandoned on its tarmac for more than a year.[12]

Now some days I have a hard time finding my car in the shopping-mall parking lot, but who forgets where they left their Boeing 747-200F for a whole year? Or, you know, *three of them?*

According to CNN, the airport's operator, Malaysia Airports Holding Bhd, placed a notice during the first week of December 2015 in Malaysia's *The Star* and *Sin Chew Daily* newspapers, announcing "If the Boeing 747-200F planes are not collected within two weeks, we reserve the right to sell or otherwise dispose of the aircraft". They said the money raised would be used to offset expenses and due debts to the airport for housing the jumbo jets for all that time.

Malaysia Airports general manager Zainol Mohd Isa, the contact person listed in the advertisement, told Bloomberg news agency the planes had been sitting on the tarmac for more than a year. Although the planes were left at KLIA at different times, and the last registered owner was known, they had not been in contact over the removal of the planes.

Further details surfaced here...[13]

"We've been in communication with the so-called owner, but they have not been responding to take away the aircraft," Zainol said. "That's why we go through this process to legalize whatever actions we want to take."

Apparently, two of the three abandoned planes had previously been leased to Malaysia Airlines from Air Atlantic Icelandic, but that company says it sold them in 2008. Since then, the aircraft appear to have changed hands several times.

With the final clues in place, I could piece together the timeline of the biggest gold heist and mass murder in history.

5 PLANES INVOLVED WITH MH370, GOLD HEIST - ASSASSINATION
2 x 777's (MH370 & MH17) + 3 x Jumbo 747's

THERE'S THAT NUMBER "537"

FOOTNOTES:
8 - https://www.forbes.com/sites/charlestiefer/2017/11/05/new-paradise-papers-disclosures-of-trump-russia-ties-warrant-immediate-congressional-hearings/2/#5560ad205df2
and
http://www.bbc.com/news/uk-41876942
and
http://www.cbc.ca/news/business/paradise-papers-leak-1.438733
9 - https://www.timesofisrael.com/jewish-investors-believed-to-be-behind-greek-patriarchate-land-buys/
10 - http://www.cbc.ca/news/world/trump-announcement-jerusalem-us-1.4435649
11 - http://www.bbc.com/news/world-41880153
12 - summarized from http://www.cnn.com/2015/12/08/aviation/malaysia-aviation-airport-abandoned-aircraft/index.html
13 - https://www.theguardian.com/world/2015/dec/09/malaysia-seeks-owners-three-boeing-747s-abandoned-airport-kuala-lumpur

CHAPTER #7 – Project Prophecy by the numbers: The murderous timeline fulfilled

Here is the sequence of events (and supporting evidence) behind the disappearance of Malaysian Airlines flight MH370 – *the biggest gold heist and mass assassination in the history of the world.*

This timeline of events -- a play-by-play description of what happened in various, seemingly unrelated incidents – along with numerological references and supporting facts that I can't believe are merely coincidences.

March 6th, 2014
Freescale Semiconductors holds a seminar in Kuala Lumpur, with at least 20 company

officers, engineers and senior technicians in attendance.

March 8, 2014 (Kuala Lumpur time) (actually March 7, 2014 in the Western World)
Numerology: 3/7/2014 (2014=2+1+4=7, making 3/7/7 – "377")
Just after midnight UTC, Malaysian Airlines flight MH370 with 239 passengers and crew took off from Kuala Lumpur's airport on a scheduled direct flight to Beijing, China.

Boeing constructs planes two at a time, working from the same spec sheet to create 'identical twins' during manufacture. According to published Boeing specifications, the two 'paired' planes MH370 and MH17 had *wireless explosives* on board, and were armed with *stealth cloaking technology* and *wireless auto-pilot technology*.

The Malaysian airliner's twin was MH17, according to The Boeing Corporation -- a Rothschild company, based in Seattle. Boeing is the manufacturer of the twin model Boeing 777-2H6(ER), and the home of Flight MH370's demise agents of darkness.

GA Telesis, a privately-owned aircraft leasing and servicing company based in Fort

Lauderdale, Florida, owns a fleet of 26 airplanes. Only one of those planes is a Boeing 777, a used Malaysian airliner that was being stored in Israel.

The owner of GA Telesis is Abdol Moabery, the son of Iranian immigrants, who lives in the posh Woodlawn Hills suburb of Los Angeles. George Soros is a friend of Moabery.

MH370's CARGO Manifest states there were two tons of MangoSteen on board. However, it was really two tons of gold, which had been smuggled in from the US military base in Thailand.

The New York Times reported that radar signals recorded by the Malaysian military appear to show the plane ascending to 45,000 feet, making a sharp turn to the left not long after it disappeared from civilian radar.

This indicates that, over the Bay of Thailand, the MH370 pilot ascended quickly to 45,000 feet and cut off the oxygen to the cabin. He maintained that altitude for 23 minutes, killing all 239 passengers and crew members on board by asphyxiation (lack of oxygen) before descending ("falling downward") and dropping "under the radar" over the Strait of Malacca.

At the same time, the Israeli Mossad came flying by in the 'twin' MH17 plane, picking up the radar signal and heading in the direction of the Indian Ocean. This was done to misdirect and fool the public into thinking MH370 landed somewhere in the vast, watery wasteland, making it extremely difficult to trace.

An immediate lock-down of Thailand and Malaysia was enforced. The Thai air force says its radar spotted MH370 heading towards the Strait of Malacca minutes after it vanished. But they didn't say anything, suggesting a military cover-up over the missing jet.

1:28 AM
MH370 spotted in the air, eight minutes after it stopped communicating. The plane turned towards Butterworth, a Malaysian city along the Strait of Malacca.

2:14 AM
Malaysia detect MH370 on their military radar, heading into the Strait of Malacca. The Thai air force later said they did not report the contact because 'it did not look like a threat'. This meant precious time was being wasted searching in the wrong area, as Malaysia ceded control to other countries in

the ongoing search operation across a wide search area, consisting of 14 sections covering an area the size of Australia

The communication systems aboard MH370 are powered up, as evidenced by the login sequence of the satellite data unit (SDU). Prior to power up, the transponder and ACARS were switched off so that the plane remained undetected.

2:29 AM
MH370 begins a descent into Banda Aceh Airport, turning from a northwest heading to a southwest heading. *New* WITN *waypoints were entered into the flight computers*, corresponding to the Maimun Saleh Airport in Sabang, Weh Island, Indonesia, which is just north of Banda Aceh.

4:46 AM
When it reached WITN, the plane turned towards the Sultan Iskandar Muda International Airport (formerly called Blangbintang Airport) at Banda Aceh, aligning with and landing on runway 17. With this approach path over the sea, the plane may have landed automatically, facilitating a night landing even by an inexperienced pilot. Since that runway has an operational instrument landing system (ILS), a B777 may be auto-landed.

As soon as it was on the ground at Banda Aceh, the precious cargo was quickly unloaded from MH370. It takes approximately 30 minutes to unload the 2 tons of gold, and to pick up medical equipment required to drain the blood from all the dead bodies onboard.

5:06 AM
MH370 takes off from runway 35, heading towards the sea, and follows the standard departure pattern towards waypoint BEDAX.

Since Putin had ordered the plane to be flown to Kazakhstan space port [13], MH370 flies north to the Yubileyniy Aerodrome within the Baikonur Cosmodrome, Kazakhstan, where it is stored until July 17th, 2014.

The blood draining will be completed in-flight by the time MH370 arrives in Kazakhstan.

The blood was divided into 3 batches of "79"and to be used for sacrificial rituals.

Numerology: 3x79=237 passengers + 2 (pilot & co-pilot) = 239

Meanwhile, MH17 continues its 'decoy' flight towards the Indian Ocean for a while before veering off, turning off its radar communications and circling back to Banda Aceh airport.

Timing is precise: As MH370 departs for Kazakhstan, MH17 arrives. After landing, it takes another 30 minutes to load the 2 tons of gold onto MH17, which then departs for the World Gold Mint in Perth, Australia.

The 2 tons of gold, to be used for negotiation purposes with the Prime Minister of Australia, are deposited and an account is set up at the World Gold Mint.

The remaining 55,300 tons of gold are to be delivered by the three 'abandoned' Jumbo 747s, later found abandoned at Kuala Lumpur International Airport. Each 747 will make 50 trips, carrying 370 tons of gold each time, over the next 5 months. At that point, the transaction is complete.

Numerology: 50x370 = 18500 x 3 = 55500 (symbolizing '555', the number they worship)

How could all of this airplane activity proceed undetected?

Pine Gap, the Earth station in the centre of Australia which is operated by both Australia and the United States, has the ability to control radar in the Southern Hemisphere. With inside help, all arrangements had now been made for the three Jumbo 747s to commence transportation of the gold.

Two of the 747s are already on the tarmac at Kuala Lumpur's airport.

The third 747 was flying in from Iran over the Maldives Islands, as witnessed by the locals. It headed to Diego Garcia, where it refuelled and proceeded to the Thai military base, where the gold was stored.

6:15am Malaysia time
Witnesses on the Maldives island of Huvadhoo report seeing a 'low-flying jumbo jet' at sunrise. They described the plane as white with red stripes, looking like a Malaysia Airlines jet. The residents stated that they sometimes see small seaplanes around the island, but this was the first time they ever saw a jumbo jet. [14]

MH370 Flies to Kazakhstan, where a surprising flurry of preparations had been taking place at the formerly-deserted site of the Yubileyniy Aerodrome, within the Baikonur Cosmodrome.

As evidenced by freely-available Google Earth and privately-obtained satellite photos viewable online at http://jeffwise.net/2015/02/23/what-went-on-at-yubileyniy, you can see :

- A number of trucks are lined up in the parking lot of the long-abandoned site
- The six-story building on the former 'space port' is being disassembled
- A large rectangular pile of dirt to the left of the building has recently been bulldozed (in several of the photos, the image resolution is so good that you can actually make out the stripes left by the bulldozer blade, as it worked back and forth horizontally)
- At the northern end of the rectangle, you can see a berm casting a shadow to the north, indicating remnants from digging on the site
- At the far northeastern corner of the area lies what appears to be a trench, with a well-defined corner on the upper right of the photo. Tread marks

> are leading out of the trench and heading toward the southeast

Looking at the pictures, I'm not sure what this dirt rectangle represents — are they building a pile of dirt, or a big hole? Either way, what really gets my attention is the size of the excavation. To give you a sense of scale, the author has superimposed a photo of an equivalently-proportioned 777 silhouette, which fits perfectly into the image of the bulldozed area.[15]

Another fact that makes this all seem particularly strange is that these 'cleanup' and excavation activities happened in the span of a couple of short winter months -- on a deserted site, in an area of Khazakstan that had sat unused, untouched and ignored for more than a decade. Plus, the flurry of preparations were completed within just two days of MH370's disappearance!

If you ask me, MH370 was flown to the space-port site and buried before the sun came up. Then it stayed buried until three weeks before July 17th, 2014, when it was resurrected to play an important role in another notorious airline international incident over Ukrainian territory.

Meanwhile, the MH370 pilot was given $10 million USD and a $500,000 villa in Bali, paid for with Bitcoin. The plane's co-pilot was flown to Dubai and looked after by Thomas and Ivan G.

For the time being, MH17 remains in Perth until the first 747 shipment arrives, which happens within 24 hours. At that point, MH17 departs for Diego Garcia, and then on to Israel or Iran.

Once MH370 and its 'ghosted twin' MH17 had caused a diversion, military leaders immediately locked down both countries in Malaysia and Thailand. That allowed the Bilderberg's henchmen to fly the three Boeing Jumbo 747s onto the military base where the gold was kept, loading up the 55,500 tons of gold and flying the gold down to Perth, where it would be re-melted at the World Gold Mint.

Numerology:
The three Jumbo 747s made 50 trips carrying 370 tons of gold each time,
for a total of 18,500 x 3 = 55,500 tons. It took 5 months to get all the gold to Perth. And mid-September 2014 was the last time I spoke to Thomas, with our conversations lasting just over 5 months in total. The number 5 keeps repeating!

While the public thought there was a 'search' going on for MH370 in the Indian Ocean, Thomas and the Swiss Jews were flying back and forth from Thailand to Perth with the gold – right in front of the world's eyes, as if they were part of the search!

This is why the Australian Prime Minister and others were constantly on TV when MH370 went missing, trying to encourage the search in the Indian Ocean. Thomas and "Swiss Jews" planned everything! It is truly amazing how they accomplished so many different goals with one massive, co-ordinated effort.

The Cost of the Hunt: MH370 Search by the Numbers

The disappearance of Malaysia Airlines Flight MH370 in March 2014 sparked a search mission that has spanned thousands of square kilometers of seabed, simultaneously absorbing millions of dollars. But the team hunting for the missing aircraft and its 239 passengers and crew has come up with few real clues as to what happened.[16]

$130 million was the total estimated cost to search 120,000 sq km -- the size of the search zone in the southern Indian Ocean. The total area, roughly 46,330 square miles, is half the size of the U.K.

And who paid for the transportation of 55,500 tons of gold for Thomas and the Swiss Jews?

The tax-payers of the countries involved! Incredible ,,,

Even the Chinese sent their largest military ship into the area to enforce the search, but to no avail -- because MH370 was sitting in the grounds of the Cosmodrome in Kazakhstan.

Now, for the conclusion of the mass-murderous activities, let's look at everything that happened three months later. On July 17th, 2014, Malaysian Airlines Flight MH17 was shot down over Ukrainian airspace, with no survivors.

Again, a reminder of significant numbers here, from Strong's Concordance at BibleHub.com

July 17th ,, #717 - Greek/Hebrew Definitions Armageddon (pronounced ar-mag-ed-dohn') of Hebrew origin; Armageddon = "the hill or city of Megiddo"

Notice the numerology of the MH17 crash, with Flight MH17, a Boeing 777, first flew on 7-17-97 and crashed on 7-17-14 -- MH17's 17th Birthday!

On July 17th, 2014, both MH17 and MH370 airliners went down together in Eastern Ukraine, with a total of 537 passengers and crew on board.

When MH17 enters Ukraine airspace, the radar records show it changes course slightly, a few degrees to the north. This is when the resurrected MH370, flying by "wireless auto-pilot" in parallel with its twin, takes over the radar screen. In reality, both MH370 and MH17 are flying in parallel ('all together'), with a Ukraine SU-25 fighter jet directly under MH370 to hide its presence from radar detection.

On cue, the Ukraine SU-25 fighter jet shoots a huge hole into the cockpit of MH17, killing the pilot. MH17 begins to fall, while the SU-25 fighter jet follows, continuing to fire rounds of ammo into MH17's fuselage as it drops. Finally, on-board wireless explosives are detonated, and MH17 explodes about 100 meters from the ground.

With closely co-ordinated timing, MH370 is also exploded, through the use of wireless explosives onboard. In a huge blue flash, it spews 4-month-old body parts and plane parts, scattering the debris over 33 kilometres as it "falls to the ground".

To witnesses of the strike, as well as to first responders at the crash site, this would have appeared like a missile had hit the plane.

The people who picked up the body parts told reporters that the body parts were already rotting and had a distinct stench. They also mentioned that the blood had been drained from the body parts they'd found.

According to news reports found on USNews and elsewhere, "A top pro-Russia rebel commander in eastern Ukraine has given a bizarre version of events surrounding the Malaysian jetliner crash -- suggesting many of the victims may have died days before the plane took off." [17]

A top pro-Russia rebel commander, Igor Girkin, described the crash site, saying "A significant number of the bodies were not fresh," adding that he was told "They were drained of blood and reeked of decomposition." Remarkably, he also claimed that a large amount of blood serum and medications were found in the wreckage.

Numerology:

MH370 had 239 passengers and crew members
MH17 - had 298 passengers and crew members
TOTAL = 537 passengers and crew members

I added it up and again almost fell out of my chair... there's that number "537" again!

Keep these references in the back of your mind, from Strong's Concordance at BibleHub.com

#537- Hebrew-Greek definition - "all together"
#5307- Hebrew-Greek definition - "fall to a violent death"

After the crash, the Dutch authorities never started clean-up operations for 4 weeks, which allowed first responders from the Ukrainian military plenty of time to collect all the pieces of MH370 that were scattered over a 33-kilometre area.

Triggered by wireless explosives onboard, MH370 was approximately 7500 meters above the ground when it came apart, looking like a missile hit it. This caused the plane's fuselage to break into pieces, all of them "falling" heavily to the ground. Some of the larger pieces caused craters 3 feet deep, which were later found to contain decomposed and rotting human body parts, drained of blood.

Mixed in with the scattered remains of both people and MH370, the twin MH17 airliner was also destroyed when it was gunned down after the Ukrainian fighter jet first shot a huge hole into the cockpit, then kept firing at MH17 until it was approximately 100 meters above the ground. At that point, wireless technology detonated the on-board explosives to finish the job.

Kiev and Western countries immediately blamed "pro-Russian" separatists and Moscow for shooting down flight MH17 with a BUK missile.

A year later, after intensive searches across miles of the Indian Ocean and other points along MH370's estimated flight path, rescue teams and world leaders seemed to be no closer to solving the plane's disappearance. To add insult to injury, and multiply the confusion, while it seemed the world knew that MH17 was shot out of the sky, no-one claimed responsibility or discovered who deserved the blame.

However, quotes from security and diplomatic personnel, first responders and the victims' families present a mysterious and suspicious picture of events.[18]

Quotes from victims' families

The mother of one victim said, "He severed all ties in Holland, it was his last flight. A flight to a new life." "He was 53".

Another from a sibling, "We believed our older brother was the best of us. We feel so sorry for him."

"The authorities never showed the bodies – only pictures of their findings. Photos were full length and he wasn't damaged, just slightly burnt. I was able to identify him."

The person who cleaned the bodies told us, "Our brother's body was in the best condition, with nothing missing. Everything was in place."

"We were not allowed to open the casket. We were told by the government, 'Nobody must see.'"

"All caskets with corpses that came back to Malaysia were not allowed to be opened."

"The Government is not telling us anything," said one victim's mother. "We just wait and hope somebody will come up with something, especially from the Black Box."

Quotes from Malaysian authorities

A Malaysian diplomat said,"Shooting the Boeing MH17 is like shooting our Country."

"We want the Facts, you know, we do not want Propaganda."

"Malaysian people blame Russia. Russia gave BUKs to separatists to shoot down MH17 because local media says so."

Malaysia's local media follows the Western media:
"The family of MH17's pilot, Captain Wan Amran, will not speak to anyone, claiming mental problems after the trauma of Wan's death."

Remarkably, no forensics analysis was ever done on the bodies! As an excuse, the CIA said that the Ukraine, being a 3rd World country, did not have the capabilities.

And from the very beginning, only one version of what happened was considered by the West... that MH17 was shot down by separatists, using a BUK surface-to-air missile launcher. The trouble with that theory is that a single air missile fired on a plane the size of a 777 Boeing would just switch off the engine. Surface-to-air missiles have just 3-5 Kilograms of high explosives.

There is evidence that MH17 was rigged with explosives. But the Russians are blaming a Ukraine fighter jet seen leaving the scene by many locals, who witnessed the crash from a distance.[19]

Eyewitness accounts at the MH17 crash site

"I heard 2 explosions, POP! Then another POP!""There were two places where planes came down. I ran into the yard... I ran into the street to see a plane very far away."The jet fired a rocket, and then from behind the clouds, I saw a plane "falling" to the ground.

One part "fell", while the other part flew off towards another village."

"You did not see a BUK missile vapour trail?" asked the reporter on the scene. "No I did not see a BUK trail. Not from either side"

"It's not only my opinion, many have seen military jets flying below civilian planes.

"There were many planes."

"I go outside and there's a plane, a military jet was flying from over there, just above the forest. About 50 meters above, I saw a passenger plane approaching from there… then the military jet flew towards the passenger plane and SHOT towards the front of the plane."

"There was a Blue Flash which turned Black. The altitude of the plane was about 100 meters above the henhouse, not high."

"I could see the engines fans and this is where the jet finished it off."

"So the plane was shot several times…then it exploded."

When more news about the crash started to surface on the following day, the gory details defied belief… except that they seemed to be coming from some pretty highly-ranked sources!

July 18 2014

Military Commander: Passengers dead long before plane took off [20]

The bodies were dead for days before the flight, smelling of rot and drained of blood, according to a top military commander at the scene.[21]

> Dutchman comments:
> "When I look at my country, the Netherlands, as an official Head of the investigation, we are part of NATO. We are part of Anti-Russian Alliance, so we are not Independent investigators. This is something the United Nations should have investigated, and not a biased government, like the Netherlands."
>
> "How can you do an investigation if the Ukraine, one of the possible murderers,

is part of the investigation, and delivered evidence that the Ukraine collected? Ridiculous!"

"Well, what it proved is that the Ukraine fired at the crash site with heavy mortars, with rockets that left craters 3 meters deep." (This was caused by MH370 Fuselage hitting the ground)

Really, you have to ask yourself, who benefits? Who gains the most, from hiding evidence and from trying to distort the investigation? It's the party who did it! Many facts have been established, but they aren't being shared with the public or the victims' relatives. The investigation remains classified.

But conflicting reports added to the horror and confusion of the families. From an MH17 crash report you can read at Independent.co.uk and elsewhere:

MH17's passengers and crew may have been conscious for the one-and-a-half minutes it took the plane to crash, investigators have said.

In its final report into the crash, the Dutch Safety Board (DSB), some were killed by serious injuries, while others are believed to have lost consciousness, but the DSB could not confirm when they died.

> "It cannot be ruled out that some of the occupants remained consciousness for some time during the one to one-and-a-half minutes for which the crash lasted," a spokesperson said.

> "The Dutch Safety Board deems it likely that the occupants were barely able to comprehend the situation in which they found themselves."[22]

And yet, we hear of bodies falling down, as witnesses described "It was raining bodies." Bodies were landing in gardens, in fields, on roofs of houses. One body crashed through the roof of an old house, landing in the bed of one of the bedrooms.

++++++++

As the drama of the plane crash grabbed headlines and the world's attention, there was still the matter of transporting all of that gold without getting caught. Once the gold was re-melted and certified on the market, it was transported by those same three Jumbo 747s into seven vaults around the world.

The vaults, located in Singapore, Hong Kong, Dubai, Zurich, London, Toronto and New York, received 7900 tons of gold each, for a total of 55,300 tons. Add the two-ton shipment that was originally transferred on MH370, and you get 55,500 tons of gold in this heist.

Numerology:

The *atomic number of gold* is 79. According to medieval magicians of Europe, gold is male and silver is female. The word 'power' is used 79 times in the New Testament, and the verb 'to curse' appears 79 times in the Old Testament.

Have you ever heard the idea that 'there are no co-incidences, and everything happens for a reason'? Okay then, since we're talking about 'significant numbers', check this out:

The Magic Number ' 7 '
Brexit collapse falls exactly on Shemitah date[23]

In 2014, Christine Lagarde, Managing Director of the International Monetary Fund since July 5th, 2011, gave a speech on "the magic number 7".

It, along with work by Jonathan Cahn, led us to the Shemitah seven-year cycle and the Jubilee year, which the globalist elites are well aware of.

What we've discovered since is that there is even more to the "magic number 7" than just years... it appears to correlate right down to months, weeks and days.

The last major market crash occurred on September 29, 2008. On that day, the Dow Jones fell 777 points, of all numbers.... its biggest one day point drop ever.
On Friday, in the aftermath of Brexit, the Dow fell over 600 points. What's interesting about Friday's date?

It was 7 years, 7 months, 7 weeks and 7 days since September 29, 2008.

And now, in my mind, the most important number to consider... the significance of "537". Let's begin with several references from Strong's Concordance at BibleHub.com

"537" - HEBREW - GREEK Definition:
Strong's #537: hapas (pronounced hap'-as)

Meaning: " ALL TOGETHER "

"5307" - HEBREW - GREEK Definition:

Strong's #5307: nap̂hal
Meaning: " TO FALL TO A VIOLENT DEATH "

5 PLANES INVOLVED IN THIS MH370 HEIST - ASSASSINATION " 537 "

A few more significant references to "537" throughout history, from ancient to modern times...

"537" B.C. - Cyrus

After the overthrow of Babylonia by the Persians, Cyrus, *who was married to Isis*, gave the Jews permission to return to their native land in 537 BC), and more than forty thousand Jews are freed and allowed to practise their sacrifice religion and begin to rebuild the 2nd Temple in Jerusalem

"537" A.D. - Phasis

The First Siege of Rome during the Gothic War lasted for a year and nine days, from 2 March 537 to 12 March 538. The city was besieged by the Ostrogothic army under their king Vitiges; the defending East Romans were commanded by Belisarius, one of the most famous and successful Byzantine generals. The siege was the first major encounter between the forces of the two opponents, and played a decisive role in the subsequent development of the war.

In a related '537' connection, Pope Vigilius (died 7 June 555) was Pope from 29 March 537 to his death in 555. He is considered the first pope of the Byzantine Papacy. While on the journey, he died at Syracuse.

"537" - Bush beats Gore by 537 votes in the 2000 US presidential election

During the hotly-contested Florida election recount in the US, during the weeks after Election Day in the 2000 United States presidential election between George W. Bush and Al Gore, the Florida vote was ultimately settled in Bush's favor -- by a margin of 537 votes.

"537" - 2012 Barak Obama re- election campaign advertisement

Referencing the 2000 election results mentioned above, Obama's campaign focused on inspiring people to get out and vote. The ad is titled "537, the number of votes that changed the course of American History". In it, Obama mentions "537, the difference between 'What was and what could have been.' So this year if you're thinking that your vote doesn't count, that it won't matter, well, back then there were probably 537 people who felt the same way. Make your voice heard. VOTE."

Shiva, the 'Goddess of Destruction' (whose sacred number is '5'), is portrayed in a commemorative statue at CERN, the CIA Headquarters in Switzerland
Shiva (or Siva) is considered the Supreme God within Shaivism, and is the creator and "destroyer" of all that is. On June 18, 2004, a 2-meter tall statue of Shiva was unveiled at CERN, donated by India.

The occultist believes "5" to be the Number of Death, and the greatest intensification of any number to be a triplicate, a "555" literally means "Highest Death".

The Bible in Basic English

1 Kings 10:14 (BBE) Now the weight of gold which came to King Solomon in one year was six hundred and sixty-six talents; 666 divided by 12 Tribes of Israel = "55.5" Talents

Finally, going back to Strong's Concordance for a numerical reference I cannot ignore, here's another 'coincidence' that is the reason I wrote this book.

"5307" - DICTIONARY OF BIBLE THEMES – 5307 ENVOY

"An official representative sent on behalf of a king or government to other kings or nations. Believers are God's envoys to his world, bearing the good news of salvation on his behalf."

Incidentally, I've had a 5-foot steel statue of *'Hermes the messenger'* in my home since 2000, and my nickname from my hockey days is 'Herby'. As details about some of the people I met in Thomas Lilley's circle of friends and beyond are becoming clearer, *I believe that I escaped death, and that I am now 'the messenger' to bring these facts to light.*

FOOTNOTES:

[13] - http://www.dailymail.co.uk/news/article-2967157/Vladimir-Putin-ordered-Russian-special-ops-steal-MH370-plane-secretly-landed-disused-space-port-Kazahkstan-expert-claims.html

[14] - http://www.veteranstoday.com/2014/04/26/mh370-evidence-of-false-flag/

[15] - Source: http://jeffwise.net/2015/02/23/what-went-on-at-yubileyniy/

16 - http://www.japantimes.co.jp/news/2016/02/21/asia-pacific/by-the-numbers-the-hunt-for-mh370/#.WUh5m5Lyvbg)

17 - https://www.usnews.com/news/world/articles/2014/07/18/rebel-leader-gives-bizarre-account-of-plane-crash)

18 - I found on You Tube Published on Jul 20, 2014 "They were falling from the SKY:" Witnesses of MH17 crash tell their stories
July 19, 2014. there are many more you tubes that have different witnesses coments

19 - https://youtu.be/2VCdjOPz2h8 , there are many more you tubeS

20 - http://www.jimstonefreelance.com/indexbkaug32014.html

21 - NewsTeam: Malaysia Airlines MH17 crash site (E32)
Published on Sep 26, 2014
Roman Kosarev arrives at the crash site of Malaysia Airlines MH17 to find that, 24 hours after the tragedy, bodies of the passengers are still there and the only people who've visited the place are journalists. Meanwhile, Harry Fear's work in Gaza City is tested when his equipment starts to fail

22 - http://www.independent.co.uk/news/world/europe/mh17-report-buk-warhead-exploded-a-metre-away-from-planes-cockpit-and-started-fatal-break-up-a6692346.html)

23 - https://dollarvigilante.com/blog/2016/06/25/magic-number-7-brexit-collapse-falls-exactly-shemitah-date.html

CHAPTER #8 – "Now that we have the gold, we need to sell it"

The last conversation I had with Thomas was in mid-September 2014, just over five months after MH370 went missing. This was also not long after the 5-month timeframe it took to deliver the gold to Perth.

Thomas told me, "Now that we have the gold, we need to sell it"

And who would do the selling? The only game in town – BitGold/GoldMoney, the one and only distributor that has access to all seven of these vaults!

It operates under SHARIA LAW.

As soon as the gold was transported to the seven vaults, BitGold/GoldMoney was created, providing delivery service through

Brinks (which Thomas told me that the Swiss Jew bankers also own, as mentioned during our conversations back in 2007-8).

In May 2015, GoldMoney is listed on the TSE (Toronto Stock Exchange), formed as a holding company following the acquisition by publicly listed BitGold Corp. of the Goldmoney business in 2015. The company subsequently changed its name to Goldmoney Inc., and had over 1,400,000 clients as of late 2016. With total customer assets of $1.8 billion representing 34.1 tonnes of gold, it is one of the largest privately owned gold reserves in the world.

As a global full reserved gold-based financial services company founded by James Turk, Roy Sebag,and Josh Crumb, GoldMoney Inc offers full reserve precious metal focused financial services, and is headquartered in Toronto, Canada and in Saint Helier, Jersey (UK). GoldMoney Inc. investors and backers include Eric Sprott, Albert D. Friedberg, George Soros, Adam Fleming, and Canadian Banks Canaccord Genuity (the Rothschilds!)[24]

Now things were starting to pick up speed on the gold front, right in line with the predictions I'd read in the NWO 7-year plan. Just before Brexit happened on June 23,

2016, China purchased 90B worth of gold, storing it in the London vault. Meanwhile, Ivan Glasenberg and Glencore started selling assets in 2016, including 40% of their agricultural business based in Regina. The agri-business stock was sold to the Canadian Pension Plan Fund for almost $3 Billion dollars.

The smoking gun

Putting the pieces of the puzzle together in January 2016, I soon realized that I'd actually figured out the 'smoking gun' of this incredible gold heist and mass-assassination!

In January 2016, I was getting calls from Nova Scotia, but I couldn't understand who they were coming from. The calls really sounded like a "hit man", and I got worried that Thomas had ordered someone to 'shake me up'… or worse.

So I contacted the police immediately, setting up a meeting with Chief Clive Weighill in Saskatoon at the end of the month.

When I arrived at the station, Chief Weighil had the top military guy from Dundurn, just 20 minutes south of Saskatoon, join in on the meeting. They told me that Dundurn has the largest storage of military equipment in North America. Anyway, I told my story to Clive and the military guy, mostly for the sake of reporting to officials and for the safety of my family.

I'd started my story by showing them my hockey records, for credibility. When I was finished the whole story, I asked them what they thought. Clive said "Good story." Military Guy said, "Wow! Those are quite the hockey records."

And that was it.

Crashing the stock market in 2016

Think about it... Thomas had said, "Now that we have the gold we need to sell it."

But in order to sell the gold, given that its stock price had been sliding since its peak in 2011, they had to crash the stock market in January 2016, to bounce the gold price back up. After all, gold has traditionally been the safe hedge from inflation and economic uncertainty, so its price usually inflates in uncertain times.

By November 2015, gold had slid to $1080 per ounce. Barrick Gold, a Canadian mining company (the largest in the world) hit a low of $8.00 per share. Canada's Minister of Foreign Affairs, John Baird, quit the government, and went to work for Barrick Gold and Hatch in November 2015.

So in January 2016 the market crashed... obviously China, Bilderbergs or the Dragons were involved. The elites simply sold their devalued stocks, and started buying gold & silver stocks instead.

> "Nobody here knows quite what to make of the latest stock market sell-off, and that, indeed, is part of the problem, for uncertainty breeds fear of loss" [25]

January got off to a terrible start, probably the worst start to a year ever. Panic about the slowdown in China and crashing oil prices sent the Dow to its worst 10-day start to a year on record (and the records go back to 1897).

With extreme fear about the meltdown in oil prices and plunging stock prices in China, investors sold off stocks in virtually all sectors. "Clearly this was an awful month. The selling was more about sentiment than a change in the actual fundamentals," said Russ Koestrich, global chief investment strategist at BlackRock.[26]

How to profit from a stock market crash

So, in this atmosphere of fear and uncertainty they'd created, the elite started buying gold and silver stocks that had recently bottomed (gold had already slid to $1,080 an ounce)... and waited patiently for them to rise, as they surely would.

In fact, it looked like they'd soon have a little extra help in controlling gold's value in the markets. Because in early March 2015, John Baird (Canada's foreign affairs minister) quit his high-profile government job in Stephen Harper's cabinet, to join Barrick Gold Corporation as an international adviser!

Although his appointment to the precious-metals giant raised questions (as did his subsequent hiring as a strategic adviser to Hatch, the engineering and consulting firm for resource companies, Baird assured reporters that his sudden move from the public sector to private firms, in the same industries he used to oversee as a government minister, didn't breach any ethical guidelines.[27]

In an unprecedented $250 million deal, a U.S. agrifood company and a Saudi Arabian investment fund took over the former Canadian Wheat Board, formed by

Parliament in 1935 to guarantee Canada's western farmers would get fair prices for their wheat and barley in markets around the world.[28]

And during the following year, the pace of massive wealth transfers between governments and a few select private companies continued to pick up speed. In early 2016, Ivan Glasenberg offloaded a 40% stake of his Glencore Agricultural Products business to the Canadian Pension Plan Fund, selling US$2.5 billion of stocks when the share price bottomed in January at $71 per share.[29]

In a massive policy shift that would surely drive up gold prices even further, Bank of Japan's Governor Haruhiko Kuroda, who had visited Thomas 3 times in 2007-08, announced his readiness to ease monetary policy further in September 2015. He seemed to shrug off growing market concerns that the bank was reaching its limits after an already massive stimulus program.[30]

But in this tumble of dramatic changes on the world stage, the best was yet to come. I laughed out loud when, for his New Year's party for 2017, US President Donald Trump announced that Hussain Sajwani, his new billionaire buddy and business partner from

Dubai, would be a featured guest at the festivities at Trump's Mar-a-Lago estate and golf course in Palm Beach, Florida.

This is the same guy Thomas had mentioned many times, as he continued trying to convince Sajwani, the founder and Chairman of global property development company DAMAC Properties, to invest in his shipment of gold. And I'd met the man three times in Thomas' office back in 2007-08, including the first time Grace hooked him up to the EPFX Bio-feedback Medical Device in 2007. From there, I was his bio-feedback practitioner on his return visits, and he had another 1-hour session on the bio-feedback device with me in early 2008.

And yes, this is the same Hussain Sajwani who Thomas confirmed had committed to buy over $600 million dollars of the gold, when he spoke with me in June 2010. So, Trump's newfound affection for the Saudi billionaire was an attention-getter for me, to say the least.[31]

A few short months later, Sajwani partnered with Trump on a golf course at a luxury development called the Akoya, not far from the heart of Dubai in the United Arab Emirates. "We made a deal with Trump as an organization; they know how to run golf courses," Sajwani told FORBES early in 2016. "We stay away from politics." [32]

While Trump was distracting the West's attention, Turkish president Recep Tayyip Erdogan survived an attempt to overthrow his government. The July 2016 attempted coup, set up by Erdogan and the CIA, supposedly reinforced his supporters, but was in reality a 'false flag' event that tightened Erdogan's grip on power even further.[33]

Erdogan would need that tight-fisted grip on his country's reactions within months, when a Russian SU-24 warplane was shot down over Turkey, supposedly for flying in restricted airspace. This created yet another public-relations disaster for Turkey's leader, especially since, only three years earlier, Erdogan had emphatically declared that a "short-term violation of airspace can never be a pretext for an attack."

There are doubts about whether the Russian plane ever crossed into Turkey's airspace at all, making the takedown appear more like an ambush. The event prompted retired Lt. Gen. Tom McInerney, former U.S. Air Force chief of staff, to tell Fox News, "This airplane was not making any maneuvers to attack the [Turkish] territory." He called the Turkish action "overly aggressive" and concluded that the incident "had to be preplanned."[34]

THOMAS GERMAIN LILLY alias Germain Grisez

Boyd's first day in Dubai, July 17th, 2007 (Thomas, Obeid, Grace, Boyd and Jihad)

And I watched as Bitcoin, another darling of Thomas' market-disrupting bag of tricks, was growing wildly in value... hypothetically, at least. In fact, in May 2017, Japan and South Korea started accepting Bitcoin as a legal currency, and it climbed above $2,000 USD for the first time that same month, triggered by increased demand by Japanese, Korean and Chinese investors.[35][36]

But I'm getting ahead of myself here. Let's look at Bitcoin's role in all of this in the next chapter... along with a staggering list of individual occurrences that are newsworthy on their own merit. More important, they demonstrate a virtual tsunami of corruption and manipulation when you understand the behind-the-scenes connections between these events!

FOOTNOTES:
[24] - summarized from https://en.wikipedia.org/wiki/GoldMoney

[25] - http://www.telegraph.co.uk/finance/12113896/Fear-and-uncertainty-are-causing-market-chaos.html)

26 - summarized from http://money.cnn.com/2016/01/29/investing/dow-january-2016-worst-month/index.html)

27 - https://www.thestar.com/news/canada/2015/06/24/john-baird-snags-yet-another-job.html)

28 - https://www.theglobeandmail.com/report-on-business/us-saudi-firms-to-buy-former-canadian-wheat-board/article23966156/)

29 - http://www.cppib.com/en/public-media/headlines/2016/CPPIB-glencore-2016/)

30 - http://www.todayonline.com/business/boj-has-ample-room-further-easing-kuroda)

31 - http://www.cnn.com/2017/01/02/politics/donald-trump-new-years-eve-speech/index.html)

32 - https://www.forbes.com/sites/kerryadolan/2017/01/03/who-is-trumps-new-years-eve-guest-and-billionaire-pal-from-dubai/)

33 - https://www.theguardian.com/world/2016/jul/23/has-turkeys-attempted-coup-really-made-erdogan-stronger)

34 - summarized from http://fpif.org/turkey-shoot-russian-plane/)

35 - http://www.cnbc.com/2017/04/12/bitcoin-price-rises-japan-russia-regulation.html)

36 - http://www.cnbc.com/2017/05/21/bitcoin-taps-fresh-record-highs-amid-rising-demand-from-japan-china.html

CHAPTER #9 – The dominoes are falling

On the surface, the take-down of Malaysian Airlines flight MH370 is an extreme and shocking act in itself. As a mechanism for concealing the gold heist, the death count alone is unforgivable.

But seeing the passenger list, with at least 20 executives and senior members from the US technological company Freescale Semiconductor on board, I couldn't get one detail out of my mind...

Why were there so many Freescale Semiconductor employees traveling together on the same flight?

It didn't take long to discover the connection.

Four days after the flight MH370 disappeared, a semi-conductor patent was approved by the U.S. Patent Office. The patent is divided in parts of 20% between five starters, one of which was the company itself, Freescale Semiconductor of Austin, Texas. The other four patent owners were Chinese employees of the company; Priding Wang, Zhijun Chen, Cheng and Li Ying Zhijong, all of Suzhou City, China.

The semiconductor company develops microprocessors, sensors, and other technologies, including stand-alone semiconductors that perform dedicated computing functions. It turns out that Freescale has been actively developing chips for military radar for years, specifically in the area of avoiding radar via "cloaking technology" (which has long been one of the objectives of the defense industry).

Here's where the diabolical part shows up...

When MH370 went missing, there were 20 Freescale Semiconductors senior technicians aboard. In the weeks immediately preceding their seminar in Kuala Lumpur, four of these men (all Chinese nationals) had become inventors and patent-rights holders to a one-of-a-kind super microchip - the Kinesis KL02.

One of the chips' abilities, for which the patent had been filed on December 21, 2012, was its highly-advanced 'Cloaking Technology'. The US Patent for the Microchip #8,671,381 B1 was finally issued on March 11th, 2014 -- just three days after MH370 vanished without a trace, with four of its primary patent-holders on board.

If a patent holder dies, the other owners share equally in dividends from the deceased. In this case, when four of the 'Five' (5) patentees were considered deceased, the patentee left alive would get 100% of the patent. As I've mentioned, that remaining patent holder is the company Freescale Semiconductor.

But who owns Freescale Semiconductor? Jacob Rothschild, the British billionaire, owns the company Blackstone, which in turn owns Freescale Semiconductors. So MH370's disappearance left the "5th" and final patent-holder, Freescale majority shareholder Jacob Rothschild, as the single remaining rights holder of the Kinesis KL02 chip.

In other words, by orchestrating the plane's disappearance, the Rothschild family exploited the airliner to gain a full patent on an incredible KL-03 micro-chip. And although a Freescale patent now exists under number US8650327, none of the names listed on the documentation actually appear on the MH370 passenger manifest released by the Malaysian authorities.

As you may know, the Rothschilds are a dynasty of financiers and international bankers of German-Jewish origin, and are one of the most influential families of bankers and financiers in all of Europe (and the world!).[37]

To understand the connection, it's helpful to know the role of 'the Illuminati' in world history.

ILLUMINATI - MAY 1st 1776

On May 1st, 1776, Adam Weishaupt, a German philosopher educated by the Jesuits, founded the Bavarian Illuminati Brotherhood, also known as the Satanic Order of the Illuminati, with plans to achieve a New World Order (NWO).

From the start, the main financier for the NWO's vision has been the House of Rothschild, a German-originated money machine founded by Mayer Amschel Rothschild, who also founded modern international finance in the 1700s. The Illuminati soon infiltrated the Freemason movement, devising a Satanic ideological tool for "natural selection and the survival of the fittest".

The name 'Illuminati', literally "the enlightened ones", refers to Lucifer, the fallen angel also characterized as the 'bringer of Light'. Lucifer is traditionally associated with the attributes Pride, Deception, and Impermanence.

Zionism, also a fundamental part of the NWO's vision, was founded in 1897 by Theodor Herzi.
The invention of Israel, financed and created as a result of the Zionist declaration and ideology, was another Rothschild crusade, brought about through the brutal colonization of Palestine and its indigenous peoples, whether Christians, Muslims or Arab Jews.

In effect, the Rothschilds have been the most active players in the creation of the State of Israel, as one of the originators of the Zionist movement itself.

Visibly, the most potent symbols of the Illuminati's power are the "All Seeing Eye", the hierarchical Egyptian Pyramid and the Devil Horn sign (frequently seen in popular culture today as a wide, two-fingered 'salute' displaying the upright index and pinky fingers). The symbols are also famous with powerful Hollywood and Western pop stars and politicians, who glorify 'pornography', sexual behavior, attitude and senseless violence as a pervasive, not-so-subtle attack to corrupt people's behavior from an early age.

The Satanic vision of the New World Order persists through the alliances of the secretive Round Table organization, first established in London during the late 1900's by Cecil Rhodes, a Supremacist 'Aryan' known as the savage British Imperialist of South Africa (which, not coincidentally, included diamond-rich Zimbabwe). Since then, the Order of Skull and Bones, the CFR, TC, and Bilderberg Group secret societies together are known as the 'Round Table' organization, playing a key part in the day-to-day manipulation of politics, banking, business, education, and the Military, namely NATO.

Rhodes, who was instrumental in the British takeover of South Africa, said the goal of the 'Round Table' was the creation of a World Government that would be controlled by
Britain. The inner elite of the 'Round Table' in the USA and UK were key administration members of World War I, and are believed to have engineered the circumstances that led to both World War I and World War II, complete with the Zionist collaborations with Nazi Germany.

Given their history, the Rothschilds and the Rockerfellers can be seen as the two most powerful families in the world, and possibly the most evil. They are behind the scenes of the world's political arenas; for example, Obama was funded and nurtured by them years in advance, along with countless other candidates, past and present. They controlled and profited widely from most (if not all) major wars, even including the Russian Revolution.

Their money and power is behind the civil unrest in Syria, Ukraine, Egypt and Venezuela, with many other countries in the pipeline. They control Big Pharma, using countless toxic vaccines as their power over life and death around the world.

Plus, the Illuminati are behind the creation of genetically-engineered GMO products, and deliberate oil tanker spillages in the hundreds. They are behind the geo-toxic engineering of our skies, with chem trails and more.

As you can see, the Illuminati control the land, sea and air. They have already created genocide into the billions... and they have not finished yet. Ultimate control over us is their unrelenting goal.[38]

For evidence of the Illuminati's continuing influence in today's world (with a particularly relevant modern connection), let's look at the 1965 involvement of the CIA and Lolo Soetoro – US President Barack Obama's stepfather.

President Obama's own work for Business International Corporation in 1983, dovetails with CIA espionage activities conducted by his mother, Stanley Ann Dunham (for further details, try a Google search for "Obama – a CIA creation"). BIC is a CIA front that conducted seminars with the world's most powerful leaders, and used journalists as agents abroad,

Soetero's work supported the 1960s post-coup takeover of Indonesia, on behalf of a number of CIA front operations that included the U.S. Agency for International Development (USAID), the Ford Foundation, and the East-West Center at the University of Hawaii.

Incidentally, Ann Dunham married Lolo Soetoro (Obama's stepfather), after they met at the East-West Center in Hawaii.

In 1965, Lolo Soetoro was called back from Hawaii by General Suharto, serving as a senior army officer in the Indonesian military to help overthrow President Sukarno by launching a bloody CIA-backed genocide.

Suharto consolidated his power in 1966, the same year that Barack Obama's real father Obama Sr., with his friend Mboya, helped to rally pro-U.S. pan-African support for the CIA's overthrow of Kwame Nkrumah of Ghana. Like Sukarno, Kwame Nkrumah was one of the "Initiate of five" founding members of the Asia-Africa Non-Aligned Movement (NAM).[39]

Obama releasing DHS (Department of Homeland Security) Prisoners:
6,000 prisoners being released early under new federal rules
October 30th 2015

More than 6,000 prisoners will be released into their communities over the next several days as part of the federal government's retroactive sentencing reductions for nonviolent drug offenders, CBS News correspondent Paula Reid reports.

Under the program, about 50,000 prisoners serving time for low-level offenses are eligible for a sentence reduction and early release. The federal sentencing reductions officially went into effect Friday.
Up to 40,000 more prisoners may be eligible for early release under this program.
Announcing the new rules last year, then-Attorney General Eric Holder said the Justice Department supported a "balanced approach" to reduce sentences for certain inmates.

"This is a milestone in the effort to make more efficient use of our law enforcement resources and to ease the burden on our overcrowded prison system," Holder said at the time.

In July, the White House announce that President Obama had commuted the prison sentences

From http://www.cbsnews.com/news/6000-prisoners-released-early-under-new-federal-rules/

Anyway, back to our story... the domino-like array of world events and massive wealth transfers showing up to support this New World Order.

Amid growing controversy, the Canadian government solidified a $14.8 billion arms deal with Saudi Arabia in February 2014, by far the largest military exports contract in Canadian history. As a result, General Dynamics Land Systems now has a 15-year contract to manufacture light-armoured military vehicles for the desert kingdom.

To put the Saudi arms deal in context, the total combined value of all Canadian military exports during the year the deal was signed amounted to $15.5 billion. So the agreement made up more than 90 per cent of the country's military export commitments that year.

Why is this a problem? Because of Saudi Arabia's questionable human rights record, potentially putting the Canadian government in violation of its own arms-trading regulations. For example, in January 2014, the United Nations released a report documenting human rights violations in the Saudi-led bombing campaign aimed at rebel Houthi forces in neighbouring Yemen. The report accused the Arab kingdom of violating international humanitarian laws by intentionally attacking civilian targets.[40]

Announced by Canada's Globe and Mail newspaper in May 2016, Barrick Gold founder Peter Munk is selling his last significant investment, Port Montenegro, the super yacht marina and resort that he built as a Mediterranean rival to Cannes, to Investment Corp. of Dubai.. The price for the resort, located on a former Serbian naval base on the Bay of Kotor, on the Adriatic Sea, is thought to be $290 million or more, though the seller and buyer are not expected to disclose the amount. [41]

In what seems to be a growing trend with politicians around the world, the public is in the dark about what Saskatchewan cabinet ministers' numbered companies are up to. And those politicians are not required to tell the public what assets those firms hold, or what they do.

For example, on April 21, 2017, Canada's CBC News revealed that Saskatchewan's Premier Brad Wall invested in Alberta energy companies he tried to lure to Saskatchewan, Experts say he should have cleared letters to Alberta companies with the province's conflict commissioner first, since out-of-province donations are not democratic or ethical.

In several cases, Saskatchewan cabinet ministers who are directors or shareholders in numbered or holding companies haven't publicly revealed what assets those companies actually hold or what those companies do. Unfortunately, a lack of public information can lead to a lack of trust by the public.[42]

And on June 22 and 23, 2016 (the same day as BREXIT was happening in Europe), the Earl and Countess of Wessex, Prince Edward and Sophie, were on a visit to Regina, Saskatchewan.[43]

Now here's a couple of examples of just how huge this big-money 'shell game' actually is, both appearing in October 2016.

First off, the head of the Canada Pension Plan Investment Board faced lawmakers for the first time in 14 years, as Prime Minister Justin Trudeau's government finalized a trillion-dollar expansion of one of the world's largest public pension funds. The new plan, rolled out from 2019-2025, would leave the fund on pace to reach $2 trillion by 2045, doubling the value of the original program.[44]

Then, as announced at RCMP headquarters in Regina, Saskatchewan in October 2016, Canada's Royal Canadian Mounted Police offered an apology and a $100 million dollar pay off as compensation for harassment and sexual abuse against female members. What a great way to keep it in the family! [45]

Remembering that Thomas Lilly also had a website that sold 'super yachts' with Bitcoin, this news item caught my eye...

On July 9th, 2011, Montenagro hosted billionaire Nat Rotchschild's birthday bash. Barrick Gold CEO Peter Munk joked about what can you give a billionaire who has everything, adding "Nat doesn't need anything, but the BEST presents in his life are the success of his business." From December 2015-July 6th, 2016, Barrick Gold stock shares on the TSX went from $8.00 to $30. [46]

In April 2016, Eric Sprott (Thomas' associate and Canada's gold expert), bet millions on gold producer Newmarket Gold Inc, a junior producer which operates three mines in Australia, as the price of gold sat stubbornly at $1200.00 (US) an ounce.[47]

When I first googled Thomas Lilly Kazansky after MH370 went missing in March 2014, Nigel Farage was the person who forwarded my message from the FOREX website to Thomas.
Thomas had Nigel call me in June 2014, asking if I wanted to invest with him, but I declined (as I did not trust Thomas).

Nigel Farage, who led BREXIT, has become one of Britain's most successful politicians.[48]

By June 23rd, 2016 (the day BREXIT happened in Europe), the price of gold had reached $1,380 US an ounce! You probably know that BREXIT is a commonly used term for the United Kingdom's withdrawal from the European Union (EU), following a government-led referendum vote held in the same year. The UK is set to leave by April 2019.

A week after BREXIT, the elite started selling off their gold investments, and started buying Bitcoin, Monero, Ethereum,

ETC Classic as well as other digital cryptocurrencies.

Meanwhile, keeping up with his mission to sweep the former government's influence on his totalitarian regime (and driving up the price of gold in the process), President Erdogan of Turkey fired hundreds of senior military staff serving at NATO in Europe and the United States following July's coup attempt in July of 2016, broadening a purge to include some of the armed forces' best-trained officials.

Erdogan defended the suspension of 28 mayors over alleged links to Kurdish militants, and fired hundreds of senior military staff serving at NATO in Europe and US. In total, Turkey's president fired or detained 50,000 generals, judges, teachers, police, and others. About 400 military envoys have been fired so far: most were dismissed from service, arrested and imprisoned, according to a Turkish military official at NATO.[49]

In fact, a lot has been going on with Turkey on the world stage lately...

Turkish President Recep Erdogan and his wife Emine Erdogan attended the Democracy and Martyrs Rally, organized by him and supported by the ruling AK Party (AKP), oppositions Republican People's Party (CHP) and Nationalist Movement Party (MHP), to protest against last month's failed military coup attempt, in Istanbul, Turkey, August 7, 2016

Turkish officials say the scale of the crackdown, which has broad popular support at home, is justified by the gravity of events on July 15, when rogue soldiers commandeered tanks, fighter jets and helicopters, bombing parliament and government buildings in their attempt to seize power. More than 240 people, many of them civilians, were killed.

But the dismissals at NATO raise questions about Turkey's strategy after the failed coup, as Erdogan seeks closer ties with the alliance's Cold War foe Russia. Turkey is a vital ally to the West in the war against Islamic State militants, and in tackling Europe's migrant crisis. It is also one of the main troop contributors to NATO's training mission in Afghanistan.

Of the 50 military staff posted to the Turkish delegation at NATO's headquarters in Brussels, only nine remain, according to the Turkish official who spoke to Reuters. Turkish military representatives were not present in recent meetings. "Turkey is not at the table," the official said.[50]

To summarize this information regarding Obama releasing prisoners and Turkey firing military staff, it appears to me that these released prisoners and future released prisoners from the USA's DHS (Department of Homeland Securities) are flown over to Turkey and trained to fight for ISIS.

Do you believe in coincidences? Neither do I. That's why it's important to remember that, during the horrific attacks in New York on 9/11 in 2001, Building 7 also contained tons of gold certificates and all the records and archives for the Department of Homeland Security, who also control all the prisons in the USA. When Thomas and the Swiss Jews created 9/11 more than 15 years ago, they made sure that Building 7 collapsed, destroying all DHS records and archives, so there was no way of tracing these criminals.

Bilal Erdogan, the man who funds ISIS

Prior to 2015, the son of Turkey's president, Bilal Erdogan, was found to be conducting an illegal cash-for-oil transfer between Turkey's ruling family and the Islamic State. Ultimately, the highly illegal bilateral trade, similar to deals Marc Reich had set up with

Iran during the 90's, continued for almost two years to support the terrorist organization.

Eventually, after the expansion of Russian bombing campaigns designed to cut off the main trade routes between Turkey and Islamic State oil producers, they began diminishing and then appeared to stop entirely. But further evidence released on WikiLeaks showed that Turkish president Recep Erdogan's son-in-law, Berat Albayrak, appeared to be continuing those 'sinister relations' between Erdogan and ISIS, through direct involvement with the monopolistic oil company Powertrans, which was still importing oil from the Isis land in Northern Iraq to Turkey in September 2015.

That's why, when the Russian SU-24 military aircraft was shot down by Turkish forces on November 24, 2015, accusations against the Turkish government - and Albayrak, specifically - became even more intense. Supporting their allegations, Russia even delivered satellite images revealing the routes of the oil from the ISIS grounds to Turkey, which paralleled similar research conducted by the ministry of Foreign Affairs of Norway. And the American government has also mentioned their awareness that the ISIS' oil ends up in Turkey.[51]

More on Erdogan's background, Donmeh connections, and why that's important:

The Dönmeh Jews: House of Saud Connections! Zionist Control Over Saudi Arabia.

Saudi Arabia is run by a corrupt and despotic Dönmeh Jewish family [52]

Crypto-Jew Recep Erdogan: Restoration of the Osman Empire with Western Technology.

Jewish control of Turkey's military, and info on the Flotilla murders [53]

Modern Turkey: a secret Zionist state controlled by the Dönmeh

Turkey's support of ISIS is more understandable. Turkey is run by secret Jews and serves the Zionist goal of a greater Israel. Like Bolsheviks and Zionists, the Dönmeh are Illuminati, i.e. Satanists, Freemasons. Erdogan is a crypto Jew.[54]

Exposing the Mossad, George Soros & Israel's role in MH370's twin jet found in Tel Aviv

When investigative journalist Christopher Bollyn, who previously exposed Israel's hand behind the 911 attacks, revealed eyewitness reports from a network of plane watchers in Europe and in Israel, it became apparent that an identical production model of the Malaysian Airlines Boeing 777 was being kept out of regular service inside a hangar at Tel Aviv Airport.

It's common knowledge in the industry that Seattle-based Boeing assembles aircraft in pairs as its standard practice. But how was one jet leased by Malaysia's national carrier, while the matching plane was secretly turned over to the Israeli government without a purchase order from state-run EL AL airlines?

The answer is, those twin Boeing jets were delivered to a middleman in October 2013, a third-party company whose top manager has a longtime connection with business magnate George Soros. The middleman delivered one of the aircraft to Malaysian Airlines in November.

Coincidentally (and you know my true feelings on that word), the timing corresponds with the appointment of Joanne McGuire, a veteran of Lockheed Martin Space Division executive, to the board of directors of Freescale Semiconductors. Remember that company, involved in the design of the Kinesis KL02 microchip, whose staffers were aboard MH370 when it left Kuala Lumpur just before it disappeared? The plan went like clockwork.[55]

More key players in the heist

Since I mentioned George Soros, let me give you a little more background on the Hungarian-born investor and business tycoon. It seems that Soros believed he was anointed by God. "I fancied myself as some kind of god," Soros once wrote. "If truth be known, I carried some rather potent messianic fantasies with me from childhood, which I felt I had to control, otherwise they might get me in trouble."[56]

Who is Abdol Moabery?

Back in 2010, Thomas Lilly had arranged for "Marli Thomas" to purchase the LIFE System from me, after I'd already left Dubai and had been out of contact with him for some time. Marli, the attractive blonde with an English accent who supposably owned 'Sparkles' Health Clinic in the Dubai Mall, told me her boyfriend was from Fort Lauderdale, Florida. Then she began showing me pictures of her so-called boyfriend who must have been related to Abdol Moabery, trying to get a reaction from me.

Thomas had set me up!

Although I didn't know this at the time, I now recognize Marli Thomas as Caroline Hyde, a news anchor with Bloomberg. And I've since discovered that the twin Boeing jets were sold to GA Telesis, an aircraft leasing and service company, based in Ft. Lauderdale, Florida. The owner of GAT is Abdol Moabery, the son of Iranian immigrants in the posh Woodlawn Hills superb of Los Angeles.

Before and after September 2001, Moabery was executive manager of electronic aircraft monitoring device manufacturer Skywatch (who counted among its partners New York City Mayor Rudolf Giuliani). Six months after 911, Moabery left Skywatch to start up GA Telesis in Ft. Lauderdale, Florida. Prior to his term at Skywatch, Moabery served in the US Navy, and then worked in executive positions for two Soros-owned aviation companies, Aviation Systems International and C-S Aviation.[57]

Boeing Corp's vice-president, Ralph "Skip" Boyce

Back in 2007-08, Thomas used to get calls from a Skip Boyce, who it turns out was Boeing Corporation's Vice-President for

Southeast Asia. He's also the former US Ambassador to Jakarta and Bangkok.

Here's more history on Boyce, direct from http://rense.com/general96/role.html ...

> Ambassador "Boyz" was the de facto dean of American envoys in Southeast Asia when anti-pedophile activist Sean Parlaman jumped off his apartment balcony in Pattaya, Thailand, according to local police on the pedophile payroll. His protection of high-ranking pedophiles in the State Department and Congress coincided with the discovery of the skeletons of 500 Indonesian boys inside a cave in Bali and intimidation of a Cambodian orphanage as a recruiting ground for sex slaves whose average age was 10 years old.
>
> Israel is neck-deep in intrigue across Asia, including nuclear deals with North Korea and Japan. The role of Israeli intelligence assets inside Muslim-dominated Malaysia is a long-running issue that involves strings of stay-behind agents left by the British colonial authority. These underground networks are descended from two strands of Jewish administrators and merchants in colonial Malaya.

First are those who have origins in the Ottoman Empire and migrated under Britain's favourable policy toward the Donmeh Jews (hidden Jews inside the Islamic community across the Arab realm, Turkey and Iran) during the Ataturk period.

Second are Baghdadi Jews involved in the Opium trade. More recent recruits are ordinary bureaucrats and military officers who are in need of a handful of shekels to pay their gambling debts.[58]

The Bilderberg Group

In 1954,"the most powerful men in the world met for the first time" in Osterbeek, Netherlands, "debated the future of the world," and decided to meet annually in secret. They called themselves the Bilderberg Group with a membership representing a who's who of the world power elites, mostly from America, Canada and Western Europe. with family names like David Rockerfeller, Henry Kissinger, Bill Clinton, Gordon Brown, Angela Merkel, Alan Greenspan, Ben Bernanke, Larry Summers, Tin Geithner, Lloyd Blankfein, George Soros, Dunald Rumsfeld, Rupert Murdock, other heads of state, influential senators, congressmen, and parliamentarians, Pentagon and NATO brass, members of European royalty, selected media figures and invited others - some quietly like Barack Obama and many of his top officials. Always represented are top figures from the Council of Foreign Relations 9CFR), IMF, World Bank, Trilateral Commission, EU, and powerful central bankers from the Federal Reserve, the ECB's Jean Claude Trichet, and the Bank of Englands Melvyn King.

For over half a century, no agenda or discussion topics become public nor is there any press coverage allowed. The few invited fourth estate attendees and their bosses are sworn to secrecy. Whatever it's early mission, the group is now "a shadow world government threatening to take away our right to direct our own destinies a disturbing reality" very much harming the public welfare. Bilderbergers want to supplant individual nation-state sovereignty with an all-powerful global government, corporate controlled, and check-mated by militarized enforcement. Along with military dominance, controlling the world's money is crucial for with it comes absolute control as the powerful 19th century Rothschild family understood. "Give me control of a nation's money and I care not who makes its laws"[59]

More on Thomas Germain Lilly

I believe Thomas was part of the Eli Lilly Pharmaceuticals family, and that he cashed in some of his Bitcoins in the fall of 2016 (as the price of Bitcoins dropped from $1,500 down to $1,000), using the money to buy stock in Boehringer, which had the monopoly on vaccinations.

For example, notice these comments I found in a recent article on Eli Lilly's purchase of pet vaccines from Boehringer for $985 Million in October 2016, as reported by IndyStar Washington Bureau's Maureen Groppe on January 31, 2017:

Lilly CEO encouraged by meeting with Trump

Three weeks after Donald Trump accused drug companies of getting away with murder on drug prices, Eli Lilly CEO David Ricks came away encouraged from a meeting he and other pharmaceutical executives had Tuesday with the new president.

"I was impressed with the president's appreciation for what our industry is, which is really a crown jewel of American enterprise," Ricks said in an earnings call with Wall Street analysts.

"We talked about a number of his policy proposals which, on balance, I think would be very good for us," he said later in an interview with IndyStar.[60]

NOVEMBER , 2017
Trump Chooses "Eli Lilly", Alex Azar for Health and Human Services Secretary
By EILEEN SULLIVAN and MICHAEL D. SHEARNOV.

WASHINGTON — President Trump nominated a pharmaceutical executive to be the next secretary of the Health and Human Services Department.

The nominee, Alex M. Azar II, served as a deputy at the department under former President George W. Bush. Until January, he was the head of pharmaceutical company "Eli Lilly's" , United States division.

Mr. Trump made his announcement in a Twitter post while traveling in Asia.

Imagine that !!!   ELI LILLY... Thomas's family company... everything unfolding on schedule...

I trust everyone understands as written in my book... Last year , Bitcoin tumbled from $1500.00 down to $1,000.00 , this is when Eli

Lilly bought Boehringer... now ELI LILLY has control of vaccinations... which is all part of the sterilization and de-populization plan. 61

By 2016, it was becoming obvious to me that one of the reasons they created ISIS, had Turkey's President Erdogan shoot down the Russian SU-24 fighter jet at the end of November 2015, and had not raised interest rates for 70 months, was in order to drive the price of gold back up!

So many of the world's 'disasters' and terrorist events had the same purpose at their core. During 2015, a relentless series of attacks in France grabbed headlines around the world again and again, including:

- the January 2015 attacks on Charlie Hebdo offices and a Jewish supermarket in Paris that killed 17 people and wounded 22
- a series of coordinated terrorist attacks in November 2015, with three suicide bombers who struck outside the Stade de France in Saint-Denis, several mass shootings (plus a suicide bombing) at cafés and restaurants, followed by
- another mass shooting at the Bataclan theatre

Not surprisingly, the Paris attacks had the subsequent effect of driving up the price of gold too, as did international incidents like the 2016 Brussels bombings and the previously-mentioned Turkish Air Force F-16 shoot-down of a Russian Sukhoi Su-24M attack aircraft near the Syria–Turkey border on 24 November 2015.

As an added boost to global gold prices, the plotters were ready to support their positions to grow their profits. On May 17, 2016, George Soros bought a US$263.7 million stake in Barrick Gold Corp, the world's largest gold miner, after its stock had bottomed out the previous October at a share price below $8.

Needless to say, huge amounts of money were being made on Gold, Silver and the British pound as a result of Brexit. I'd say it's pretty easy to make billions when your buddies control the voting results!

Check out this news item as reported by Bloomberg's Nariman Gizitdinov from July 2016, and you'll see what I mean...

Brexit Bet Makes Kazakhstan Better Than Soros

> Move over George Soros, Kazakhstan is claiming the title as the most prescient speculator in the pound.
>
> The former Soviet republic's central bank bet against the currency before Britain's surprise decision to leave the European Union last month, Governor Daniyar Akishev said in an interview Friday. Soros, who famously broke the Bank of England in 1992, netting a profit of $1 billion, didn't repeat that wager in the historic Brexit referendum, according to a spokesman.[62]

Not to be outdone, the Rothschilds announced in August, 2016 that they'd be selling all their US dollars and buying physical gold, silver and Bitcoin, calling it "The Biggest Monetary Experiment in the History of the World."[63]

What would Donmeh Jews want with blood?

"The Freemason lodges are witchcraft gatherings of the Children of Israel. One of the ceremonies, for instance if someone wants to be accepted as a new member, or rise in rank... he has to somehow bring one of his sons or daughters, or his wife or one of his male or female relatives, and put them on the table and slaughter them with his own hands as a sacrifice to Satan, in order to rise in the ranks of the Freemasons. My brothers, this exists until today."[64]

Blood libel
From Wikipedia, the free encyclopedia

Blood libel (also **blood accusation**)[1][2] is an accusation[3][4][5] that Jews kidnapped and murdered the children of Christians in order to use their blood as part of their religious rituals during Jewish holidays.[1][2][6]

Historically, these claims – alongside those of well poisoning and host desecration – have been a major theme of the persecution of Jews in Europe.[4]

Blood libels typically say that Jews require human blood for the baking of matzos for Passover.

https://en.wikipedia.org/wiki/Blood_libel

And to back up the blood reference above with an astonishing coincidence, have you noticed what you find when you cross-reference the number 79 (the atomic number of gold) with its appearance in the Bible?

Here's what Chapter 79 of the Psalms has to say, from an easy-to-find online reference by the US Conference of Catholic Bishops

> Psalms, Chapter 79 - A psalm of Asaph
>
> O God, the nations have invaded your inheritance;
> they have defiled your holy temple;
> they have laid Jerusalem in ruins.a
> **"They have left the corpses of your servants as food for the birds of the sky, the flesh of those devoted to you for the beasts of the earth."**
> **"They have poured out their blood like water all around Jerusalem,"**
> and no one is left to do the burying.
> "Where is their God?"
> Before our eyes make known to the nations **that you avenge the blood of your servants which has been poured out.**
> Let the groaning of the imprisoned come in before you; in accord with the greatness of your arm preserve those doomed to die.[65]

Don't doubt that the events I've described are extremely relevant today, especially with respect to current events in Russia,

Kazakhstan and the Middle East. Incidentally, notice the number of Catholic communities in Kazakhstan as of February 2013...

Pope Welcomes Kazakhstan's Efforts to Promote Inter-Religious Understanding

Pope Benedict XVI welcomed the efforts of President Nursultan Nazarbayev to promote inter-religious and inter-cultural understanding on Feb. 6 and gave his apostolic blessing to Kazakhstan's initiatives in this field.

"By a twist of fate Kazakhstan became the second home for thousands of Catholics. Today, 79 Catholic communities operate in the country," Mami said.[66]

While it may seem encouraging to see Kazakhstan developing an "inter-religious understanding", there's more going on than meets the eye of casual observers. Check out the observations I found in this article (I've edited some of the outdated references, since it was originally posted in 2009). This is also well worth looking into today, to see further results from Nazarbayev's line of thinking!

Is Kazakhstan the "Seat of Satan"?

Kazakhstan has good relations with Israel. President Nazarbayev presides over what has been called one of the most corrupt satanic regimes in central Asia. Known to have rubbed elbows with Bill Clinton, George W. Bush, and even Dick Cheney, Nazarbayev made international headlines in 2009 when he proposed a single world currency.

Astana (SATAAN), the first capital of New World Order, is being built in the 21st century, and as Kazakhstan's president, Nursultan Nazarbayev's vision, it perfectly represents where the world is headed. The city, being built from scratch in a remote and deserted area of the Asian steppes, is astonishing. It's a futuristic occult capital, embracing the New World Order while celebrating Sun Worship, the most ancient religion known to man.

Conceived by Britain's most prolific architect, Lord Norman Forster, this giant pyramid is dedicated to "the renunciation of violence" and "to bring together the world's religions". Norman Foster has said that the building has no recognizable religious symbols, to permit the harmonious reunification of confessions. In reality, the pyramid is a temple for the occultist's only 'true' religion: Sun worship.

The Republic of Kazakhstan in Central Asia is in the process of building the world's first "Alien Embassy" according to some local media reports. Apparently, the authorities have already allocated a large plot of land in the city of Almaty for this ambitious project.

Kazakhstan's government believes open contact with aliens is imminent, and by being the first nation to specifically create such facilities, they are convinced they will reap enormous financial and economic rewards. The Kazakhstan government also sees this as a chance to demonstrate their nation's forward thinking policies.[67]

I guess even with the mindset and beliefs of Kazakhstan's president, the country may serve a strategic purpose for some global powers... but to what ends?

A U.S. partnership with Kazakhstan can keep Chinese and Russian ambitions in check

The November 30, 2016 telephone call between President-elect Donald J. Trump and President Nursultan Nazarbayev of Kazakhstan was a shocker, concentrates on building relationships with key countries in key regions. Kazakhstan is in the heart of Eurasia, bordering both Russia and China: the two main headaches of American foreign policy.[68]

Oops... maybe I've answered my own question above... especially since it points to more motivations behind the Malaysian Airlines disasters. But if this is the way these groups operate, are the results we're seeing actually the results we're wanting?

(The following article is so powerful, I've included it here in its entirety, with thanks to http://www.texemarrs.com/082014/jews_rule_world_special_article.htm)

Satanic Jews Revenge: Two Malaysian Airliners Missing or Destroyed

The Jewish elite were outraged when in 2001, Prime Minister Mahatir of the economically prosperous Southeast Asian nation of Malaysia bravely stood up and told a large global conference of leaders, "The Jews rule the world."

The assembled leaders were stunned to hear one of their own fearlessly stand up to Israel and the Jews. "They rule by proxy," said Prime Minister Mahatir. Though they are only a small group, he explained, "The Jews have now gained control of the most powerful countries and they, the tiny community, have become a world power."

Mahatir warned that the few countries in the world still free of Zionist control must fight back and be intelligent in confronting them. "We need guns and rockets, bombs and warplanes," he said, and "tanks and warships for our defense."

In the guise of a so-called "War on Terrorism," said Mahatir, the Zionist Jews now "attack and kill us, invade our lands, bring down our governments."

Mahatir's disclosure and warning brought the world's Jewish-controlled media down on his head. The truth was unveiled, and the Jews were boiling in anger. The Mossad's official motto is By Way of Deception, and here the Malaysian Prime Minister had publicly branded the Jews for what they are. No longer could they silently and stealthily kill, control, and dominate. Their ruthless and brutal conduct was no longer a secret.

Jews Seek Revenge

And so the Jews, who are proven to be insanely methodical and coldly calculating in seeking revenge, could naturally be expected to attack and punish Malaysia. It was only a matter of time and opportunity.
Malaysian Airlines Reputation Tarnished

Malaysian Airlines is now ruined. Few wish to ride this company's once highly praised jet aircraft. What a blow to Malaysia and its reputation. Israel has taken its revenge, simultaneously killing two birds at once, smearing both Malaysia and its historic enemy, a free and independent Christian Russia.

Remember what I revealed first here, that Ukraine is ancient Khazaria, original homeland for the fake "Jews" who now populate both Israel and the U.S.A.

Goal: A Jewish, New World Order

This is the Jews' horrible goal, and they believe that America's leaders are too greedy and fearful to stop them. Indeed, the American elite are helping them in their ungodly quest for a Jewish New World Order. The Jews are also convinced that the people of America are too stupid to know what is happening. By way of Deception is the Israeli Mossad motto. By proxy the Jews do indeed rule the world. And the once, great America is today their muddy footstool.[69]

And this leaked report from March 18, 2014, Israel acknowledges that Jews are in fact Khazars.

Khazars - A Warlike Turkic People— and a Mystery

It is well known that, sometime in the eighth to ninth centuries, the Khazars, a warlike Turkic people, converted to Judaism and ruled over a vast domain in what became southern Russia and Ukraine.

Many have speculated that the Khazars became the ancestors of Ashkenazi Jews. In 2012, Israeli researcher Eran Elhaik published a study claiming to prove that Khazar ancestry is the single largest element in the Ashkenazi gene pool. Israel seems finally to have thrown in the towel, acknowledging that European Jews are in fact Khazars.[70]

Finally, to tie these observations together, remember that Simon Elliot, the man I met in Dubai as Al-Baghdadi, is the son of Jewish parents and a Mossad agent. It's impossible to imagine those facts don't play a part in his involvement with Thomas Lilly, the gold heist, and the mass murders of hundreds of people on the Malaysian Airlines flights. In the next chapter, we'll see more proof of how the numbers all add up.

FOOTNOTES:

[37] - summarized with details from http://beforeitsnews.com/politics/2014/03/rothschild-takes-down-malaysian-airliner-mh370-to-gain-rights-to-a-semiconductor-patent-getting-rid-of-those-who-stood-in-his-way-2607888.html

[38] - https://en.wikipedia.org/wiki/Adam_Weishaupt

39 - summarized from
http://www.voltairenet.org/article166741.html and

http://www.voltairenet.org/article166759.html

40 - summarized from
http://www.ctvnews.ca/politics/canada-s-arms-deal-with-saudi-arabia-what-to-know-1.2858230

41 - https://www.theglobeandmail.com/report-on-business/international-business/european-business/mining-magnate-peter-munk-selling-superyacht-marina-in-montenegro/article29817069/

42 -
http://www.cbc.ca/news/canada/saskatchewan/holding-companies-saskatchewan-cabinet-ministers-1.4078627

43 -
http://www.cbc.ca/news/canada/saskatchewan/prince-edward-and-sophie-s-visit-to-regina-2016-1.3649016

44 - http://business.financialpost.com/executive/c-suite/canada-pension-chief-to-testify-amid-trillion-dollar-boost/wcm/9d91792f-3f78-40a8-8736-b79b9d651342

45 - http://www.cbc.ca/news/politics/rcmp-paulson-compensation-harassment-1.3793785

46 -
http://www.telegraph.co.uk/news/worldnews/europe/montenegro/8627610/Montenegro-hosts-billionaire-Nat-Rothschilds-birthday-bash.html

47 - summarized with details from
https://www.theglobeandmail.com/globe-investor/investment-ideas/analysts-like-newmarket-

the-popular-new-kid-in-the-gold-industry/article29531653/

48 - https://www.ft.com/content/02cad03a-844f-11e4-bae9-00144feabdc0?mhq5j=e2

49 - summarized with details from http://www.reuters.com/article/us-turkey-nato-exclusive-idUSKCN12C16Q

50 - http://uk.reuters.com/article/uk-turkey-nato-exclusive-idUKKCN12C16Z

51 - summarized with details from http://www.zerohedge.com/news/2016-12-05/wikileaks-documents-reveal-sinister-relations-between-erdogan-and-isis?page=1

52 - https://socioecohistory.wordpress.com/2015/04/14/the-donmeh-jews-house-of-saud-connections-zionist-control-over-saudi-arabia-part-2/

53 - http://new.euro-med.dk/20151207-crypto-jew-recep-erdogan-restoration-of-the-osman-empire-with-western-technology.php

54 - https://www.henrymakow.com/2015/11/modern-turkey-a-secret-zionist.html

55 - summarized with details from http://rense.com/general96/role.html

56 - summarized with details from http://articles.latimes.com/2004/oct/04/opinion/oe-ehrenfeld4

57 - includes summarized details from http://rense.com/general96/role.html

58 - http://rense.com/general96/role.html

59 - summarized from Stephen Lendman's review of Daniel Estulin's book "The True Story of the Bilderberg Group" found at http://www.globalresearch.ca/the-true-story-of-the-bilderberg-group-and-what-they-may-be-planning-now/13808

60 - http://www.indystar.com/story/money/2017/01/31/lilly-ceo-joins-pharmacuetical-chiefs-meeting-trump/97275982/

61 - https://www.nytimes.com/2017/11/13/us/politics/alex-azar-health-human-services-trump.html

62 - https://www.bloomberg.com/news/articles/2016-07-08/kazakhstan-beats-soros-after-dumping-pounds-on-day-before-brexit

63 - http://www.zerohedge.com/news/2016-08-16/lord-rothschild-greatest-experiment-monetary-policy-history-world

64 - summarized from http://www.jerusalemonline.com/news/middle-east/israeli-palestinian-relations/al-aqsa-mosque-lecture-the-jews-use-childrens-blood-for-passover-matzos-13903?amp=1

65 - http://www.usccb.org/bible/psalms/79

66 - http://astanatimes.com/2013/02/pope-welcomes-kazakhstans-efforts-to-promote-inter-religious-understanding/

[67] - summarized from https://seeker401.wordpress.com/2009/06/30/is-kazakhstan-the-seat-of-satan/

[68] - from http://nationalinterest.org/feature/the-world-frets-over-the-taiwan-call-trumps-talk-kazakhstan-18659

[69] - from http://www.texemarrs.com/082014/jews_rule_world_special_article.htm

[70] - summarized from http://blogs.timesofisrael.com/leaked-report-israel-acknowledges-jews-in-fact-khazars-secret-plan-for-reverse-migration-to-ukraine/

CHAPTER #10 – The tale of the numbers: 5, 555 & 17

To understand how so many of these events and connections came to be obvious to me in hindsight, it's helpful to realize the importance of the numbers involved – with their prominence throughout history, philosophy and the world's religions. We're going to go a little heavy on the numerology here too, but rest assured that it will all add up to more answers, too (pun intended).

To begin, many experts believe that the number 5 is considered sacred in context of Lord Shiva.[71]

> Different reasons to this theory include the idea that Lord Shiva's body consists of five mantras, called 'Panchabramans', namely Sadyojata, Vamadeva, Aghora, Tatpurusa and Isana. These five mantras represent the five faces of Lord

Shiva, and are often associated with the five senses, the five elements, the five organs of perception and the five organs of action. It is said that the five elements are the five senses of Lord Shiva, with Sky being his ears, wind being his body, fire represented by his eyes, water as his tongue and land as his nose.

Some experts also say that Lord Shiva was five faced, inspiring the evolution of the five swaras (musical notes) of Carnatic music. The most common mantra of Lord Shiva, 'Om Namah Shivay', also has five syllables, another manifestation of the sacred number.

Also, consider the five temples in southern India where Lord Shiva has his throne, namely:

1. Kanaka Sabhai (golden throne) – Chidambaram
2. Velli Sabhai (silver throne) – Madurai
3. Ratna Sabhai (gem throne) – Tiruvalangadu
4. Taamira Sabhai (copper throne) – Tirunelveli
5. Chitra Sabhai (Artistic throne) – Tirukkuttralam

These are all referred to as 'Sabhas', and considered the throne or seat where a ruler, king or judge sits to hear the prayers and grievances of the people.

The number 555

Now, accentuating the power of the number '5', let's consider how '555' signifies the energy of change. Traditionally, it's a sign of positive changes bringing you into greater alignment with your soul purpose, and with greater love, vitality and abundance.

But I recently realized that it also has a strong meaning of releasing the past. 555 is about life choices, and also speaks about expressing the truth of your brilliant authentic light as an individual. It's about being open, adaptable, and willing to learn lessons as you journey through life -- one step at a time, aligning more fully with your highest soul truth, your freedom, and your authentic vibration.

So next time you see 555, know that the angels are with you and speaking to you about changes. There are big changes in store for you... but you're meant to be an active participant in them.

In other words, it's a call for you to positively change your life in an uplifting and empowering way, rather than a warning that the rug is about to be pulled out from under you!

That's why, to make the most of these times of accelerated changes, it's important to keep asking your angels for guidance, clear direction and support. 555 means divinely guided changes are unfolding, so keep moving forward on your path one step at a time.

Occultists recognize what they regard as the immense inherent spiritual power of numbers. Astrology is highly mathematical, and its most important use is to clothe events in time. Occultists seek to plan and time events according to what they consider to be the most favorably disposed time.

Experts in numerology use the numbers to determine the best time for major moves and activities in life. Numerology is used to decide when to invest, when to marry, when to travel, when to change jobs, or relocate. Prime Minister

Tony Blair of England declared his next UK election to be for 5/5/05, "Mr Blair's position as Prime Minister gave him the chance not just to choose the date, but to make the first play for votes of the campaign." "Mr Blair attempts to become the first Labour leader to win three(The heightened Power of '3' x 5) successive terms in power."

(from *http://www.timesonline.co.uk/article/0,,2-1555776,00.html*)

President Bush began this war at 05:50 Baghdad time, on March 20th, 2003(the Feast Day celebration, eve of eve of Ostara), according to occult considerations, March 20th, 2003 was Day "555" since the attacks on 9/11. The Illuminati intended the attacks of 9/11 to be the first blow struck for the appearance of Antichrist; The occultist believes "5" to be the Number of Death, and the greatest intensification of any number to be a triplicate, a "555" literally means "Highest Death".

Members of secret societies, such as Masonic Lodges of the Grand Orient, in their highest levels use the words "unknown superiors" to describe the force that guides them and their efforts. When the Illuminati was formed on

Walpurgisnacht (eve of May 1st), 1776, five men gathered in a cavern deep beneath Ingolstadt in Bavaria and made contact with what they said were "unknown superiors."

One of these five men was Dr. Adam Weishaupt. The name Adam Weishaupt is profound in the sense that his name means "first man to know the superiors." Here let it be noted that the five founders of the Illuminati used witchcraft rituals known as "The greater and lesser keys of Solomon", which involved the "Pentacle of Invocation." The pentacle is a three-dimensional, five-pointed star, and the number five became sacred to the Illuminati. We must also note that the Rothschild family consisted of five sons of one Moses Amschel Bauer, who took the name Rothschild, because it means "Red Shield." Much later, a man named John D. Rockefeller also had five sons to control the American branch of Illuminism. The Illuminati and all of witchcraft is obsessed with the Pentacle of Invocation, and is it any wonder that the Washington Monument in Washington D.C. is exactly 555 feet high? Is it any wonder that we have a five-sided death house, known as the Pentagon?

(from *http://www.greatdreams.com/five/five.htm*)

Also in the video Hoggard talks about the number 5 in the Bible.
  * Antichrist is mentioned 5 times in Scripture
  * satan mentioned 55 times
  * Devils are mentioned 55 times

Lucifer has a "5" point plan in Isaiah 14.
1) I will ascend into Heaven.
2) I will exalt my throne above the stars of God.
3) I will sit also upon the mount of the congregation in the sides of the north.
4) I will ascend above the heights of the clouds.
5) I will be like the most high.

Rev 9:1 And the "5th" angel sounded, and I saw a star (stars have 5 points) from heaven unto the earth: and to him was given the key of the bottomless pit."

Every year, in Sydney, Australia, the Spring Equinox falls on the 21st of September and exactly at 5:55 the sun lines up to perfection casting it's shadow to make it appear that the sun quenches it's thirst by taking a drink at the " Fountain of Life".

555 is incorporated into the Free Masonic architecture and buildings world-wide and holds the key of being ENLIGHTENED.

Binary Code and Ancient Calenders use # 101 symbol = " 5 "

Square of Saturn & Free Masons
A magic square consisting of 9 smaller squares, which when added up horizontally, vertically or diagonally total 15. It is often used as a talisman where the qualities of the planet Saturn are required.

"15" ... 1 + 5 = 6 ... '666'

4	9	2
3	5	7
8	1	6

The Number 17

MH370 landed on runway 17 at Iskandar Muda International Airport (formerly called Blangbintang Airport) at Banda Aceh, where it unloaded the 1st 2 tons of gold.

I wore #17 when I scored those 5 goals in 3:07 on Oct. 7th, 1972
(10th month, 7th day: 10 + 7 = 17).

My linemates, Tommy and Lanny, wore #8 and #9 (8 + 9 = 17).

Valeri Kharlamov, my Russian hockey player idol, wore #17.

So, after digging further into the number 17's appearances throughout history, I wanted to mention some of the other references for you to discover. Some are eye-opening, and some are just fun to notice.[72]

Properties of the number 17

Symbolism

17 is the number of the Son of Man, according to Abellio.

It's also the symbol of the man participating in both worlds, celestial and terrestrial, representing "the junction between the material world and the spiritual world".

Saint Augustin declares: "In the number seventeen, as in its multiples, we find an admirable sacrament".

As explained in the Book of the Balance, including his most famous *'Theory of the balance in Nature'* by Jâbir Ibn Hayyân (alchemist and Sufi), the form of anything in the world is 17. The number 17 represents the base of the theory of the Balance, and must be considered as the rule of the balance of each thing.

17 is also an ominous number for Italians, similar to the number 13 in Occident. Thus, in Italy, there is no bedroom 17, no 17th floor, etc. This is because the number 17, when written as the Roman numeral XVII, is considered as the anagram and the numerical value of the Latin expression 'VIXI', which means "I lived". Therefore, by extension, it also means "I am dead"... clearly an unpopular association!

References to the number 17 in the Bible

There are scores of references to the number seventeen in the Bible, so I'll summarize some of them in this section.

- Seventeen people and nations are present at the Pentecost:
- Galilee
- Parthians
- Medes and Elamites
- peoples from Mesopotamia, Judaea and Cappadocia; Pontus and Asia; Phrygia and Pamphylia; Egypt; and the parts of Libya round to Cyrene
- residents of Rome
- Jews and proselystes alike
- Cretans, and
- Arabs. (Ac 2,7-11)

Joseph was seventeen years old when he was sold by his brothers and escorted into Egypt. *(Gn 37, verse 2)*

The seventeen Judges between the death of Josuah until the rule of Samuel: Othonial, Aod, Samgar, Jahel, Deborah, Barac, Gideon, Abimelech, Thola, Jair, Jepheth, Abezan, Ahialon, Abdon, Samson, Eli and Samuel.

Rehoboam, son of Solomon, reigned seventeen years in Jerusalem. *(1 K 14, verse 21)*

Jehoahaz, son of Jehu, reigned seventeen years in Isarel to Samaria. *(2 K 13, verse 1)*

The Ten Commandments of God were given in 17 verses, to the twentieth chapter of the book of Exodus.

Jacob lived seventeen years in the country of Egypt. *(Gn 47, verse 28)*

The Pentateuch contains 5852 verses (or 17x7x7x7+7+7+7 verses). 1533 verses of the Genesis can be also expressed as 17x70+7x7x7, or 17x7+707+707. The book of the Exodus contains (17+17) x (17+17) + 57 verses (or, simply, 1213 verses). By the way, it is 17x7 shorter than 666 + 666.

The 17th book of the *New Revised Standard Version* of the Bible is the shortest.

Occurrences

The number 17 is used 13 times in the Bible. But if we count also all the numbers having "17" or "seventeen" in their manner to be written, but which are not equal to 17, the four following references would also be retained: Jg 8,14 with sixty-seventeen; 1 Ch 7,11 with 17200; plus Ezr 2,39 and Neh 7,42, both with 1017. In that case, the number 17 would be used 17 times in the Bible.

Just as a side note, do you remember how $130 million was spent on MH370 search? Coincidentally, the number 130 is also used 17 times in the Bible.

In 17 places in the New Testament, God is called the God Unique. The verb 'to pay' is used 17 times in the NT, as is the word 'manna' and the verb 'to kneel'.

In the Revelation of John, 7 is used 53 times and designates 17 different elements: 7 Churches of Asia, 7 spirits, 7 candelabras, 7 seals, etc.

In the Bible, there are 17 numbers that are multiples of 17.

General

Jesus traveled seventeen years in preparation before His public ministry.

The prayer of the Rosary of the Virgin Mary is composed of 17 Pater and 153 Ave Maria (and the sum of the 17 first numbers gives 153).

Jewish law counts seventeen blessings.

According to a passage of the Talmud, it is written that the complete Torah initially included 17 books.

The apostle James wrote his Epistle seventeen years after the crucifixion of Jesus Christ.

There are seventeen liturgical gestures (rak'a) in the Islamic tradition, which compose the five daily prayers. Seventeen words also compose the call to the prayer.

One of the appearances of the Virgin Mary occurred on January 17, 1871 (1+8+7+1=17) at 17 hours, in the village of Pontmain, having 17 hamlets. This appearance, proceeding in 17 phases, occurred 17 years after the date of the blooming of the Mystery of Mary, which inspired promulgation of the dogma of the Immaculate Conception.

It was believed that the Sky was divided into 17 celestial layers.

The Ark of Noah was on the Ararat mount, at an altitude of 17,000 feet.

The mummy of the king Toutankammon was wrapped in 17 cloths.

The Parthenon is 17 columns in length.

The Alhambra, the splendid Moor palace which inspired Escher, has 17 types of mosaic (in fact, that's all possible types).

Henry IV celebrated his marriage a second time on December 17, 1600 in the cathedral St. John in Lyon. His wife, Mary Medicis, arrived with approximately 5000 Italians in 17 galleys.

The first woman of Henry VIII had 17 children who died before reaching their 1st year.

Shakespeare wrote 17 comedies (during the 17th century).

Hamlet reigned 17 years.

The Great Lodge of England, which made the speculative Masonry, was founded in 1717.

The French revolution occurred in 1789 (8+9 = 17).

The number 17 has a particular importance in the tradition of trade corporations that recognize 17 companions initiated by Ali, 17 owners of Muslim corporation founders initiated by Selman-i Farsi, and 17 major corporations.

Two interesting musical references… Beethoven wrote 17 quartets, and the first performance of Handel's Water Music occurred on July 17, 1717.

In Muslim folklore, the symbolic number 17 appears especially in the legends, in particular in the 17 advices murmured to the ear of the king during his coronation, and in the 17 components of the banner.

In Lebanon, there are officially 17 religions: 5 Islamic groups, 11 Christian groups (4 Orthodoxs, 6 Catholics, 1 Protestant) and 1 Judaic.

For the ancient Greeks, 17 represents the number of consonants of the alphabet; it is divided in 9 (number of the dumb consonants) and in 8 (number of the semivowels or semi-consonants). These numbers were also in relation with the musical theory and the harmony of the spheres.

The age of the universe is about 10^{17} seconds.

The symbol indicating the constant which would be the most famous in mathematics is the 17th letter of the original Greek alphabet, pi.

The Japanese poetry Haiku contains 17 syllables.

The first atomic bomb, prepared by 1700 persons, was released on Hiroshima with 17 seconds of delay.

Gandhi was assassinated on January 30, 1948 at 17h17.

November 17, 1972 (1972 = 17x116) marked the return of General Peron in Argentina, after 17 years of exile.

Two of the most important earthquakes in 1994 and 1995 occurred on January 17: January 17, 1994 in California (Los Angeles), and January 17, 1995 in Japan (Kobe). In both cases, the latitude was 34° (2 x17), and the longitudes were respectively -118° and 135° (- 118 + 135 = 17).

In India, they speak 17 languages.

Seventeen days separate the feast of the Presentation of Mary (November 21) from the feast of the Immaculate Conception (December 8).

17 is the eighth prime number and, by theosophical reduction, 17 gives also 8 (1 + 7 = 8).

FOOTNOTES:
[71] - summarized from http://www.theshivaexperience.com/five-as-the-lucky-number/

[72] - summarized from http://membre.oricom.ca/sdesr/nu17.htm

CHAPTER #11 – What do the Vikings, the Roman Empire, the CIA, and CERN have in common? *(Hint: it's not a joke)*

They say everything happens for a reason. And while those reasons may not always be obvious, there's definitely a driving force behind events happening around us. The following connections bring some of those purposes and meanings to light, and show that things happening in the world today had their beginnings long before you and I were born!

Let's start with a notoriously secretive organization who operates behind the scenes of countless governments around the world... the CIA.

CERN Identified as secret entrance to subterranean CIA Headquarters beneath Lake Geneva in Switzerland

CERN in Switzerland is the largest and most advanced nuclear and particle physics laboratory in the world, and security at the top-secret facility is the most stringent on Earth. So it's the perfect place to hide the entrance to the one and only Central Intelligence Agency (CIA).

According to David Chase Taylor's newsy article from September 2015, hard evidence previously confirmed that Switzerland is in fact harboring the CIA. However, exactly where CIA Headquarters is located within Switzerland has remained a mystery—until now.

In short, CERN serves as the secret entrance to CIA Headquarters, which is located in the underwater Alpine canyons of Lake Geneva, a lake so deep it can only be explored by Russian Mir submarines, known for their ability to dive up to 6,000 meters (19,685 feet).

Today, CIA Headquarters beneath Lake Geneva is only accessible via:

- underground trains from CERN, and

- submarines which travel through a 275 kilometer (170 mile) subterranean tunnel which evidently begins in Genova, Italy, and ends in Lake Geneva

CERN's LEP Tunnel, which is 26.659 kilometers (16.6 miles) in length, passes through Switzerland and France, likely en route to CIA Headquarters. It appears that CERN's LEP Tunnel is political cover for the subterranean tunnel, offering daily commuter trains access to shuttle CIA personal from the suburbs of Geneva, Switzerland, to the CIA's underwater headquarters.

The idea that CERN is the secret entrance to CIA Headquarters beneath Lake Geneva is backed up by the fact that as of 2013, CERN had 2,513 staff members and 12,313 fellows, associates and apprentices, a majority of which are likely CIA personal. And since approximately 15,000 people commute to CERN and/or CIA Headquarters on a daily basis, they must do so via secret underground trains, as there are no major parking lots at CERN as seen in the aerial view of CIA Headquarters in Langley, Virginia. A secret tunnel essentially allows persons arriving in Geneva access to CIA

Headquarters without ever being seen in public.

In fact, because CERN doubles as the entrance to CIA Headquarters beneath Lake Geneva, there are a number of secret tunnels which enable CIA personal with the right identification (e.g., an RFID chip) entrance into the subterranean compound. This may have been where the marriage between the RFID chip and the "Mark of the Beast" was made, as the number "666" is depicted within the logo of CERN.

And yes, that number „666" has an actual physical connotation to the known entrances to CERN, namely:

> 1. Entrance "A": Access for all CERN personnel at specific times (Switzerland)
> 2. Entrance "B": Access for all CERN personnel at all times. Often referred to as the "Main Entrance" to CERN (Switzerland)
> 3. Entrance "C": Access for all CERN personnel at specific times (Switzerland)
> 4. Entrance "D": For so-called goods reception at specific times (Switzerland)
> 5. Entrance "E": Access for French-resident CERN personnel at specific times. Named "Porte Charles de Gaulle" in recognition of de Gaulle's alleged role in the creation of CERN (France)
> 6. Entrance "Inter-Site Tunnel": Reportedly for equipment transfer to and from CERN sites in

France by personnel with a specific permit. This is the only permitted route for such transfers (France)

While we're on the subject of logos, in the original coat of arms of Geneva, a 'Jesuit' symbol adorns the shield consisting of the letters "IHE". As depicted in the book "Greenland Theory: Apocalypse Now", the Jesuits (i.e., the Society of Jesus) are the largest religious order in the Catholic Church who are known as God's Marines". Interestingly, the Jesuits take their orders from the "Black Pope" which appears to be the voice of the Roman Empire in Greenland. Consequently, it's highly likely that a majority of the personal working at CERN and CIA Headquarters are Jesuits.

By the way, if you recognize the name CERN, maybe it's because it's also the home of the World Wide Web, which began as a CERN project named ENQUIRE, which was allegedly initiated by Tim Berners-Lee in 1989 and Robert Cailliau in 1990. Since virtually all banking, commerce, communication, drone warfare and travel are now controlled by computers. In other words, CERN is the internet hub or motherboard of entire world, and whatever agency has power over said CERN essentially rules the world.

Not coincidentally, CERN is home to the world's largest supercomputer, used by the CIA to conduct 24/7 electronic espionage and surveillance, as well as control the underworld (e.g., deflate/inflate currencies, manipulate global markets, execute drone attacks, etc.). This notion was foreshadowed in the novel "Angels & Demons" (2000) by Dan Brown which portrays antimatter created at CERN being used in a weapon against the Vatican. In reality however, CERN is being used as a weapon against all of humanity.

In short, CERN is ultimately responsible for any future apocalyptic-like event that could theoretically destroy planet Earth (e.g., asteroid attack, biological pandemic, nuclear terror attack, World War III, etc.) which is exactly what one would expect from the Central Intelligence Agency (CIA). [73]

And here's where the symbolism becomes more intense, if you know what you're looking for. Back on June 18, 2004, a 2-meter tall statue of Shiva was unveiled at CERN. Shiva is considered the Supreme God within Shaivism, and is known as the creator and destroyer of all that is.

Shiva's sacred number is "5" which equates to the "Ж symbol (i.e., "Chi") (there are '537' mountains that exceed 3,000 meters in the Swiss Alps)

Is the Roman Empire still alive and well?

As for the Roman Empire's connection to all of this, consider how GreenlandTheory.com's "Greenland Theory: Apocalypse Now" (2014) explores the unrecognized but mighty conspiracy which has been hidden from humanity for ages, unfortunately to the detriment of all life forms which have inhabited planet Earth. Briefly, the Roman Empire, commonly referred to as Ancient Rome, evidently faked its own death 715 years ago and now excerpts command and control over all 206 nations of the world though its primary proxy state of Switzerland (home of the CIA) which was coincidentally formed in c.1300 AD, approximately 715 years ago.

The collective histories depicted in the Bible and in the cultures commonly referred to as Ancient Egypt, Ancient Samaria, Ancient Greece, Ancient Babylon, Ancient Rome and the Vikings are the comprehensive historical evolution of the same line or lineage of "man" which originated from Minos of Crete in Greece.

'Who rules the world?'

"5" Nordic Leaders Trolled President Trump With a Soccer Ball Orb poke fun at Trump's

OSLO (Reuters) - World leaders don't generally troll each other, but the prime ministers of the five Nordic countries are giving it a shot.

Sweden's Prime Minister Stefan Lofven (L-R), with his counterparts Lars Lokke Rasmussen of Denmark, Erna Solberg of Norway, Juha Sipila of Finland and Bjarni Benediktsson of Iceland hold a soccer ball during their meeting in Bergen, Norway May 29, 2017. Picture taken May 29, 2017. They just posted a photograph of themselves clasping a soccer ball - a droll take on a photo of U.S. President Donald Trump, Saudi King Salman and Egyptian President Abdel Fattah el-Sisi holding a glowing orb that went viral last week.

That orb was an illuminated globe at the Global Centre for Combating Extremist Ideology in Riyadh, the opening of which the three leaders were attending on May 21. Eerie lighting gave the photo an aura of comic-book villains plotting world domination, an image that proved irresistible to the Twitterati.

And, apparently, it was just as irresistible to Lars Lokke Rasmussen, Juha Sipila, Bjarni Benediktsson, Erna Solberg and Stefan Lofven, the prime ministers of Denmark, Finland, Iceland, Norway and Sweden respectively.

At a meeting in Bergen, Norway, to discuss cooperation among their countries, the five heads of government came up with their own version of the photo, and stuck it on social media. On her Facebook page, Norway's Solberg made the comparison explicit.

"Who rules the world? Riyadh vs Bergen," Solberg wrote under the Trump photo and the photo of her and her fellow Nordic leaders.

"Don't know what those in the upper photo were thinking," she wrote. "In the lower one are the five Nordic prime ministers, holding a ball with the sustainability goals. We're hoping they'll be a roadmap for the future."

Sweden Poised to Become Leading Scandinavian Cashless Society through Bitcoin

Sweden Poised to Become Leading Scandinavian Cashless Society through Bitcoin

Sweden is fast-moving to follow through on its plans to become the world's first cashless society.

While this is seen as a good sign for digital currencies on a new progressive frontier, it brings issues, such as privacy concerns, when every transaction is surveyed. Nevertheless, the country is still rooting for Bitcoin as the answer to provide anonymity similar to the traditional cash system.

Potential profits in cashless

As seen by many of Sweden's financial institutions, companies make no profit from the use of cash, as it lacks harvestable personal data and it has to be physically managed. Due to this problem, finance is potentially changing to cashless transactions, with Sweden leading the way.

Reports show that 900 of Sweden's 1,600 bank branches no longer store cash, and they will no longer accept cash deposits. There is a gradual decrease in numbers of ATMs, and the circulation of the Swedish krona fell from 106 bln in 2009 to 60 bln in 2016. [74]

So the idiom "When in Rome do as the Romans" is literally and figuratively true as evidence of Rome's domination and rule over the world is readily evident in the architecture, calendar, currency, flags, names, numerology, universities and symbols currently representing almost every single entity on Earth. After all, "Rome wasn't built in a day" -- meaning the idea that it takes a long time to do an important job could not be more true, as all the world is now ruled by modern day Rome.[75]

Finally, it turns out that conventional energy sources aren't the only types of energy the Illuminati-inspired New World Order wants to control. Looking back on my days as a biofeedback practitioner, this helps explain why the devices had such a dramatic effect on both people and animals!

The Power of Loosh

Loosh is an energy generated by all organic life in varying degrees of purity, the clearest and most potent coming from humans- engendered by human activity which triggers emotion, the highest of such emotion being Love/Loosh. Something, somewhere (or both, in millions, or uncountable) requires, likes, needs, values, collects, drinks, eats, or uses as a drug, a substance identified as

Loosh. This is a rare substance, and those who possess Loosh find it vital for whatever it is used for.[76]

From 'Parasites on the Loosh'...

The fundamental understanding that we are an energy source for some form of inter-dimensional parasites is becoming more and more predominant. After all, it fits not only ancient and even current religious and spiritual teachings, but every form of social and psychological framework as well. We're being used and abused.

But by whom, ultimately, and why?

There's clearly a contrary current at play working against the instinctive creative and loving force most of us are tapped into and endeavor to manifest in our lives. We have not just opposition, but apparently a seemingly coordinated or similarly "inspired" enemy of mankind continually acting contrary to our best interests.

A simple perusal of the abusive systems at large in the human societal fabric paints a very clear picture. Whether its false education and controlled media that only stifle and misdirect or the engineered highly toxic social, geological, technological and essential resource manipulation we see escalate at an exponential rate, humanity and our planet are under attack and at a serious crossroads. Just how these parasitic forces operate, and indeed manage us, in order to provide the energetic food source they need to live on, is essential to our empowerment.

Rather, it was simply Monroe's identifying, and hence naming, of a metaphysical, alchemical phenomenon that has always existed (spiritual energy simply is) and - probably since many centuries ago, perhaps even millennia - was developed and exploited as a dark, multidimensional occult art and skill, utilized by secret societies and institutionally for social programming and mind control, and raised to a zenith in our electronic era.

Capitalized upon by the secret services and black-ops, and exploited as a social engineering utility by the interdimensional Negatives, "loosh" essentially is of the earth planes (lower dimensions) and the trauma energy of the human and animal emotional body (for example, via the cruelty imposed upon and endured by the animal kingdom, and the brutality of the abbatoir).

As negative emotional energy, especially the energy of pain, trauma, stress, abuse, and suffering, or as Georgi very rightly described it, as "dreadful loosh," it contains the heightened molecular content and organic /hormonal adrenalin-cortisol cascades, coursing through the quantum dynamics of blood, body, and brain systems. Under such intense extremity of trauma, the blood and flesh is, for the Negative Entities, thus highly 'enriched' and hence highly prized, their brand of premium gold caviar diamond steak, as it were. (There is a passage in the Old Testament where the gods rush in from afar, salivating at the aroma of burning human flesh. The so-called "God" or "Gods" in the O.T. - Old Testament - were/are mostly Negative Entities.)

Not only is this negative loosh highly coveted, but most crucially of all, it is absolutely necessary for probably most Negative Entities, for enabling and facilitating existence in the Earth planes, as well as for the ability to hold the human form so they don't slide into shapeshifting.

Apparently, because of the vibrational difference in frequency levels, there is a fundamental physiological incompatibility which our negative loosh neutralizes for them, and which even enhances their energetic stamina and function in the Earth and lower dimensions.

Vibration and frequency, in them, in humans, and animal Earthlings, are key to loosh's entrapment dynamics and emancipation from it.[77]

The World's Firm

Our world is run by a demonic cabal, a conglomeration of the most depraved consciousness on the planet.

These narcissists are the pillars of a corrupt establishment and are shameless in their lusts, lying, scheming and murdering their way up the greasy pole of power.

The sociopathic rulers and their ilk are the gate-keepers of the 'Loosh rote', supervisors of the farm and, service to self (STS) is the only game they play.

The 'Loosh Rote'

Earth is a farm, set up for the sole purpose of harvesting the energy of fear and suffering from living creatures.

Quote from Robert Monroe, *Far Journeys*

"From experience, the Collectors have evolved an entire technology with complimentary tools for the harvesting of the Loosh from the Type 4M [i.e. human] units."

The most common have been named: love, friendship, family, greed, hate, pain, guilt, disease, pride, ambition, ownership, possession, sacrifice - and on a larger scale, nations, provincialism, wars, famine, religion, machines, freedom, industry, trade, ...to list just a few.

Loosh production is higher than ever before...

As Morpheus says in the Matrix, 'we are all batteries...' and I would add, on tap 24/7.

Just imagine a mind parasite sending us into a past trauma... for half a pint of abandonment with a shot of jealousy thrown in! The psycho's in power run the 'loosh farm' as a business, where profit and loss is governed by how much energy is generated and collected from mankind and the animal nations, physically and energetically.

Amplification of suffering

The shootings at Aurora in Colorado and Sandy Hook took place on ley lines, amplifying the human misery for a mega loosh collection... this is why so much death and mayhem happens upon the power lines of earth's magnetic grid.

The major football stadiums are built upon the grid, and think of all the 'ra... ra' energy, pure testosterone and adrenaline in action at a game. The raw 'loosh' of the intoxicated fans, amplified by a ley line, is a feast for something.

You've got to hand it to the Firm, they've got us all wrapped up.

Their bought-and-paid-for media hangs right in there and inundates us with cruelty and bloodshed, lewd Saturnalia's, buzzing with spells and symbols at the Superbowl and Olympics, and all the while pumping out fear-based propaganda of war... of shock and awe.

The Firm knows how to program our psyches with poverty and loss, wanton cruelties, false flags and lies, so we will continuously produce emotional misery and torment. The loosh rote is big business for the devil's pimps.

> Peter Singer, the author of Animal Liberation, believed that the meat industry deliberately devised the slaughtering process to increase suffering in animals... as another way of increasing the 'loosh harvest' for the diabolical owners of the farm
>
> Loosh is most readily obtainable in the game of 'us versus them' and none of us are immune to conflict. But we can make a start to mitigate its effects by refusing to be drawn in to the divisive nature of the game.[78]

The more I found out about Loosh, the more I understood the theories and rumors of vast FEMA camps being built throughout the USA. Foreseeing their purpose, The U.S Federal Emergency Management Agency (FEMA) is planning to imprison US citizens in concentration camps... at undetermined times, whether the imprisonments occur at random intervals or (more effectively) in a simultaneous 'human roundup'.

Typically described as following the mass imposition of martial law in the United States after a major disaster or crisis, some versions of the theory suggest only suspected dissidents will be imprisoned. But in more extreme versions, large numbers of US citizens will be imprisoned for the purposes of extermination, as a New World Order is established. The FEMA camps 'conspiracy theory' has existed since the 1980s, but it has picked up greatly in popularity since late 2000.[79]

Minister of Indigenous and Northern Affairs Carolyn Bennett speaks during a news conference on the Missing and Murdered Indigenous Women and Girls inquiry in Ottawa, Monday, February 15, 2016.
(Adrian Wyld/THE CANADIAN PRESS)

Missing and murdered indigenous women toll 'way bigger' than 1,200: minister
by KATHRYN BLAZE BAUM AND TAVIA GRANT, The Globe and Mail
Published Monday, Feb. 15, 2016 6:04PM EST
Last updated Wednesday, Feb. 17, 2016 10:11AM EST

The number of missing and murdered indigenous women in Canada is "way bigger" than 1,200, the federal Indigenous Affairs Minister says, provoking scrutiny of a commonly cited official figure ahead of a national inquiry into the tragedies.

A 2014 RCMP report found there were 1,181 police-recorded cases of murdered and missing aboriginal women across all jurisdictions in Canada from 1980 to 2012 – 164 missing and 1,017 homicide victims.

In an e-mailed statement to The Globe and Mail on Monday, the office of federal minister Carolyn Bennett indicated her remarks were based on concerns voiced by survivors and victims' families – not on new data. "The families believe that the number of missing and murdered indigenous women and girls is higher than 1,200," her office said.

The RCMP did not respond to requests for comment Monday on whether its number may be understating the problem.

"It's bigger than 1,200," Dr. Bennett said in Ottawa. "Way bigger than 1,200." [80]

FOOTNOTES:
[73] – summarized from http://saviorsofearth.ning.com/forum/topics/babylon-falling-cern-identified-as-secret-entrance-to-subterranea

[74] - https://cointelegraph.com/news/sweden-poised-to-become-leading-scandinavian-cashless-society-through-bitcoin

[75] - summarized from https://sites.google.com/site/greenlandtheory/home

[76] - summarized from http://www.urbandictionary.com/tags.php?tag=super%20love

[77] - summarized from http://www.theeventchronicle.com/metaphysics/galactic/archons-parasites-loosh/#

[78] - https://www.bibliotecapleyades.net/ciencia/ciencia_conscioussociopol197.htm

[79] - with details summarized from https://en.wikipedia.org/wiki/FEMA_camps_conspiracy_theory

[80] - http://nationalpost.com/news/politics/number-of-missing-murdered-indigenous-women-way-bigger-than-1200-minister-says

CHAPTER #12 – Russian deals, Middle East atrocities, and Bitcoin today

Now, on to Bitcoin (remember, the Swiss Jews have the code for the 'blockchain')...

Knowing that Thomas' partner, Richard Leibel, mentioned that he'd been programming the blockchain computer code for years, the idea that Gavin Andresen, a leader of the Bitcoin community would make a dramatic (or embarrassing) announcement at CoinDesk's Consensus 2016 conference, saying that he was standing behind 'Craig Wright's' claim that he was actually Satoshi Nakamoto, the pseudonymous creator of the crypto-currency. This seemed like a shameless grab for headlines. Unsubstantiated, but newsworthy.

From the article "Where is Gavin Andresen? The Quiet Exile of Bitcoin's Former Face standing behind Craig Wright's claim

"It was a very bizarre moment," said Eric Lombrozo, a Bitcoin Core developer since 2011 who witnessed the announcement... because the overwhelming consensus from the technical community was, as Lombrozo put it: "There is absolutely no way he's Satoshi."[81]

As of August 23, 2017, one Bitcoin was worth $4,300 USD. To compare, one Ethereum was valued at $235. In other words, Bitcoin – Richard Leibel's brainchild – has become one of the world's biggest business stories... and a fantastically profitable investment for some, as a replacement for the currency it's designed to replace.

Just down the road from CERN lies the small city of Zug, Switzerland. Bitcoin Crypto Valley is also the home of GLENCORE and Ivan Glasenberg (remember, the guy who called me to tell me Thomas had a stroke in September, 2014).

Crypto Valley Zug:
Canton of Zug – Home of Innovation

The Swiss canton of Zug offers a unique area to live and create. Where innovation, traditional values, multicultural mindset, economy and nature meet.

Zug offers well educated knowledge workers, stability and an excellent infrastructure with a high standard of living, high security and a beautiful clean environment

Zug also offers a unique level of creativity, a robust platform for innovative growth due to an unusually open mindset of local stakeholders (government, education, tax authorities, Venture Capital, etc.), and an easily accessible network to many leading global companies headquartered based in the canton.

Thriving Fintech Ecosystem

Cryptocurrencies, Blockchain, Digital Identities/ Certificates, encryption algorithms and other innovative technologies drive the social and economic process of digitalization. They foster the free and uncomplicated B2B and B2C exchange of goods and value. They support stability, trust and security in the web and in the economy.
(from https://steemit.com/cryptocurrency/@steven

maiso/crypto-valley-zug-switzerland-home-of-the-future)

Ivan Glasenberg keen to tell the world he is back on top *(from http://on.ft.com/2mhYvkm)*

Hard-charging boss has restored Glencore to profit after a turbulent period

4-Traders Homepage > Equities > London Stock Exchange > Glencore   GLEN JE00B4T3BW64
United Kingdom GLENCORE (GLEN)
Delayed Quote. Delayed - 07/12 11:35:09 am
315.00   GBp +2.14%
12:13p FTSE down as defensives, Pearson and M&S fall; Carillion crumbles
06:24a GLENCORE : Sells 20,000 Tons of Cobalt Product to Chinese Firm
07/06 Tesla shares drift lower as Model S fails to ace some safety test..

from http://www.4-traders.com/GLENCORE-PLC-8017494/news-twitter/Ivan-Glasenberg-keen-to-tell-the-world-he-is-back-on-top-835552276173422593/

Well, after Thomas and the Swiss Jews pulled off the biggest Gold Heist · Assassination in the History of the World and created Bitcoin, Ethereum, Monero, ETC Classic etc...

"Ivan says he's back on top!"

Just like Kazakhstan being the big winner when Brexit took place, they all look like HEROES... WOW! Not difficult when the cards are completely stacked in their favour.

Who started the wildfire at Fort McMurray, the costliest disaster in Canadian history?

The Fort McMurray wildfire was Canada's news story of 2016. When the fires were set in Northern Saskatchewan last summer and a lot of Indians had to be brought to Saskatoon in order to survive, I did not give it too much thought, until my friend found pieces of sodium sulphate thoughout the forest and in the lakes to keep the fire burning...

When the fire that destroyed Ft. MacMurray, Alberta swept through the community, destroying approximately 2,400 homes and buildings and forcing the largest wildfire evacuation in Albertan history in spring 2016, my friend Karen sent me the satellite link showing how quickly the fire surrounded Ft. MacMurray. It continued to spread across northern Alberta and into Saskatchewan, consuming forested areas and impacting Athabasca oil sands operations. [76]

The fire started at approximately 5:45AM just south of Ft. Mac, and by 7:00AM, it surrounded the entire city like a horseshoe. I quickly emailed this info to Ivan, just to let him know that we knew.

I checked the same satellite link about 4 hours later, and the times were changed. Someone had manipulated the satellite info!

Why would a disaster like the Fort McMurray wildfire be connected to the diabolical death-dealers in Thomas' network?

An article that appeared on the PowerLine blog in August 2016 provides a clue...

Memo sheds new light on Clinton – Russia uranium scandal

The future demand for Uranium & Graphite is huge. Nuclear to be used for good & evil purposes. Graphite for graphene to use for electric car batteries.

There just happens to be a lot of Uranium under Lake Athabasca and throughout northern Alberta and Saskatchewan. Saskatchewan has graphite which is a surface mineral...
When a fire or any disaster occurs, the government brings in their first responders.

These first responders are also their 'cover-up' guys, in case anything needs to be removed from the site that may cause suspicion.[82]

Why Bitcoin mines are moving to Iceland

Bitcoin runs on computers. Massive computing power. And they're pumping out millions of dollars worth of bitcoin in Iceland.

Why Iceland?   ICELAND , HOME OF THE VIKINGS ,,,,, (remember the 3 abandoned 747's used to transport the Gold to Perth,, 2 of them came from Icelandic Air)

Because with its permanently-cool arctic temperatures, 100% renewable energy, and data cable connections to both sides of the Atlantic, Iceland is a "sweet-spot" location for companies to cut costs and make their endeavours profitable -- by basing the massive power-consuming, heat-producing computers there to run the Bitcoin 'mining' process that makes it all work.

Bitcoin mining is the process of solving complex mathematical equations with a hi-speed computer, in order to generate the digital crypto-currency. By design, the cryptographic algorithms become exponentially more complicated as more computers join the global 'mining' network.

With the continent's abundance of dual-source energy in the form of geothermal and hydroelectric supplies readily available, Iceland provides cheap, stable and abundant energy to operate and scale huge data-processing centres for cryptocurrency generation. In addition to offering up to 80% savings on energy costs alone, Icelandic 'Bitcoin farms' substantially reduce the carbon footprint of the companies that choose to locate operations there.[83]

Here's a cute story about a Bitcoin tradition, that also highlights just how much the crypto-currency's value has skyrocketed in just a few years.

> **Bitcoin Pizza Day: Celebrating the $20 Million Pizza**
>
> Monday marks the seven-year anniversary of the first Bitcoin transaction, in which a Florida man paid for two pizzas with the cryptocurrency. The day has become part of folk law, not because of the transaction, but more the price; 10,000 Bitcoins, or--going by the current BTC value--$20 million for the two pizzas. (See also: New

Bitcoin Price Record: Over $2,000 Per Coin)

On May 22, 2010, now known as Bitcoin Pizza Day, Laszlo Hanyecz agreed to pay 10,000 Bitcoins for two delivered Papa John's pizzas. Organized on bitcointalk forum, the Florida man reached out for help. "I'll pay 10,000 bitcoins for a couple of pizzas.. like maybe 2 large ones so I have some left over for the next day," Hanyecz wrote.[84]

Barry Silbert #1 is the brother of Allan Silbert who was the guy who ran or owned the Bitcoin exchange back in 2014 that purchased the Villa in Bali with Bitcoin for the MH370 Pilot and is doing well...

Below is a recent article... fast forward!

MAY 30, 2017
BITCOIN
"3" People Set to Make a Killing from the Bitcoin Boom, by Jeff John Roberts

#1
Barry Silbert, Venture Capitalist
Fortune Brainstorm TECH 2014
Barry Silbert is another long-time player in the bitcoin scene, who made big bets when most people laughed that the currency was

for kooks. One of his bets saw him obtain 48,000 bitcoins in a second auction held by the U.S. Marshals Service in 2014. At that time, bitcoin prices had fallen to around $350, which means Silbert's stake could now be worth around $110 million.

Silbert is currently focused on building a rival financial product to the Winklevoss ETF, and likely owns a lot more than the 48,000 bitcoins he won at auction.

REMEMBER BARRY SILBERT !!!!!!

$500,000 Bali Villa is Biggest Bitcoin Purchase Ever *(this is where they put the pilot of MH370)*

March 20, 2014 12:00 GMT is the largest purchase ever made with cryptocurrency. ***(The new home for MH370 Pilot)***

Sold through the bitcoin-only BitPremier luxury marketplace, the fully-managed property in the delMango Villa Estate sold for in excess of $500,000 though the exact price and identity of the buyer involved remain unknown.

BitPremier was founded by Alan Silbert, who is the brother of Barry Silbert, a major bitcoin investor and founder of the Bitcoin

Investment Trust. Barry Silbert is also the founder of SecondMarket and has invested in his brother's BitPremier venture.

Alan Silbert told CoinDesk that the purchaser of the property in Bali was an early bitcoin adopter from the US and that the sale represented "by far the largest" sale to date on the marketplace, which launched 10 months ago.

#2
Satoshi Nakamoto, Bitcoin Inventor - Richard
Since his 2008 white paper, which described a new type of software tied to a digital currency, the man known as Satoshi has stood as the soul of bitcoin.
But no one can say for sure he is.
Satoshi has not spoken publicly for years, but he is believed to control large numbers of bitcoin wallets from the currency's early days. Some reports say he controls more than 5% of all bitcoin in circulation, which means his net worth could be in the billions.
It remains to be seen if Satoshi will emerge one day and distribute that wealth (maybe by endowing a bitcoin university?) or if Satoshi and his riches will remain invisible and out of reach forever.

#3

Uncle Sam - Rothchilds

The early idealists of bitcoin saw it as an anarchy-currency free of the control of national governments. Alas, the U.S. government didn't get the memo. Since 2016, the Internal Revenue Service has been stepping up a campaign to identify bitcoin investors and slap them with capital gains tax. Right now, the agency is locked in a legal fight with the popular cryptocurrency exchange Coinbase, and is demanding information about millions of customer accounts. The IRS is annoyed because it says only 802 people declared bitcoin income in 2015—even though the value of the currency has increased dramatically from its 2013 value of $13. [86]

Putin was involved from the beginning of the 7 year plan ,,, after all, he ordered MH370 to fly to and be stored at the cosmodrome in Kazakhstan...

> June 6, 2017, 11:16 AM CST
> **ETHEREUM - RUSSIA**
> **A Vast Blockchain Experiment Could Change Russia**
> **By Leonid Bershidsky**
> June 6, 2017, 11:16 AM CST
>
> Russian President Vladimir Putin and his economic team have long been under the

impression that, to wean the country off its oil dependence, they needed a major leap in some specific area of technology that wasn't yet dominated by Western, Chinese or Japanese tech giants. Their latest hopes are being pegged to the Ethereum blockchain platform.

At last week's St. Petersburg Economic Forum, Putin talked to Vitalik Buterin, the founder of Ethereum. Buterin's family emigrated from Russia to Canada when he was six. There, the math whiz got interested in Bitcoin while still in his teens. A $100,000 fellowship from Peter Thiel's foundation launched him on the Ethereum project.

Though Buterin's platform does host the ether currency, which has risen in value to more than $260 from $8 so far this year, it's far more ambitious than that. Buterin thinks of his project as the safe medium for all sorts of transactions that can be validated through a distributed system, the way Bitcoin transactions are. This includes bets, option deals, insurance contracts, the government registration of property rights and copyright -- pretty much any kind of deal that requires validation or that can be automatically executed when certain conditions become right. Ethereum provides a universal blockchain upon which various projects can be built.

Russia has brilliant engineering brains, and it could try to lure back talented Russians like Buterin and those who work in Silicon Valley. But it's not easy to find the "blue ocean" areas not infested with international sharks like Apple, Google and Alibaba. In the past decade, technological bets placed by Russian leaders have suffered from being overly audacious or too far behind the competition.

The search for a promising moonshot resumed when Putin became president again. Last year, he hit on Elon Musk's hyperloop idea as something Russia could put into practice. Russia's expanse, after all, calls for a hyperloop-style solution. At the 2016 St. Petersburg Economic Forum, Putin promised support to a company called Hyperloop One, and indeed, Kremlin-linked investors soon arrived for the start-up. Then the project ran into trouble amid bitter recriminations between co-founder Shervin Pishevar and former chief technology officer Brogan BamBrogan. The company still exists and proposes projects in a number of countries -- it opened a test track in Nevada earlier this year -- but Russia doesn't appear to be a priority for the U.S. firm despite the Russian investment.

Lately, Ethereum has become the arena for a boom in capital-raising through the sale of digital tokens which can be used within a certain application, such as the Gnosis prediction market, which raised $12 million in 15 minutes in that way.

Though large global companies got there first -- the Enterprise Ethereum Alliance, formed to promote the technology in various business environments, includes UBS, JP Morgan, Microsoft, Intel and other giants -- Russia has a chance to be ahead of others.

Like other central banks, the Russian one is testing blockchain technology: Last year, a consortium of large Russian banks it formed for the purpose processed the first transactions through the Etherium platform. With Putin's support, which means everything in today's Russia, the central bank, run by Putin favorite Elvira Nabiullina, can more aggressively move the country's financial sector to the blockchain.

Buterin has also offered his platform to Russia's vast government sector, stressing its anti-corruption potential: The system is inherently transparent. I'm not sure the Putin elite is excited about this aspect of the blockchain, but Putin himself might be interested in the potential for greater control that it creates. The brief meeting between Putin and Buterin last week might open exciting prospects for the latter. His vast country of birth is the most impressive field for controlled experiments any techie could dream of; in Putin's system, decisions can be made fast, and mistakes can be forgiven in the name of Russia's great leap forward. Summarize: Ethereum has been Putin's plan since the NWO began it's 7 year plan in 2008.

Russia is planning to move the economic and financial power away from the USA and become the leader of the NWO and have the capital in ASTANA, KAZAKHSTAN.[87]

DONALD TRUMP, CHABAD-LUBAVITCH AND THE OLIGARCHS
Submitted by David Livingstone on Sat, 04/08/2017 - 18:55
CHABAD-LUBAVITCH

Global Security has hypothesized that Donald Trump may be a Manchurian Candidate planted by the Russian mafia in collusion with the Russian government.[1] Using a network of hackers and Internet trolls controlled by the Russian mob, the Russian government was able to influence the 2016 US Presidential election in favor of Trump. The basis of Trump's cooperation in the plot has been alluded to in 35-page report, known as the Trump Dossier, first reported by CNN and then published by BuzzFeed on January 11, 2017, which alleges that Russia has gathered damaging intelligence on Trump which it is using to blackmail Trump. In fact, a series of studies by the Financial Times has shown how after he suffered a string of six successive bankruptcies, Trump was bailed out by Russian crime lords.

Despite his alignment with the racist right, Trump has professed ultra-right views on Israel. His connections with Israel also extend to his broad ties with the Russian mafia, many of whom hold dual citizenship in Israel. The Russian mafia is closely associated with is a Hasidic movement that derived originally from Sabbateanism. The Zohar and the Kabbalah of Rabbi Isaac Luria, are frequently cited in Chabad works. Although the Chabad Lubavitcher movement is often listed as a part of Orthodox Judaism, it has often been condemned as heretical by traditional Jews. Rabbi David Berger, a highly popular figure in Modern Orthodox circles, wrote The Rebbe, the Messiah, and the Scandal of Orthodox

Indifference, criticizing Lubavitcher messianism as "precisely what Jews through the generations have seen as classic, Christian-style false messianism." His views are shared and supported by many prominent Orthodox authorities. In the 1980's and early 1990's, Rabbi Eliezer Menachem Schach, a leader of the strictly Orthodox Jews in Israel who wielded powerful influence over the country's politics for more than two decades, waged a campaign against the Lubavitcher movement. The messianic claim, Rabbi Schach said, was "total heresy," adding that those making it "will burn in hell."[2]

Lubavitch messianism involves the belief in the coming of the Messiah and a goal of raising awareness that his arrival is imminent. In addition, the term also refers more specifically to the hope that Rabbi Menachem Mendel Schneerson (1902 –1994), known to many as the Rebbe, could himself be the Messiah. Schneerson was a Russian Empire-born American Orthodox Jewish rabbi, and the last Lubavitcher Rebbe, and considered one of the most influential Jewish leaders of the 20th century.[3] Schneerson transformed the Chabad-Lubavitch movement, that almost came to an end with the Holocaust, into one of the most influential movements in world Jewry, with an international network of thousands of educational and social centers, known as Chabad Houses. Chabad's goal, explains Sue Fishkoff, author of The Rebbe's Army, is to reach every Jew in the world. Chabab seeks out the support of the rich, famous and powerful, including celebrities like Bob Dylon, Jon Voigt, Whoppi Goldberg and Al Gore.[4] Schneerson's grave attracts thousands of Jews and non-Jews for prayer.

Schneerson spoke of the position of the United States as a world superpower, and would praise its foundational values of "'E pluribus unum'—from many one", and "In God we trust."[5] Schneerson was visited by Presidents, Prime Ministers, Governors, Senators, Congressmen and Mayors. Notable among them are John F. Kennedy, Robert Kennedy, Franklin D. Roosevelt, Jr., Ronald Reagan, Jimmy Carter, Jacob Javits, Ed Koch, Rudy Giuliani, David Dinkins and Joe Lieberman.[6] In 1978, the US Congress asked President Carter to designate Schneerson's birthday as the national Education Day USA. It has been since commemorated as Education and Sharing Day. In 1994, he was posthumously awarded the Congressional Gold Medal for his "outstanding and lasting contributions toward improvements in world education, morality, and acts of charity."[7]

President Bill Clinton spoke these words at the ceremony:

The late Rebbe's eminence as a moral leader for our country was recognized by every president since Richard Nixon. For over two decades, the Rabbi's movement now has some 2000 institutions; educational, social, medical, all across the globe. We (the United States Government) recognize the profound role that Rabbi Schneerson had in the expansion of those institutions.
Schneerson took great interest in the affairs of the state of Israel, where he was a major political force, both in the Knesset and among the electorate.[8] Although he never visited Israel, many of Israel's top leadership made it a point to visit him. Prime Minister Menachem Begin who came to visit him before going to Washington to meet President Carter. Ariel Sharon who had a close relationship with Schneerson. Yitzhak Rabin. Shimon Peres and Benjamin Netanyahu also visited and sought Schneersons advice. Benjamin Netanyahu said that while serving as Israel's ambassador to the United Nations in 1984, Schneerson told him: "you will be serving in a house of darkness, but remember, that even in the darkest place; the light of a single candle can be seen far and wide..." Netanyahu later

retold this episode in a speech at the General Assembly, on September 23, 2011.[9]

OLIGARCHS

Natan Sharansky, the Chairman of the Jewish Agency said that Chabad Lubavitch was an essential connector to Soviet Jewry during the Cold War.[10] Shimon Peres has stated that it's to Schneerson's credit that "Judaism in the Soviet Union has been preserved."[11] These Russian Chabad-Lubavitcher Jews composed a substantial portion of the country's notorious "oligarchs." As James Henry indicated in The American Interest, "one of the most central facts about modern Russia: its emergence since the 1990s as a world-class kleptocracy, second only to China as a source of illicit capital and criminal loot, with more than $1.3 trillion of net offshore 'flight wealth' as of 2016." Following the collapse of the Soviet Union, the state's industry was privatized largely into the hands of a handful of well-connected buyers. Simultaneously, neoliberal "market reform" policies were introduced by Boris Yeltsin, and designed and financed by senior Clinton Administration officials, neoliberal economists, and USAID, World Bank, and IMF officials.

According to Henry:

By the late 1990s the actual chaos that resulted from Yeltsin's warped policies had laid the foundations for a strong counterrevolution, including the rise of ex-KGB officer Putin and a massive outpouring of oligarchic flight capital that has continued virtually up to the present. For ordinary Russians, as noted, this was disastrous. But for many banks, private bankers, hedge funds, law firms, and accounting firms, for leading oil companies like ExxonMobil and BP, as well as for needy borrowers like the Trump Organization, the opportunity to feed on post-Soviet spoils was a godsend. This was vulture capitalism at its worst.[12]

As revealed by Karen Dawisha in her highly acclaimed Putin's Kleptocracy, during the time Yeltsin's chosen successor, Vladimir Putin, was deputy mayor of St. Petersburg, he was alleged to be involved with the local Mafia, ex-KGB apparatchiks and bureaucrats in schemes involving the diversion of municipal funds, illegal arms shipments, the food shortage scandal of 1991, the local gambling industry, and money laundering for the Cali drug cartel through the Real Estate Board of St. Petersburg. And when he moved into the Kremlin, Putin put his old mafia contacts to use. Mark Galeotti, a Russian organized crime expert and professor at New York University, asserted in a recent lecture at the Hudson Institute that Putin's Russia is "not so much a mafia state as a state with a nationalized mafia."[13]

According to a classified cable from the U.S. embassy that was published by Wikileaks, in 2010, José Grinda Gonzalez, Spain's national court prosecutor, following a decade-long investigation, briefed U.S. officials in Madrid, informing them that the Kremlin used "organised crime groups to do whatever the government of Russia cannot acceptably do as a government."[14] Putin's Kremlin has used organized crime to carry out arms smuggling, assassinations, raising funds for black ops, or fomenting subversion in the former Soviet regions. Moscow relied heavily on local organized crime structures in its support for separatist movements in Transdniester, Abkhazia, South Ossetia, Crimea, and the Donbas. Grinda said the mafia now exercised tremendous control over sectors of the global economy. Gonzalez claimed the KGB and its SVR successor had deliberately created the Liberal Democratic party of Russia (LDPR), which worked hand in hand with mafia groups.[15]

Grinda said he agreed with claims made by former FSB officer Alexander Litvinenko. "A significant part of Russian organised crime is organised directly from the offices of the Kremlin," the International Business Times quoted Ben Emmerson, a prominent British attorney who represents the family of slain Russian defector Aleksandr Litvinenko, as saying.[16] According to Litvinenko, Russia's intelligence and security services control the country's organised crime network – with Gonzalez citing the federal security service (FSB), foreign intelligence service (SVR) and military intelligence (GRU).[17]

Organized crime in Russia uses legal businesses as fronts for illegal activities and for setting up illegal product lines. The expansion of organized crime in Moscow, for example, occurred through buying real estate, and through gaining controlling shares of banks and other enterprises. Grinda's 488-page petition to the Central Court in Madrid filed in 29 May 2015 depicts links between the criminal enterprise and top law-enforcement officials and policy makers in Moscow, including some of Vladimir Putin's closest allies, Viktor Zubkov, the chairman of gas exporter Gazprom who was prime minister and first deputy premier from 2007 to 2012, and Zubkov's son-in-law, former

Defense Minister Anatoly Serdyukov. Shortly after his rise to power, Putin exploited his influence over the Russian legislature to create an oil and gas monopoly under Gazprom, Russia's largest company, as a state-controlled operation that has exclusive rights to export natural gas from Russia.[18]

Litvinenko wrote two books, Blowing Up Russia: Terror from Within and Lubyanka Criminal Group, in which he accused the Russian secret services of staging the Russian apartment bombings and other terrorism acts in an effort to bring Putin to power. November 23, 2006, Litvinenko died from what was established as a case of poisoning by radioactive polonium-210. Shortly before his death, former FSB officer Alexander Litvinenko claimed that Simeon Mogilevich, believed to be the "boss of bosses" of most Russian Mafia syndicates in the world, has allegedly had a "good relationship" with Vladimir Putin since the 1990s, and has contacts with al Qaeda to whom he sells weapons.[19] In the year he was murdered, Litvinenko was investigating suspicions that Roman Abramovich was involved in money-laundering and illegal land purchases.[20]

Born in Kiev, Mogilevich earned an undergraduate economics degree from Lviv

University, and specializes in sophisticated, virtually undetectable financial frauds. A 1998 FBI report reportedly said Mogilevich's organization had "approximately 250 members," and was involved in trafficking nuclear materials, weapons, and more, as well as money laundering.21 In early 1990, Mogilevich and his top associates settled in Israel, where they received Israeli citizenship. Mogilevich "succeeded in building a bridgehead in Israel" and "developing significant and influential [political] ties," according to an Israeli intelligence report. In Europe and Russia, the "corruption of police and public officials has been part of the Semion Mogilevich Organization's modus operandi," says a classified FBI document.[21]

The corruption apparently extends to the Russian security system. In 1998, the German national television network ZDF reported that the BND had entered into a secret contract with Mogilevich to provide information on the Russian mob. His reported ties to the BND and also expolice officers in Hungary keep him informed of police efforts to penetrate his organization.[22] Mogilevich is on one of the FBI's top 10 most wanted fugitives. Between 1993 and 1998, Mogilevich caught the FBI's attention when he allegedly participated in a $150 million scheme to defraud thousands of investors in a Canadian company, YBM Magnex, based just outside Philadelphia, which supposedly made magnets. Russian mafia is suspected of having a sizable investment in General Motors via its interest in Canadian auto parts maker Magna International.[23]

Mogilevich is now a citizen of Israel as well as Ukraine and Russia. Close to 25% of the 200 richest people in Russia are Jewish, according to a report by Russian banking website lanta.ru. The report found that of the country's 200 billionaires, 48 are Jews and own a combined net worth of $132.9 billion. Among the 48 Jews who made the list, 42 are Ashkenazi and together have a net worth of $122.3 billion, even though they comprise only 0.11% of the population. The wealthiest Ashkenazi is Mikhail Fridman, who has a net worth is $17.6 billion and is Russa's second richest man. The Ashkenazi billionaires include Viktor Vekselberg (net worth of $17.2 billion), Leonid Michelson (net worth of $15.6 billion), German Khan (net worth of $11.3 billion), Mikhail Prokhorov (net worth of $10.9 billion), and Roman Abramovich (net worth of $9.1 billion).[24]

A 2012 article in the Jerusalem Post titled "At Putin's side, an army of Jewish billionaires" mentioned three Russian-Jewish billionaire oligarchs in particular who are close to Putin: Mikhail Fridman, Moshe Kantor and Lev Leviev.[25] Under Putin, the Hasidic Federation of Jewish Communities of Russia (FJCR) became increasingly influential within the Jewish community of Russia, partly due to the influence and support of businessmen close to Putin, notably Lev Leviev and Roman Abramovich.[26] Leviev is an Uzbeki-born Israeli citizen and devout Lubavitcher. Known as the "King of Diamonds," Leviev has come under scrutiny by the US government and international media for, among other things, both his partnership with a Chinese business group believed to have funded North Korea and his possible role in developing West Bank settlements.[27]

Chris Hutchins, a biographer of Putin, describes the relationship between Putin and Abramovich as like that between a father and a favorite son. Abramovich was the first person to originally recommend to Yeltsin that Putin be his successor.[28] Abramovich is the primary owner of the private investment company, Millhouse LLC and is best known outside Russia as the owner of Chelsea Football Club, a Premier League football club. In 1996, acquired the oil company Sibneft, for about $US100 million, and sold it to Gazprom for $US13 billion a decade later. His $5.6-billion legal dispute with a former business partner, Boris Berezovsky, nicknamed the "Godfather of the Kremlin," uncovered evidence involving illicit activity including protection rackets, contract killings, arms dealings.[29] Abramovich is a chairman of the Federation of Jewish Communities of Russia (which is allied with Putin's administration), and donates money to the Chabad movement.[30]

KOSHER NOSTRA
Trump's mentor Roy Cohn, who was also a mob consigliere, introduced Trump to clients including "Fat Tony" Salerno, boss of the Genovese crime family, the most powerful Mafia group in New York, and Paul Castellano, head of what was said to be the second largest family, the Gambinos. According to an article by Pulitzer Prize-winning reporter David Cay Johnston in Politico, Salerno and Castellano dominated the construction firms that Trump hired to build his Trump Tower and Trump Plaza buildings, buying concrete from them at an inflated price to keep the unions under control. An indictment on which Salerno was convicted in 1988 and sent to prison, where he died, listed the nearly $8 million contract for concrete at Trump Plaza as one of the acts

establishing that S&A was part of a racketeering enterprise. Michael Chertoff, the chief prosecutor in the indictment, called the Genovese and Gambino crime families "the largest and most vicious criminal business in the history of the United States."[31]

In 1987 Donald Trump purchased his first casino interests when he acquired 93% of the shares in Resorts International, which evolved from a CIA money-laundering front company set up by CIA chief Allen Dulles in the 1950's. Resorts International has a sordid history which began in the early 1950's when it evolved from a CIA and Mossad front company which had been established for the purpose of money laundering the profits from drug trafficking, gambling, and other illegal activities. The appropriation by the mafia of casinos like those operated by Resorts International was the result of a decision by the Meyer Lansky Syndicate to expand operations outside Las Vegas.[32] On October 30, 1978, The Spotlight newspaper reported that the principle investors of Resorts International were Meyer Lansky, Tibor Rosenbaum, William Mellon Hitchcock, David Rockefeller, and one Baron Edmond de Rothschild.[33]

Trump found himself in financial trouble when his three casinos in Atlantic City were under foreclosure threat from lenders, he was Bailed out by senior managing director of N.M. Rothschild & Sons, Wilber Ross, who Trump would later appoint to Secretary of Commerce. Ross, who is known as the "King of Bankruptcy," specializes in leveraged buyouts and distressed businesses. In the late 1970s, Ross began 24 years at the New York City office of N.M. Rothschild & Sons, where he ran the bankruptcy-restructuring advisory practice. Along with Carl Icahn, Ross convinced bondholders to strike a deal with Trump that allowed Trump to keep control of the casinos.[34]

Ross has had direct financial ties to several leading oligarchs from Russia and the Former Soviet Union. As of February 2017, Forbes magazine lists Ross as one of the world's billionaires, with a net worth of $2.5 billion. Ross has been Vice Chairman and a major investor since 2014 in the Bank of Cyprus, the largest bank in Cyprus, one of the key offshore havens for illicit Russian finance. His fellow bank co-chair was appointed by Putin. Since the 1990s, Cyprus has served as one the top three offshore destinations for Russian and former Soviet Union flight capital, most of it motivated by tax dodging, kleptocracy, and money laundering.[35]

The Financial Times FT investigation showed that Trump joined forces with the Bayrock Group, a New York property developer founded by Tevfik Arif, newcomer to the US from the Soviet republic of Kazakhstan. Jewish philanthropist Alexander Mashevich's "Eurasia Group" was a strategic partner for Bayrock. Mashevich, who holds both Kazakh and Israeli citizenship, served as president of the Euro-Asian Jewish Congress (EAJC) until 2011. The EAJC is one of the five regional branches of World Jewish Congress (WJC). In 2011, Mashevich announced his intention to found a Jewish version of Al-Jazeera, to "represent Israel on an international level, with real information."[36]

Together with two other prominent Kazakh billionaires, Patokh Chodiev (aka "Shodiyev") and Alijan Ibragimov, Mashkevich reportedly ran the "Eurasian Natural Resources Cooperation." In Kazakhstan these three are sometimes referred to as "the Trio." The Trio recently attracted the attention of many investigators and news agencies, including the September 11 Commission Report, the Guardian, Forbes, and the Wall Street Journal. The litany of the Trio's alleged activities include resource grabbing, money laundering, bribery, and racketeering. In 2010, Arif and other members of Bayrock's Eurasian Trio were arrested together in Turkey during a police raid on a suspected prostitution ring, according to the Israeli daily Yediot Ahronot. At the time, Turkish investigators reportedly asserted that Arif might be the head of a criminal organization that was trafficking in Russian and Ukrainian escorts, allegedly including some as young as 13.[37]

As Bayrock's COO and managing director, Tevfik Arif hired Felix Sater, the son of a reputed Jewish-Russian mobster. Although Trump has denied knowing him, Sater appeared in photos with Trump, and carried a Trump Organization business card with the title "Senior Advisor to Donald Trump." Sater reportedly emigrated with his family to the United States in the mid-1970s and settled in "Little Odessa." During the 1970s and 1980s, the United States expanded its immigration policies, allowing Soviet Jews, with most settling in a southern Brooklyn area known as Brighton Beach (sometimes nicknamed as "Little Odessa"), which is where Russian organized crime began in the US.[38] The investigative reporter Robert I. Friedman revealed in his book Red Mafiya: How the Russian Mob Has Invaded America that the

"Russian" mafia was in fact more Jewish than Russian. Sater had already served time prison for stabbing a man in the face with the stem of a margarita glass. Sater pled guilty in 1998 to one count of racketeering for his role in a $40 million stock fraud scheme involving the Genovese and Bonanno crime families.[39] Sater's Bayrock Group was based in Trump Tower. According to a certified US Supreme Court petition, Sater's FBI handler stated that Sater's father was a boss for the crime syndicate of Simeon Mogilevich.

Bayrock and Trump joined forces to pursue deals around the world, from New York, Florida, Arizona and Colorado in the US to Turkey, Poland, Russia and Ukraine. Their best-known collaboration was Trump SoHo, which was featured in Trump's television show The Apprentice. Jody Kriss, a former Bayrock finance director, has claimed in racketeering lawsuits against his former employer that Bayrock's backers included "hidden interests in Russia and Kazakhstan."[40] Most of the Bayrock-Trump projects either never materialized or were complete failures. SoHo was foreclosed by creditors and resold in 2014 after more than $3 million of customer down payments had to be refunded. Bayrock's Trump International Hotel & Tower in Fort Lauderdale was foreclosed and resold in 2012, while at least three other Trump-branded properties in the United States, in addition to many other concept projects pursued by Bayrock, from Istanbul and Kiev to Moscow and Warsaw, never happened.

Trump and Bayrock partnered with the Sapir Organization, led by the now-deceased Tamir Sapir and his son Alex, in the development of Trump SoHo. During the Cold War, Tamir Sapir, who was born to a Jewish family Tbilisi, Georgia, emigrated to the US where he sold electronics to KGB agents from a storefront in Manhattan. Sapir was ranked on Forbes Magazine's list of billionaires and was a donor to Chabad Lubavitch.[41] Sapir's executive vice president and top aide, Fred Contini, pled guilty in 2004 to "participating in a racketeering conspiracy with the Gambino crime family for 13 years."[42] Alex Sapir's business partner Rotem Rosen is a former lieutenant of Lev Leviev.[43]

All the while, Sater also served as a government informant on the mob and mysterious matters of national security. Sater's lawyer, Robert S. Wolf, while not addressing Sater's relationship with Trump stressed Sater's work for the government, saying he saved lives, including by providing "significant intelligence with respect to nuclear weapons in a major country openly hostile to the United States."[44] Sater, who met Rebbe Schneerson several times as a child, is an active member of Chabad-Lubavitch, and in 2014 was named Man of the Year by Chabad of Port Washington, NY. Sater's rabbi, who presented him the award, explained that it was partly in response to a closed-door meeting he was invited to attend with Sater at the federal building in New York, where dozens of intelligence officers from many agencies praised Sater as a "national hero." One officer, the rabbi explained, said Sater "probably saved tens of thousands of US lives, maybe even millions… through the brave work that he's done." In his own words, Sater explained that his effort aimed of achieving Tikkun Olam.[45]

TRUMP TOWER
Trump Tower has received press attention for including among its many residents tax-dodgers, bribers, arms dealers, convicted cocaine traffickers, and corrupt former FIFA officials. A typical example involves an illegal gambling operation that reportedly took up the entire 51st floor run by the alleged Russian mobster Anatoly Golubchik and Vadim Trincher, a dual citizen of the United States and Israel, Trincher's son Illya, Hillel

Nahmad, the son of a billionaire art dealer and heir of a descendant of a Jewish Lebanese art family, and another follower of Chabad-Lubavitch.[46]

"This is the top of the top of the top in organized crime in Russia," according to the prosecutor.[47] The ring answered to Russian mob boss Alimzhan Tokhtakhounov, whose organization the Interpol believes to be tied to Semion Mogilevich.[48] Tokhtakhounov, who holds both Russian and Israeli citizenship, is one of the world's most notorious Russian mafia bosses, known as the "Little Taiwanese." In 2008, Forbes named him the world's third most wanted, after Osama bin Laden and el Chapo. He is accused of bribing of judges in the 2002 Winter Olympics, where a Canadian figure-skating team were denied their gold medal.[49] Seven months after he was busted in 2013, he appeared near Trump in the VIP section of the Miss Universe pageant in Moscow. Tokhtakhounov operated out of Trump Tower, just three floors down from Trump's penthouse, what prosecutors called "an international gambling business that catered to oligarchs residing in the former Soviet Union and throughout the world."[50]

The indictment filed by against the gambling ring was filed Preet Bharara, then the US attorney in Manhattan. Bharara earned a reputation of a "crusader" prosecutor who for seven years was one of "the nation's most aggressive and outspoken prosecutors of public corruption and Wall Street crime."[51] Following the 2016 election, Bharara claimed that Trump asked Bharara to remain as U.S. Attorney, and Bharara agreed to stay on. However, he was eventually fired, after refusing to resign, as a result of Attorney General Jeff Sessions' request for all remaining 46 US Attorneys appointed during President Obama's administration to resign.

Trump had reportedly personally sold five separate condos in Trump Tower to David Bogatin. David's brother Jacob Bogatin was CEO of a fraudulent company YBM Magnex International, supposedly a world-class manufacturer of industrial magnets, was founded by the Mogilevich. And Vyacheslav Ivankov, another key Mogilevich lieutenant in the United States during the 1990s, also lived for a time at Trump Tower, and reportedly had the private telephone and fax numbers for the Trump Organization in his personal phone book.[52]

In all but a handful of cases, Trump's Mar-a-Lago Club in Palm Beach, FL, which describes itself as "one of the most highly regarded private clubs in the world," sought to fill the jobs with hundreds of foreign guest workers from Romania and other countries. Trump uses a recruiter based in upstate New York, Peter Petrina, to find foreign workers for his resorts, golf clubs and vineyard. Petrina is of Romanian descent and has an office in Romania. Trump pursued more than 500 visas for foreign workers at Mar-a-Lago since 2010, while hundreds of domestic applicants failed to get the same jobs.[53]

Trump's son Donald Trump Jr. made that very claim at a real estate conference in New York in 2008, saying "Russians make up a pretty disproportionate cross-section of a lot of our assets." Donald Trump Jr. added, "we see a lot of money pouring in from Russia."[54] A Reuters review found that at least 63 individuals with Russian passports or addresses bought as much as $98.4 million worth of property in seven Trump-branded luxury towers in southern Florida. The buyers include Alexander Yuzvik, a former executive in a Moscow-based state-run construction firm involved in construction projects of the FSB and GRU; Andrey Truskov, co-owner of Absolute Group, the biggest wholesale electronic business in Russia; and Alexey Ustaev, the founder and president of St. Petersburg-based Viking Bank, one of the first private investment banks established in Russia after the fall of Communism.[55]

The second Financial Times article places Trump in the middle of a money laundering scheme, in which his real estate deals were used to hide not just an infusion of capital from Russia and former Soviet states, but for laundering hundreds of millions looted by oligarchs. One of the people who said he brought Russian money into Trump projects was Sergei Millian, head of the Russian-American Chamber of Commerce (RACC). The Financial Times quotes former Russian MP Konstantin Borovoi in identifying the chamber as a front for intelligence operations during Soviet times. Borovoi, who is also an expert on the KGB, said "The chamber of commerce institutions are the visible part of the agent network... Russia has spent huge amounts of money on this."[56] As explained by James S. Henry writing The American Interest, "All this helps to explain one of the most intriguing puzzles about Donald Trump's long, turbulent business career: how he managed to keep financing it, despite a dismal track record of failed projects."[57]

Millian came under suspicion as part of a wider FBI probe due to US intelligence concerns that Russia was activating networks long thought defunct after the end of the cold war.[58] Millian boasted in an interview with Russian state news agency Ria Novosti that he had built extensive ties with Trump and his organization, of how Russia-US relations would improve under his presidency. "I can assure you he is very positive and friendly," he told Ria Novosti.[59] One of the RACC's main backers is Mikhail Morgulis, a prominent Soviet émigré who also serves as Belarus honorary consul to the US. Morgulis told the Financial Times Millian explained to him he was helping Trump and the Republican party. "We have soft power and we are trying to change relations now," Mr Morgulis said.[60] For Konstantin Zatulin, head of the Russian parliament's CIS affairs committee and a vocal advocate of expanding Russian power, the accusations hint of McCarthyism. Nevertheless, Zatulin conceded, "While the west was playing with James Bond . . . we turned our attention to gaining respect," said Mr Zatulin. "When the west thought the cold war competition was over, they lost respect for their opponent. Now they are waking up to this again."[61]

RUNNING FOR PRESIDENT
Trump's personal counsel, Michael Cohen, along with Trump's Russian mob-affiliated Lubavitcher business associate Felix Sater, and Ukrainian lawmaker Andrii V. Artemenko, delivered a "peace" plan for Russia and Ukraine to former national security adviser Michael Flynn before Flynn was asked to resign. The plan involved lifting sanctions on Russia in return for Moscow withdrawing its support for pro-Russia separatists in eastern Ukraine. It would also allow Russia to maintain control over Crimea, which it annexed in 2014.[62]

Retired United States Army lieutenant general Michael T. Flynn, was Trump's initial choice National Security Advisor, before finally being forced to resign after questionable contacts with the Russian government and revelations that he lied about them to the vice president and the FBI. In 2013, as director of the Defense Intelligence Agency (DIA), Flynn travelled to Moscow where he became the second director of the DIA to be invited into the headquarters of the GRU, though he will later boast of being the first. "Flynn thought he developed some rapport with the GRU chief," a former senior U.S. military official said.[63] Records show that Flynn collected nearly

$68,000 in fees and expenses from Russia-related entities in 2015. The bulk of the money, more than $45,000, came from Russia Today, when he was invited to a gala in Moscow in honor of RT, to participate in a panel on "Geopolitics 2015 and Russia's changing role in the world."[64] Flynn, who had made semi-regular appearances as an analyst on RT after he retired from government service, sat next to Putin, and at the same table as Green Party candidate Jill Stein.

Flynn was also paid $11,250 that year by the American subsidiary of a Russian cybersecurity firm, Kaspersky Lab, and another $11,250 by a U.S. air cargo company affiliated with the Volga-Dnepr Group, which is owned by a Russian businessman. Kaspersky Lab, which makes some of the world's most popular anti-virus software, has long suspected by US intelligence of being used to assist Russian espionage efforts. However, in December 2016, a top Kaspersky Lab official was arrested by Russian authorities and accused of spying for American companies and intelligence services. In 2007 Volga-Dnepr was removed from a list of approved UN vendors following corruption allegations against two Russian officials who steered contracts to the firm.[65]

In March 2016, Trump hired Paul Manafort who has worked in presidential politics since the 1976 Republican convention. Manafort has spent the majority of his recent career with pro-Russian groups in the Ukraine. He's also been forging some intricate business deals for Oleg Deripaska, a close ally of Putin who has been denied entry into the United States due to alleged ties with organized crime.[66] According to Forbes magazine, Deripaska is Russia's sixth-wealthiest man, with an estimated fortune of $13.3 billion.[67] In 2000, he and Roman Abramovich created a partnership and founded RUSAL, the largest aluminum company in the world.[68] In 2010, the Financial Times published a story exploring Deripaska's business relations with Sergei Popov and Anton Malevsky, alleged heads of Russian organized crime groups.[69] Starting in 2005, Manafort negotiated a $10 million annual contract with Deripaska to influence politics, business dealings and news coverage inside the US, Europe and former Soviet republics in favor of Putin's government. Manafort told Deripaska he was pushing policies as part of his work in Ukraine "at the highest levels of the U.S. government — the

White House, Capitol Hill and the State Department."[70]

One of Manafort's biggest clients was the shady pro-Russian Ukrainian billionaire Dmytro Firtash. By his own admission, Firtash maintains strong ties with Ukrainian/Russian mob boss Semion Mogilevich.[71] Firtash and a partner owned half of RosUkrEnergo (RUE), which was founded in 2004 and emerged as Ukraine's sole gas importer in 2006 to 2009. Ukraine's security service in 2005 said may be indirectly controlled by Semion Mogilevich. Russia's state-run Gazprom owned half of RUE, and there are the reports that, as a 50-50 partner, Firtash made his billions as Putin's handpicked surrogate.[72]

Manafort stepped down as Trump's campaign manager in August of 2016 in response to press investigations into his ties not only to Firtash, but to Ukraine's previous pro-Russian Yanukovych government. Bankers close to Putin granted Firtash credit lines of up to $11 billion, which helped Firtash to back Yanukovich who won power and went on to rule Ukraine for four years. The relationship had great geopolitical value for Putin: Yanukovich ended up steering the Ukraine away from the West and towards Moscow until he was overthrown in February 2014.

"Firtash has always been an intermediary," said Viktor Chumak, chairman of the anti-corruption committee in the previous Ukrainian parliament. "He is a political person representing Russia's interests in Ukraine."[73] Yanukovych is mentioned in the unverified Trump Dossier that went public just before the inauguration. He was said to have assured Putin that no one would ever trace alleged cash payments to Manafort back to the Russian president.[74]

Additionally, Trump recently recruited Carter Page, who is well familiar with Russian politics, as one of his foreign-policy advisors. Page, who maintains close ties to a number of prominent Russian politicians and businessmen, worked to open a Merrill Lynch office in Moscow.[75] Page is the founder and managing partner of Global Energy Capital, a New York investment fund and consulting firm specializing in the Russian and Central Asian oil and gas business. His partner in that venture is former Gazprom executive, Sergei Yatsenko. By his own admission, his "e-mail inbox filled up with positive notes from Russian contacts" who were enthusiastic at the prospect of strengthening ties with the US. Page is known as a staunch defender of Russia's ambitions as well as a routine critic of current US policymakers. In January 2017,

Page, whose name appeared repeatedly in the Trump Dossier, was under investigation by the FBI, CIA, NSA, ODNI, and FinCEN.

JARED KUSHNER
In 2015, Trump's son-in-law and chief adviser Jared Kushner, who has strong ties with the Lubavitchers, purchased the former New York Times Building in Manhattan from Leviev. Kushner, who married to Trump's daughter Ivanka after she converted to Judaism, had become what the Times described as Trump's "de facto campaign manager."[76] He was principal owner in his family's real estate company Kushner Companies, and of Observer Media, publisher of the weekly, on-line New York Observer. The Kushner's were friends with Israeli Prime Minister Netanyahu, who stayed at their home in New Jersey, sleeping in Jared's bedroom.[77] Trump's foundation has donated thousands of dollars to Chabad institutions, and Haaretz also reported that the foundation of Jared's parents gave $342,500 to Chabad institutions and projects over a 10-year period.[78] "Israel wasn't a political discussion for him; it was his family, his life, his people," said Hirschy Zarchi, rabbi at the Chabad House at Harvard, where Jared was a member.[79]

May 27th, 2017
Russian ambassador told Moscow that Kushner wanted secret communications channel with Kremlin
Russian ambassador told Moscow that Kushner wanted secret channel with Kremlin
Sergey Kislyak reported to his superiors in December that Jared Kushner, President Trump's son-in-law and adviser, asked him about setting up a communications channel between the transition team and the Kremlin using Russian facilities in the United States.

By Ellen Nakashima, Adam Entous and Greg Miller May 26

Jared Kushner and Russia's ambassador to Washington discussed the possibility of setting up a secret and secure communications channel between Trump's transition team and the Kremlin, using Russian diplomatic facilities in an apparent move to shield their pre-inauguration discussions from monitoring, according to U.S. officials briefed on intelligence reports.

Jared's father, Charles Kushner, was a real-estate titan and one of the most important Democratic donors in the country. He was arrested on charges of tax evasion, illegal campaign donations, and witness tampering in 2004 and was eventually convicted on all charges and sentenced to two years in federal prison.[80] In 2004, Charles Kushner was investigated for hiding violations of federal limits on campaign contributions. He then hired a prostitute in order to blackmail one of the case's key witnesses, whose wife then informed investigators of his attempts at obstructing justice.[81]

As Director of the United States National Economic Council, Trump appointed Gary Cohn, who is currently the president and COO of Goldman Sachs, the investment bank for which Trump took Hillary Clinton and Ted Cruz to task for their connections. On January 27, 2017, the Kushners invited Cohn, Department of the Treasury appointee Steve Mnuchin and several members of the President's cabinet for a Shabbat meal, along with Rabbi Levi Shemtov, from the local Chabad-Lubavitch house, which is only a few blocks away from their home. Also attending were Department of Commerce pick Wilbur Ross and his wife Hilary Geary Ross, and Strategic Communications Director Hope Hicks.[82]

Shemtov heads the Central Committee of Chabad-Lubavitch Rabbis. Shemtov serves the daily governmental and diplomatic needs of the international Chabad-Lubavitch movement, flying to Buenos Aires, Moscow and other capitals. Shemtov is often at the White House, Pentagon, United States Department of State and other venues in official Washington, and maintains close relationships with numerous members of the US Congress, senior Administration officials and leaders in the international community, including a number of heads of state and government.[83]

Steve Mnuchin Second-generation Goldman Sachs alumnus and Skull and Bones member. Cohn and Mnuchin, who have known each other for fifteen years, worked together on building deals years earlier. After leaving Goldman Sachs, Mnuchin invested in Hollywood blockbusters and worked at hedge funds including that of George Soros, who Trump ads have attacked. Mnuchin's business partner, Australian billionaire James Packer, is a close friend and confidant of Israeli Prime Minister Benjamin Netanyahu, whose gifts to the Netanyahu family were being investigated by the Israel Police.[84] Mnuchin told the New York Times in May 2016: "I was there at the beginning when he decided to run for president, and I've been a supporter and quiet adviser behind the scenes to him."[85]

Kushner has acted as a liaison with dozens of influential figures, including Henry Kissinger, Paul Ryan, Rupert Murdoch, and, until recently, Roger Ailes, founder and former Chairman and CEO of Fox News.[86] Jared and Ivanka are close friends with Rupert Murdoch's former wife Wendi Deng, who was rumored to be dating Putin.[87] They are also friends with the wife of Abramovich, Dasha Zhukova, who Ivanka invited to Trump's inauguration.[88] All of them were guests in August 2016 on medial mogul David Geffen's $200 million yacht off the coast of Croatia, and a few weeks later at the US Open.[89]

MESSIAH
Russia, reported the BBC, "has, for the time being, supplanted the United States as a key player in crisis management in Syria."[90] On 19 October 2015, Putin and Netanyahu agreed to allow Gazprom to develop the Leviathan gas fields with major concessions from Israel.[91] "We discussed the continued coordination between our two militaries in the region, which already works quite well," Netanyahu told reporters at a joint press conference in the Kremlin with Putin after they met again in June 2016. "We talked about the challenges to all civilized countries such as terrorism and radical Islam," Netanyahu added. According to an English

translation of Putin's words by the Tass News Agency, the Russian leader stated: "We spoke about the necessity to pool efforts to counter international terrorism. Israel knows only too well what it means and it is fighting against terrorism. In this sense, we are unconditional allies."[92]

According to the Jewish Telegraphic Agency, Putin is popular amongst the Russian Jewish community, who see him as a force for stability. In 2016, Ronald S. Lauder, the president of the World Jewish Congress, also praised Putin for making Russia "a country where Jews are welcome."[93] Russia's chief rabbi, Berel Lazar, of the Chabad-Lubavitcher, said Putin "paid great attention to the needs of our community and related to us with a deep respect."[94] As noted by Joshua Keating, "One of the more intriguing aspects of contemporary Russian Jewish life is the close relationship between the Kremlin and Chabad, also known as Lubavitch."[95] In 1992, Lazar became acquainted with Putin confidant Lev Leviev, who introduced him to Boris Berezovsky and Roman Abramovich. Putin set up a Kremlin-affiliated Jewish structure called the Federation of Russian Jewish Communities. In 1999, Putin's ally Leviev established the new organization, which was chaired by Abramovich. Lazar, an

American citizen and a native of Milan, Italy, was quickly granted Russian citizenship and appointed chief rabbi of the new federation.[96]

Lazar is sometimes referred to as "Putin's Rabbi," appears frequently at Putin's side at public events, and is the leader of the Federation of Jewish Communities (known by its Russian acronym FEOR). Chabad members are a small fraction of Russia's small Jewish community. Adolf Shayevech, a prominent figure in the Jewish community since the late Soviet period, was considered chief rabbi until 2000, and still claims the title. The Russian Jewish Congress, the country's largest secular Jewish organization, also recognizes Shayevech. However, FEOR had received government support, which has restored dozens of synagogues and built Jewish community centers throughout the country. "Eighty percent of all synagogues, the rabbis are Chabad," said Rabbi Alexander Boroda, the organization's chief spokesman.[97] Jason Greenblatt, a former Trump Organization lawyer and now a special representative for international negotiations at the White House, met with Lazar in the summer of 2016.[98]

At the 2006 International Conference of Shluchim, attended by Alan Dershowitz, Lazar told the story supposedly related to by Putin, that when he was a young child, he grew up in a very poor family, but his next neighbours who were Hassidic Jews were extremely kind to him. "He realized," recounts Lazar that, "not only were they kind to a child that wasn't Jewish, but they were kind to a child in a time and place when it was dangerous to do that." In a 2014 meeting with Lazar and chief rabbis from Israel, Europe and Russia, Putin said he "supports the struggle of Israel," was noted as a "true friend" and ally of Benjamin Netanyahu, and pledged to combat anti-Semitism and "Holocaust denial" in Russia. During the meeting the Sephardic Chief Rabbi of Israel, Yitzhak Yosef, said of Putin's rule in Russia: "according to the Jewish tradition, your leadership is decided by the kingdom of G-d, King of the world, and therefore we bless you: Blessed is the One who gave of His glory to flesh and blood."[99]

Rabbi Hillel Weiss, the spokesman for the nascent Sanhedrin, which is composed of right-wing Zionists, claimed that the American media, "tried to create a man-made reality in which Trump could not win. In the end, it did not work. Hashem is moving us towards a greater Jerusalem, and anyone who goes against that, is destined to fail." Rabbi Yosef Berger, who oversees the final resting place of King David on Mount Zion, told Breaking Israel News. "The gematria (numerology) of his name is Moshiach (Messiah). He is connected to the Messianic process which is happening right now. When he promised to move the American Embassy to Jerusalem, he attached himself to the power of Moshiach, which gave him the boost he needed. If you separate from Jerusalem, disaster will follow." Rabbi Berger added, "As the spiritual descendant of the Biblical nation of Edom, America has a very important role to play in the Messiah. But in order to be suited for that role, America had to be humbled."[100]

Orthodox scholars and rabbinic authorities generally believe that rebuilding of the Third Temple of Jerusalem, should occur in the era of the Messiah. The revived Sanhedrin contacted Trump, who has promised to recognize Jerusalem as the capital of Israel, and Putin who expressed desire for the same, to join forces and fulfill their Biblically-mandated roles by rebuilding the Jewish Temple in Jerusalem. The revived Sanhedrin, also known as the Nascent Sanhedrin, was established in 2004. It represents the sixth attempt in recent history, after Rabbi Jacob Berab in 1538, Rabbi Yisroel of Shklov in

1830, Rabbi Aharon Mendel haCohen in 1901, Rabbi Zvi Kovsker in 1940 and Rabbi Yehuda Leib Maimon in 1949. The Nascent Sanhedrin regards itself as a provisional body awaiting integration into the Israeli government as both a supreme court and an upper house of the Knesset, while the Israeli secular press regards it as an illegitimate fundamentalist organization of rabbis.

The current Nasi of the Sanhedrin is Chabad-Lubavitcher Adin Steinsaltz, who has been hailed by Time magazine as a "once-in-a-millennium scholar."[101] Its long-term aims are to build the third Jewish temple on the Temple Mount. The most immediate and obvious obstacle to realization of these goals is the fact that two historic Islamic structures which are thirteen centuries old, namely the Al Aqsa Mosque and the Dome of the Rock, are built on top of the Temple Mount. Al Aqsa is the third holiest site in Sunni Islam. Muslims believe that Muhammad was transported from the Sacred Mosque in Mecca to al-Aqsa during the Night Journey, known as the Isra and Mi'raj.

During Putin's third official trip to Jerusalem in 2012, an Israeli bystander called out in Russian, "Welcome, President Putin." Putin approached the man, who explained the importance of the Temple Mount and the Jewish Temple. Chadrei Charedim, an Orthodox Hebrew news site, reported that Putin responded, "That's exactly the reason I came here – to pray for the Temple to be built again."[102] The Jerusalem Embassy Act, passed in Congress in 1995, initiated the move of the embassy, but has been vetoed by every American president since. The Sanhedrin calls on Trump to withhold the veto after he takes office. "We are poised to rebuild the Temple. The political conditions today, in which the two most important national leaders in the world support the Jewish right to Jerusalem as their spiritual inheritance, is historically unprecedented," Rabbi Weiss told Breaking Israel News.[103]

[1] "Donald Trump - The Manchurian Candidate?" Global Security.
[2] Joel Greenberg. "Rabbi Eliezer Schach, 103; Leader of Orthodox in Israel." New York Times (November, 2001).
[3] Bari Weiss. "Crowdsourcing the High Holy Days." Wall Street Journal (October 2, 2014).
[4] Fishkoff Sue. The Rebbe's Army. (New York: Knopf Doubleday, 2003), p. 12.

[5] Menachem M. Schneerson. "The Difference Between Faith and Trust." Chabad.org (January 15, 1981).

[6] "No One There, But This Place Is Far From Empty." New York Times. (January 14, 2009).

[7] "Public Law 103-457." Thomas.loc.gov.

[8] Ari L. Goldman. "Rabbi Schneerson Led A Small Hasidic Sect To World Prominence." New York Times (June 13, 1994).

[9] The Light of Truth at the UN, (video) Excerpt: Prime Minister Netanyahu at the General Assembly, Chabad.org (September 23, 2011).

[10] Mordechai Lightstone. "Natan Sharansky Praises Work of Chabad at Federation General Assembly." Chabad Lubavitch World Headquarters.

[11] Joseph Telushkin. Rebbe (HarperCollins, 2014), p. 566.

[12] James S. Henry. "The Curious World of Donald Trump's Private Russian Connections." The American Interest. Volume 12, Number 4 (December 19, 2016).

[13] Brian Whitmore. "Putinfellas." Global Security (May 03, 2016).

[14] Ibid.

[15] "US embassy cables: Russia is virtual 'mafia state', says Spanish investigator." The Guardian (February 8, 2010).

[16] Brian Whitmore. "Putinfellas." Global Security (May 03, 2016).
[17] Mark Galeotti. "Putin Welcomes the Return of the Russian Mafia." Newsweek (July 28, 2016).
[18] Brandon Martinez. "Putin, Oligarchy and Alt-Media Delusion." Non-Aligned Media (April 1, 2016); "Duma approves Gazprom export bill." BBC News (July 5, 2006).
[19] Lyndsey Telford, Edward Malnick and Claire Newell. "Listen: Alexander Litvinenko's apparent warning before his death." Telegraph (January 23, 2015)
[20] Luke Harding. "Litvinenko investigating Abramovich money-laundering claims, court told." The Guardian (March 16, 2015).
[21] Robert I. Friedman. "The Most Dangerous Mobster in the World." Village Voice (May 26, 1998).
[22] Ibid.
[23] "Russian Organized Crime." Global Security (accessed March 20, 2017).
[24] Itamar Eichner. "Jewish World." Ynet (February 11, 2014).
[25] Gil Stern & Stern Shefler. "At Putin's side, an army of Jewish billionaires." Jerusalem Post (June 26, 2012).
[26] Yossi Mehlman "No love lost." Haaretz, (December, 11 2005); Phyllis Berman Lea

Goldman. "Cracked De Beers." Forbes (15 September 2003).

[27] Massed Hayoon. "Trump and His Advisors Are Connected to a Self-Professed Friend of Putin." Pacific Standard (January 21, 2017).

[28] Richard Sakwa. The Crisis of Russian Democracy: The Dual State, Factionalism and the Medvedev Succession. (Cambridge University Press, 2011). p. 135.

[29] Martin Fricker. "Roman Abramovich revealed: The dangerous world of Roman and Russia's oligarchs." Mirror (November 5, 2011); Peter Pomerantsev. "The Hidden Author of Putinism." The Atlantic (November 7, 2014).

[30] M. Goldman. The Piratization of Russia: Russian Reform Goes Awry. (Routledge, 2003). p. 132.

[31] David Clay Johnston. "Just What Were Donald Trump's Ties to the Mob?" Politico (May 22, 2016).

[32] F. William Engdahl. "A Mafia Don with a Pompadour." New Eastern Outlook (March 20, 2016).

[33] J.C. Collins. "How Rothschild Inc. Saved Donald Trump (FREEPOM)." Philosophy of Metrics (June 21, 2016).

[34] "What You Need To Know About Commerce Secretary Pick Wilbur Ross,

Trump's Billionaire Pal". Fortune Magazine. (November 20, 2016).

[35] James S. Henry. "The Troubling Russian Connections Of Trump Nominee Wilbur Ross." The National Memo (February 27, 2017).

[36] "Russian billionaire to found 'Jewish Al-Jazeera'." Jerusalem Post (April 7, 2011).

[37] James S. Henry. "The Curious World of Donald Trump's Private Russian Connections." The American Interest. Volume 12, Number 4 (December 19, 2016).

[38] Stephen L. Mallory. Understanding Organized Crime. (Jones and Bartlett Publishers, 2007), pp. 73-87.

[39] "Russian Organized Crime." Global Security (accessed March 20, 2017).

[40] Rosalind S. Helderman and Tom Hamburger. "Former Mafia-linked figure describes association with Trump." Washington Post (May 17, 2016).

[41] "Tamir Sapir, 67, OBM." ColLive (September 29, 2014).

[42] "Russian Organized Crime." Global Security.

[43] Ben Schreckinger. "Trump's mob-linked ex-associate gives $5,400 to campaign." Politico (August 26, 2016).

[44] Rosalind S. Helderman and Tom Hamburger. "Former Mafia-linked figure

describes association with Trump." Washington Post (May 17, 2016).

[45] Felix Sater. "Felix Sater - Man Of The Year: Chabad of Port Washington" 12:28. YouTube (August 8, 2014).

[46] Hillel Nahmad has posted several comments at Chabad.org: Tzvi Freeman. "Going Over." Chabad.org (March 5, 2013); Lazar Gurkow. "A People of Three-Thousand Years." Chabad.org (July 16, 2012).

[47] Rebecca Rosenberg. "Art gallery was 'mobbed'" New York Post (April 25, 2013).

[48] Andrew E. Kramer & James Glanz. "In Russia, Living the High Life; in America, a Wanted Man." New York Times (June 1, 2013).

[49] Andrew Dampf. "Taivanchik Hearing Ordered to Stay Put." The St Petersburg Times. The Associated Press. (13 August 2002).

[50] David Corn & Hannah Levintova. "How Did an Alleged Russian Mobster End Up on Trump's Red Carpet?" Mother Jones (September 14, 2016).

[51] Benjamin Weiser & William K. Rashbaum. "With Preet Bharara's Dismissal, Storied Office Loses Its Top Fighter." New York Times (March 10, 2017).

[52] James S. Henry. "The Curious World of Donald Trump's Private Russian

Connections." The American Interest. Volume 12, Number 4 (December 19, 2016).

[53] "Russian Organized Crime." Global Security (accessed March 20, 2017).

[54] Rosalind S. Helderman. "Here's what we know about Donald Trump and his ties to Russia." Washington Post (July 29, 2016).

[55] Nathan Layne, Ned Parker, Svetlana Reiter, Stephen Grey & Ryan McNeill. "Russian elite invested nearly $100 million in Trump buildings." Reuters (March 17, 2017).

[56] Catherine Belton. "The shadowy Russian émigré touting Trump." Financial Times (October 31, 2016).

[57] James S. Henry. "The Curious World of Donald Trump's Private Russian Connections." The American Interest. Volume 12, Number 4 (December 19, 2016).

[58] Catherine Belton. "The shadowy Russian émigré touting Trump." Financial Times (October 31, 2016).

[59] Ibid.

[60] Ibid.

[61] Ibid.

[62] Megan Twohey & Scott Shane. "A Back-Channel Plan for Ukraine and Russia, Courtesy of Trump Associates." New York Times (February 19, 2017).

[63] Greg Miller, Adam Entous and Ellen Nakashima. "National security adviser Flynn

discussed sanctions with Russian ambassador, despite denials, officials say." Washington Post (February 9, 2017).

[64] Rosalind S. Helderman and Tom Hamburger. "Trump adviser Flynn paid by multiple Russia-related entities, new records show." Washington Post (March 16, 2017).

[65] Ibid.

[66] Jim Wolf. "U.S. revoked Deripaska visa – State Dep't official." Reuters (May 11, 2007).

[67] "Deripaska, Mogilevich Hired Top U.S. Lobbyists, WSJ Says." Moscow Times (April 18, 2007).

[68] Jeanne Whalen. "Aluminum Shake-Up May Loom in Russia." Wall Street Journal (September 25, 2003).

[69] Catherine Belton. "Rusal: A lingering heat." Financial Times (January 25, 2010)

[70] Jeff Horwitz and Chad Day. "AP Exclusive: Before Trump job, Manafort worked to aid Putin." AP News (May 22, 2017).

[71] James S. Henry. "The Curious World of Donald Trump's Private Russian Connections." The American Interest. Volume 12, Number 4 (December 19, 2016).

[72] Robert Kolker. "Will Trump Rescue the Oligarch in the Gilded Cage?" Bloomberg (February 15, 2017).

[73] Stephen Grey, Tom Bergin, Sevgil Musaieva and Roman Anin. "SPECIAL REPORT-Putin's allies channelled billions to Ukraine oligarch." Reuters (November 26, 2014).

[74] Robert Kolker. "Will Trump Rescue the Oligarch in the Gilded Cage?" Bloomberg (February 15, 2017).

[75] Dustin DeMoss. "From Russia With Love: Trump's Alliances With Putin." Huffington Post (June 30, 2016).

[76] Michael Barbaro & Johnathan Mahler. "Quiet Fixer in Donald Trump's Campaign: His Son-in-Law, Jared Kushner." New York Times (July 4, 2016).

[77] Jodi Kantor. "For Kushner, Israel Policy May Be Shaped by the Personal." New York Times (February 11, 2017).

[78] "Report: Trump, Kushner foundations have donated thousands to Chabad." Jewish Telegraph Agency (January 10, 2017).

[79] Jodi Kantor. "For Kushner, Israel Policy May Be Shaped by the Personal." New York Times (February 11, 2017).

[80] Allison Kaplan Sommer. "Meet the Kushners: The Feuding Real Estate Dynasty That Links Donald Trump and Chris Christie." Haaretz (March 1, 2016).

[81] Andrew Ross Sorkin. "Donald Trump's Pick for Fund-Raiser Is Rife With

Contradictions." New York Times (May 9, 2016).

[82] Kaileen Gaul. "The Kushners break bread with Team Trump: Jared and Ivanka welcome several members of the President's cabinet for the first big Shabbat meal at their new DC home." Daily Mail (January 28, 2017).

[83] Fishkoff Sue. The Rebbe's Army. (New York: Knopf Doubleday, 2003), p. 185.

[84] Allison Kaplan Sommer. "The Hollywood Connection Between Trump's Treasury Pick and Billionaire at Center of Netanyahu Scandal." Haaretz (November 30, 2016).

[85] Andrew Ross Sorkin. "Donald Trump's Pick for Fund-Raiser Is Rife With Contradictions." New York Times (May 9, 2016).

[86] Lizzie Widdicombe. "Ivanka and Jared's Power Play." The New Yorker (August 22, 2016).

[87] Sierra Marquina. "Rupert Murdoch's Ex-Wife Wendi Deng Is Dating Vladimir Putin." US Weekly (March 31, 2016).

[88] Susanne Craig, Jo Becker & Jesse Drucker. "Jared Kushner, a Trump In-Law and Adviser, Chases a Chinese Deal." New York Times (January 7, 2017).

[89] Anneta Konstantinides. "Who cares about the tennis? Ivanka Trump sits with

wife of Russian oligarch as she and husband Jared join Wendi Deng, Karlie Kloss, billionaire Clinton-backer David Geffen, Princess Beatrice and Democratic activist at the US Open." The Daily Mail (September 12, 2016).

[90] Jonathan Marcus. "Putin and Netanyahu: A complex diplomatic dance." BBC (March 9, 2017).

[91] "Putin and Netanyahu to strike deal on Levianthan gas field." The Australian. (October 19, 2015.

[92] Tovah Lazaroff. "Putin to Netanyahu: Israel, Russia 'unconditional allies' in war against terror." Jerusalem Post (June 7, 2016).

[93] "Ronald S. Lauder: Russia's fight against anti-Semitism isn't just good for Jews – it's good for Russia as well." World Jewish Congress. (November 1, 2016).

[94] Lev Krichevksy. "In Putin's return, Russian Jews see stability." The Jerusalem Post. (October 10, 2011).

[95] Joshua Keating. "Putin's Chosen People." Slate (November 28, 2014).

[96] Konstanty Gebert. "Putin's Jews." Moment (November/December, 2015).

[97] Joshua Keating. "Putin's Chosen People." Slate (November 28, 2014).

[98] Scott Shane & Andrew Kramer. "Trump Team's Links to Russia Crisscross in

Washington." New York Times (March 3, 2017).
[99] Chaim Lev & Ari Yashar. "Putin: 'I support the struggle of Israel'." Arutz Sheva (July 10, 2014).
[100] Adam Eliyahu Berkowitz. "Trump Upset Victory Divinely Sent to Begin Messianic Process: Rabbis." Breaking News Israel (November 9, 2016).
[101] Richard N. Ostling. "Giving The Talmud to the Jews." Time (18 January 1988).
[102] Adam Eliyahu Berkowitz. BIN EXCLUSIVE: Sanhedrin Asks Putin and Trump to Build Third Temple in Jerusalem. Breaking News Israel (November 10, 2016).
[103] Ibid.[88]

MESSAGE FROM MOSCOW... 2016

Thomas used to say this sentence all the time... "I don't have an AXE to Grind with You!"

When I first listened to Gabe Zolna, I believed Thomas was the one who sent this message below...

This message from MOSCOW was recently emailed to Gabor Zolna on YouTube:

October 20th, 2016
I'm afraid "The Race for the Whitehouse" this is the very last one for the USA as a sovereign country if you ask me. It's factually over with two opposing candidates who have both been maneuvered, yes! Maneuvered because to me, it looks perfectly orchestrated by the higher ups who have, **"AN AXE TO GRIND AGAINST THE PEOPLE."**[89]

This from Google definitions... this is more to do with the destruction of America which is taking place... this is only to make the public aware that Trump and Pence are totally controlled by the Jesuits... Because Trump's partner is Sajwani and Trump obviously got to know Thomas as he probably helped connect the two... and also I believe Trumpence defines the two fraudsters very well... moving in the direction of the Jesuits...

Trumpence - Definition
(derived from the names Donald Trump and Mike Pence)
The punishment or fate a society deserves to receive, e.g. "The American people received their trumpence when they decided hate and ignorance was more affective and important than love and understanding."

Trump - Pence
Trumpence - (Meaning, Definition)
The amount of return on investment on a con job, e.g. "I knew it was too good to be true, but I thought it was worth trumpence."
1.) Something that is fallaciously splendid.
2.) Falsehood, empty talk.

FOOTNOTES:

[81] - summarized from http://www.coindesk.com/where-is-gavin-andresen-the-quiet-exile-of-bitcoins-former-face/

[82] - summarized with details from https://en.wikipedia.org/wiki/2016_Fort_McMurray_Wildfire

83 - summarized from http://www.powerlineblog.com/archives/2016/08/memo-sheds-new-light-on-clinton-russia-uranium-scandal.php

84 - summarized from http://www.ibtimes.co.uk/geothermal-gold-why-bitcoin-mines-are-moving-iceland-1468295

85 - http://www.investopedia.com/news/bitcoin-pizza-day-celebrating-20-million-pizza-order/

86 - http://www.haaretz.com/world-news/u-s-election-2016/1.706420

87 - https://www.nytimes.com/2016/05/10/business/dealbook/donald-trumps-pick-for-fund-raiser-is-rife-with-contradictions.html?mcubz=0

88 - Breaking Bread Together: Jared Kushner and Ivanka Trump Welcome Members of President Trump's Cabinet for Their First Big Shabbat Meal at New D.C. Home | BCNN1 - Black Christian News Network

89 - summarized from *https://books.google.ca/books?id=huLqAwAAQBAJ&pg=PA58*

CHAPTER #13 – The first Jesuit pope & the Dead Pools

This is the first time in the history of the world that we have a Jesuit pope!

And based on their hidden agenda, as well as their own history, that fact alone should strike fear in the hearts of millions. So to begin, let's look a little closer into the background of the Jesuit "Society of Jesus".

Who are the Jesuits?

The Jesuits call their group 'the Society of Jesus', a Roman Catholic order of priests and brothers founded half a millennium ago by the soldier-turned-mystic Ignatius Loyola. On the surface, their claimed intention is to seek and "find God in all things," dedicating themselves to the "greater glory of God" and the good of all humanity

In fact, with 17,000-plus priests, brothers, scholastics and novices worldwide, the Jesuits are the largest male religious order in the Catholic Church, comprised of pastors, teachers, and chaplains, plus doctors, lawyers, and astronomers, among many other roles in Church and society. In their varied ministries, they seek to care for the whole person: body, mind, and soul, and to nurture "men and women for others." [90]

On the whole, it sounds like noble intentions for a generous benefactor. But the first clue to the potential for diabolical implementation of those good intentions shows up when you look at the four vows every Jesuit must agree to when they join the order. I've highlighted the suspicious part in the clip below, taken directly from the Jesuit website at http://jesuits.org/aboutus...

> **Four Vows Of A Jesuit**
> "As members of a religious order, Jesuits take three vows — of poverty, chastity and obedience — **and a fourth vow of obedience specifically in regards to the worldwide mission. In other words, Jesuits must be ready to accept whatever mission the Pope requires, a vow that is reflective of our broader dedication to the universal Church, and to the greater**

good of all people from all faiths and cultures." [91]

The problem here is that the Jesuits are not genuinely supporting the goals they've identified for themselves. They're actually 'crypto-Jews', masking their real identity (and their real purposes) behind a publicly acceptable front!

In case you need a refresher, here's a quick definition to describe 'crypto-Jews'...

> **Crypto-Judaism** is the secret adherence to Judaism while publicly professing to be of another faith; practitioners are referred to as "crypto-Jews" (origin from Greek kryptos - κρυπτός, 'hidden'). [92]

For example, the Dönmeh (Turkish: Dönme) were a group of crypto-Jews in the Ottoman Empire who converted publicly to Islam, but were said to have retained their beliefs.[93]

"Before the Lord does anything, He tells his plans to His servants the Prophets'.-Amos **3:7** [94]

To push this example over the tipping point, I'll mention the Shemitah phenomenon, along with the biblical notion known as the recurring Jubilee Year in this ancient Judaic practice. The previous Jubilee began on September 23, 2015 and ended on October 2, 2016.

You should know that it has been proven that the Shemitah has governed the timing of cataclysmic events on Earth during the past century. There have been several periodic economic collapses and financial crashes during that time, which have aligned perfectly with the Shemitah cycle.[95]

As a clue to understanding why the passengers of MH370 were never coming back, Thomas had prompted me by saying "You need to know where money originates from, that's the key."

And while goldsmiths in England had been craftsmen, bullion merchants, money changers and money lenders since the 16th century, they were not the first to act as financial intermediates. In the early 17th century, the scriveners were the first to keep deposits, for the express purpose of re-lending them.[96]

Fast-forward to this year, and you can see how centuries of Shemitah-scheduled economic events have culminated in the 2017 world-wide bank crisis happening right now! Countries are printing money everywhere at alarming rates, which has never happened before on this scale in world history

The trouble is, history also shows us that when a country attempts to print its way out of debt, the country fails and collapses. What happens when the whole world does it instead?

Today, in 2017, the US national debt is pegged at close to 18 trillion dollars (the greatest level of national debt in world history), but the total debt of all liabilities is actually more than ten times greater. In fact, it is greater than the amount of all goods and services on the entire the planet.

We have been set up to fail!

In the Middle East, ISIS is beheading Christians -- just as the Bible predicted. As the Russians are move into the Middle East, USA forces are pulled out, giving the Russians what they've been trying to achieve for a hundred years -- control of the world's oil supply.

America has signed a peace treaty with Iran, a country that vows to destroy Israel and America. In this treaty, our bankrupt nation is giving our enemy 160 billion dollars. Nothing in this treaty stops Iran from building a bomb, or developing ICBMs that can strike Israel and America! It seems the US is giving aid and comfort to it's own enemies, supplying them with means to destroy the country.

This chaotic assortment of world events could be setting the stage for World War III.[97]

Why is the US federal government in Washington called District of Columbia?

Washington DC was founded in 1871 by the organic act of congress, which means that the US Congress, with no constitutional authority to do so, created a separate form of government for the District of Columbia. It's located on a 10 mile square parcel of land, and has its own police force, its own mayor, and its own taxes.

As it's set up, the District of Columbia is not beholden to any state of America. It's run by the federal government, as a federal district under the exclusive jurisdiction of the congress, and the District is therefore not a part of any US state. This was done because the Act was passed when, in 1871, the nation was essentially bankrupt, weakened financially by the aftermath of the civil war.

So the Rothschilds, the international banking family who wanted to gain a stranglehold on the coffers of America, cut a deal with Congress which immediately placed the country in debt. At the same time, the Act formed a corporation known as 'THE UNITED STATES'. (No, my caps-lock key didn't get stuck, the capitalization is exactly as it appears in the Act, which raises an important point).

This corporation, owned by foreign interests, replaced the original "organic" version of the constitution with a new document, changing the "for" in its title to "of" in the new version. In other words, the original Constitution drafted by the founding fathers, was written with the wording "the Constitution for the United States of America".

Birth certificates, drivers licenses, SSN's, bank statements are all written in capital letters, which means you have registered, submitted or applied to be part of the UNITED STATES OF AMERICA, corporation as a fictitious character.

The altered version reads: "THE CONSTITUTION OF THE UNITED STATES OF AMERICA", with the name in all capitals actually representing a fictitious corporation. So it's not the same document you might think it is, since capitalization — not an insignificant change when one is referring to the context of a legal document.

In other words, the new, altered Constitution serves as the constitution of the corporation and NOT that of America.[98]

How did the District of Columbia get its name?

The Jesuit, John Carroll, who was probably the richest man in America in the 1700's, allowed funding to construct D.C. (which was nicknamed "Rome on the Potomac"). The owner of the land for the new district used to be Frances Pope, and his priest was Jesuit Andrew White.

The Carroll family, who were run by the Pope, the Jesuits of Rome and the freemasons, were key in the American Revolution. John Carroll founded the Jesuit college Georgetown University in 1879.[99]

Where did the name "Columbia" come from?

To name the new District, the Jesuit-influenced founders decided to use "Columbia", which is the name of the 'Goddess of Creation', 'War and Destruction', and also known as the Goddess of 'Death and Pain'.

Incidentally, the statue on top of the Capitol Building, crowned with pentacles and called the "Statue of Freedom", is actually the Greek goddess Persephone, meaning "She who destroys the Light". She is the Queen of the underworld.

Anyway, with their symbols firmly in place in the 10-square-mile plot of land that seats the whole country's leadership, all rule comes from the "District of Columbia", run by the Gnostic Priesthood of Babylon, and under the 'Masonic Rule'.

In fact, added Masonic symbolism is found in the layout of the District of Columbia streets, the Washington monument (Obelisk 666' tall , divide by 12" = 555), the Pentagon, and on the back of the one-dollar federal reserve note.

To mention even more of the names I've already highlighted in this book, some of the Gnostic Priesthood include:

Illuminati, Skull & Bones Society, Hospitalizers, Knights of Malta, Knights of Columbus, Knights of the Round Table, Oddfellows, Society of Jesuits, Jesuit

Priesthood, Club of Rome, Knights Templar, York Rite Temple, Shriners, Inner Temple Bar, International Temple Bar Association, Barristers Inn, Zionists, Jesuits, Jesuits Brotherhood, Milner Group (aka Milners Kindergarten), Round Table Group, Rhodes Crowd, Rhodes Scholars, the Times Crowd, all soles group, cliveden set, the society of the elect, the association of helpers, Junta of three, the secret society of Cecil Rhodes, Chatham House crowd, Commonwealth of Nations, Royal Institute of I international Affairs, Trilateral Commission, Bilderberg Group, Council of Foreign Relations (CFR) Magistrates, Bar Attorneys.

Since 1873, the Global Elite of the so-called "Bohemian Club" has held secret meetings in the ancient Redwood forests of California, with members including former US Presidents Eisenhower, Nixon and Reagan. The Bush family maintains a strong involvement. Each year at "Bohemian Grove", members of this all-male club put on Red, Black and Silver robes, and conduct an Occult Ritual and worship a great stone owl, sacrificing a human being in effigy to the figure known as the Great Owl of Bohemia.[100]

The Georgia Guidestones – Shrouded meaning behind the modern-day 'American Stonehenge'

There's a huge granite monument on one of the highest hilltops in Elbert County, Georgia, looking like a modern-day equivalent to the ancient oracle's monuments in Britain. Alternately referred to as The Georgia Guidestones, or the American Stonehenge, it's engraved with 10 Guides, or commandments, in eight different languages on the four giant stones supporting the common capstone.

The origin of that strange monument is shrouded in mystery, but it is an important link to the Occult Hierarchy that dominates the world in which we live. Although no-one knows the true identity of the man, or men, who commissioned its construction, a well-dressed, articulate stranger visited the office of the Elberton Granite Finishing Company in June 1979 and announced that he wanted to build an edifice to transmit a message to mankind.

He identified himself as R. C. Christian (a pseudonym), saying he represented a group of men who wanted to offer direction to humanity. The messages engraved on the Georgia Guidestones deal with four major fields: (1) Governance and the establishment of a world government, (2) Population and reproduction control, (3) The environment and man's relationship to nature, and (4) Spirituality.

According to a book written by the man who called himself R.C. Christian that was available in the public library in Elberton, the monument he commissioned was erected in recognition of Thomas Paine, along with the occult philosophy he championed. In fact, the Georgia Guidestones are used for occult ceremonies and mystic celebrations to this very day.

THE MESSAGE OF THE GEORGIA GUIDESTONES

1. **Maintain humanity under 500,000,000 in perpetual balance with nature.**
2. Guide reproduction wisely - improving fitness and diversity.
3. Unite humanity with a living new language.
4. Rule passion - faith - tradition - and all things with tempered reason.
5. Protect people and nations with fair laws and just courts.
6. Let all nations rule internally resolving external disputes in a world court.
7. Avoid petty laws and useless officials.

8. Balance personal rights with social duties.
   9. Prize truth - beauty - love - seeking harmony with the infinite.
   10. Be not a cancer on the earth - Leave room for nature - Leave room for nature.

The American Stonehenge's references to establishing a world court and uniting humanity with a living new language foreshadow moves to create an International Criminal Court and a single world government. But the most unsettling message contained in the Georgia Guidestone's "10 commandments" is the first one on the list...

Because limiting the population of the earth to 500 million will require the extermination of nine-tenths of the world's people!

This sounds way too familiar, much like one of the components of the 14-year plan (double SHEMITAH) document Thomas handed me to read in 2008, in Dubai. You can see pictures of the Georgia Guidestones monument at http://www.radioliberty.com/stones.htm [95]

After discovering all of this info and remembering the man I'd met in Dubai, could it be that Thomas is the General of the Jesuits? ... R.C. Christian?

Or perhaps he's actually The Black Pope? Either way, I believe the total amount of people's deaths related to Thomas is approximately 777 (and yes, there's that number again!)

Thomas often used to speak of Melchizedek, the High Priest of God and the king of peace in Abram's time. When I researched that name further, the references to the Hebrew word naphal floored me! as #5307 in Hebrew/Greek definition refers to Naphal

"...there were Nephilim (Giants) on the earth in those days"

On their return to Moses and the people of Israel, the spies complained that the land was defended by what they described as the "sons of Anak ".

These men were Bullies and Tyrants and as a consequence very much Anti-God and "His way of love."

#5307 comes from the root word in Hebrew for 'Nephilim' which comes from the word 'Naphal' (naw-fal') , which is the Prime Root word in 'Hebrew' that means "to Fall", inferior inheritance, fugitive, someone pitied, someone prayed for, someone judged, to smite out, to throw down.

"these children of Adam were to be blessed of God, to be Kings on the Earth and subdue the Earth in the model of God himself. But they fell short of this and became unacceptable to God. God felt that he could not continue to have children raised in this evil mould any longer and determined to destroy these people and cast down the cause of this evil; SATAN and his Ways.

The Dead Pools

When you consider the large number of highly suspicious deaths surrounding the 537 people aboard MH370 & MH17, along with 125 Scientists, 75 High-Level Bankers, 3 Investigative Journalists, and Autumn Radke (CEO of Bitcoin S.E. Asia), it's easy to feel that something strange is going on.

That's why I decided to write this book in the first place. And to finish up, I'd like to show you how unusual this list of new members in these NWO-inspired "Dead Pools" appear at first glance. When you look much deeper, the list is an even less probable result of random chance.

In addition to the mass-murdered Malaysian Airlines passengers, the Dead Pool includes a Denver banker who supposedly shot himself 8 times in his head and torso with a nail gun; the Infectious Disease scientist who was stabbed 196 times; 3 investigative journalists who all work in explosive areas and died within 24 hours…the list goes on and on.

Statistically, it makes no sense… unless they were all intended deaths, carried out with diabolical purpose and precision.

For example, take a look at just one of many lists I've seen, this one direct from Hillarydaily.com, and see how insane this dead pool really is:

Dead Scientists 2004-2015

Alberto Behar, 47, Robotics expert at the JPL 47-year-old NASA scientist Alberto Behar died instantly when his single-engine plane nose-dived shortly after takeoff Friday from Van Nuys Airport. He worked on two Mars missions and spent years researching how robots work in harsh environments like volcanoes and underwater. As part of the NASA team exploring Mars with the Curiosity rover, Behar was responsible for a device that detected hydrogen on the planet's surface as the rover moved. According to the Daily Mail, his death in a plane crash happened in 2014 in LA, California. While plane crashes do happen and scientists do die, Behar's name has now been added to a very long list of scientists and astronomers who have met their untimely ends prematurely, leading us to ask, did Behar know something that 'they' don't want the rest of society to find out?

John Rogers, Tropical Disease expert with the National Institutes of Health

Martin John Rogers was found "near" his wrecked car down in an embankment in western Maryland on Thursday, September 4, 2014, after disappearing on August 21, 2014 when he left home for work at the world-renowned research center near Washington, D.C. No word yet on the cause of death, an autopsy will be performed to determine the manner of death, according to LA Times' The Baxter Bulletin.

Here is where the mystery comes in. According to the report, the search for Rogers didn't start until a "few days after he failed to show up for work," but on the day he disappeared he is seen on a surveillance camera, and used a credit card at a Motel 8 a few hours after he left home. Two days later there is a report of a sighting of Rogers on a "local trail," which authorities have deemed "likely credible." While the search for Rogers is over, the search for answers regarding his disappearance and death continues.

Glenn Thomas, AIDS and Ebola expert and spokesperson for the World Health Organization
Ebola expert Glenn Thomas was among the 298 people who were killed when Malaysia Airlines flight MH17 was shot down and crashed in Ukraine. It is understood he was one of more than 100 researchers who were aboard the flight on their way to an international Aids conference in Australia. Among the other delegates aboard the plane was Joep Lange, a leading AIDS researcher and former president of the International AIDS Society (IAS)

Mark Ferri, 59, Nuclear engineer
The renowned American engineer was found dead in his hotel room in Salford in 2013, after his heart suddenly stopped working. Mark Ferri, 59, from Tennessee, had completed two degrees in engineering as well as an MBA, before becoming a nuclear engineer. At an inquest into Mr Ferri's death at Bolton Crown Court, it was heard that the dad-of-one was visiting Manchester on business on September 18 – the day of his death.

It was said Mr Ferri had been under stress from his job. His wife, Michaela, told the inquest: "He said a number of times, this job is killing me." Mr Ferri was originally due to return to the US a week earlier to see his family, but was asked to remain in the UK for an extra week. On September 5, Mrs Ferri spoke to her husband and said that 'he didn't sound right'. She said: "He said it was just his work and they were giving him additional assignments, and he was feeling overwhelmed and he didn't think he would be able to complete them".

Professor Carol Ambruster, 69, University professor and Astronomy and Astrophysics Officers had found nothing in Ambruster's life or history that appeared suspicious. Philly.com reported; Carol W. Ambruster, 69 was found by her roommate in the kitchen of her apartment in the 5500 block of Wayne Avenue, Germantown with a knife in her neck about 9 p.m., police said. She also had been stabbed in the chest.

Ambruster, a tenured professor in the department of astronomy and astrophysics at Villanova, retired in 2011. Ambruster attended Northeastern University, where she majored in physics, and received her doctorate in astronomy from the University of Pennsylvania in 1984. Her research interests included stars and the history of astronomy.

Anne Szarewski, 53, pioneered the cervical cancer vaccine

Doctors are still at a loss to explain Dr Anne Szarewski's death in 2013 at her Hampstead home in August. Doctors are still at a loss to explain what exactly caused the brilliant researcher's death. She was found with high levels of an anti-malarial drug in her bloodstream, but doctors said this was not thought to have caused her death. The scientist, who pioneered the cervical cancer vaccine, was found dead by her husband at their £2million home, after he warned she was 'heading for a crisis' by working too hard

Dr Anne Szarewski, 53, a university lecturer whose discovery has saved thousands of lives, was begged to slow down by her husband, who was becoming increasingly concerned about the pressure she was putting on herself. In August he found her dead in their four-bedroom home in West Hampstead, north London, after he spent two hours drilling through a door she had locked from the inside. Dr Szarewski is credited with discovering the link between the human papillomavirus and cervical cancer, leading to a vaccine for HPV – the first-ever vaccine against any form of cancer

– which is now routinely given to girls across the country.

Shane Todd, 31, Phd in electrical engineering with expertise with GaN (Gallium Nitride)
Dr. Todd felt increasingly uncomfortable with the work he was doing with the Chinese company Huawei, to the point Shane told his family that he was being asked to compromise US security and he feared for his life. Shane was working on a "one of a kind" machine, with a dual use in commercial and in military application, requiring expertise in the area of GaN (Gallium Nitride).

Shane refused to do what he was being asked to do and turned in his sixty day notice at IME. He found a good job with a company in Virginia, and bought a ticket to fly back to the US on July 1, 2012. Shane was killed late June 22nd, or 23rd, right after his last day of work.

Shane's death was so unusual that CBS 48 Hours did a show on it:

48 HOURS: DID A SON DIE PROTECTING AMERICAN SECRETS? A FAMILY'S QUEST FOR THE TRUTH

http://www.cbsnews.com/news/48-hours-did-a-son-die-protecting-american-secrets-a-familys-quest-for-the-truth/

Dr. Richard Holmes, 48, Weapons expert
Dr Holmes is believed to have worked on the production of chemical protection suits for troops. In 1991 he was the joint author of a scientific paper about an RAF chemical and biological protection system.

The scientist resigned from Porton Down last month, but it is unclear why. But the weapons expert, who worked with Dr David Kelly at the Government's secret chemical warfare laboratory, has been found dead in an apparent suicide.

In circumstances strongly reminiscent of Dr Kelly's own mysterious death nine years ago, the body of Dr Richard Holmes was discovered in a field four miles from the Porton Down defence establishment in Wiltshire. It is not yet known how he died.

Melissa Ketunuti, died January 2013
Firefighters found the charred body of murdered pediatrician Melissa Ketunuti, who was hog-tied, strangled and set on fire in her basement.

Dr. Kentunuti worked at Children's Hospital of Philadelphia, and dedicated her whole life to being a doctor and helping kids with cancer. According to the Philadelphia Inquirer, she earned a doctorate in medicine from Stanford University, and had initially considered working as a surgeon internationally.She worked on an AIDS research fellowship in Botswana through the National Institutes of Health. She also completed internships at Johns Hopkins Hospital and New York University.

Professor Dr. Richard Crowe, 60

Professor Dr. Richard Crowe died May 27, 2012 in an off-road accident in Arizona. Dr. Crowe came to UH Hilo 25 years ago, and helped launch the University's undergraduate astronomy program. His numerous publications and co-authored works added significantly to the body of astronomical literature. He regularly trained UHH student observers with the UH 24-inch telescope on Mauna Kea, and conducted many research programs on that telescope. In 2005, he won the AstroDay Excellence in Teaching Award for his efforts. In 1991, Dr. Crowe was selected as a Fujio Matsuda Research Fellow for his scholarly work on pulsating variable stars. Crowe was also active in the community. He was a longtime member of the Rotary Club of Hilo Bay.

Gelareh Bagherzadeh, Molecular scientist
Gelareh Bagherzadeh died Jan. 17, 2012 when she was shot outside her home. Detectives investigating the murder of the Iranian molecular scientist, who was gunned down in her car as she drove home, and thet believe she was followed or that someone was waiting for her. Bagherzadeh was struck by a single bullet that entered the passenger door window, as she talked on her cell phone with her ex-boyfriend. Bagherzadeh was a molecular genetic technology student at M.D. Anderson Cancer Center in Houston and also active in promoting Iranian women's rights.

James S. Miller, 58, Professor
Professor James Steven Miller died as a result of being attacked during a home invasion. Miller came to Goshen College to teach in 1980, the same year he completed his doctorate degree in medical biochemistry at Ohio State University. He received his undergraduate degree in chemistry in 1975 from Bluffton (Ohio) University. The Goshen College Board of Directors granted Professor Miller tenure in June 1985. He primarily taught upper-level courses taken by students in nursing, pre-medical and other health-related tracks.

Zachary Greene Warfield, 35,
Engineer/Analyst

Zachary Greene Warfield died July 4 in a boating accident on the Potomac River. Zack was a co-founder and a member of the Board of Directors for Omnis, Inc., a McLean, VA-based strategic consulting firm for the intelligence, defense and national security communities. He spearheaded major research initiatives and, in addition to helping steer the company, was directly involved in numerous projects, including analytic training and technology consulting.

Prior to founding Omnis, Zack was an engineer and analyst for the U.S. Government and private industry. As a science and technology analyst, he assessed missile and space systems, managed technical contracts, and investigated Iraq's Weapons of Mass Destruction (WMD) program as a member of the Iraq Survey Group, serving in Baghdad on two separate occasions. As an engineer, he worked on aerospace projects for the National Aeronautics and Space Administration (NASA), the Defense Advanced Research Projects Agency (DARPA), and private industry. Most notably, Zack designed critical guidance systems that ensured a successful landing for the Mars Exploration Rovers, Spirit and Opportunity; his name is inscribed on one of the rovers, and remains on Mars today.

Jonathan Widom, 55, Professor

Professor Jonathan Widom died July 18, 2011 of an apparent heart attack. He was a professor of Molecular Biosciences in the Weinberg College of Arts and Sciences at Northwestern University. Widom focused on how DNA is packaged into chromosomes — and the location of nucleosomes specifically. Colleagues said the work has had profound implications for how genes are able to be read in the cell, and how mutations outside of the regions that encode proteins can lead to errors and disease.

Fanjun Meng, 29, and Chunyang Zhang, 26

Fanjun Meng and Chunyang Zhang drowned in a Branson hotel swimming pool. Both were from China and working in the anatomic pathology lab at the University of Missouri-Columbia. Meng was a visiting scholar and his wife, Zhang, was a research specialist, according to information at the university's website. Meng was working on research looking at a possible link between pesticides and Parkinson's disease. Police said the investigation is ongoing as to the cause of the drowning but had said earlier there was no sign of foul play.

Andrei Tropinov, Sergei Rizhov, Gennadi Benyok, Nicolai Tronov and Valery Lyalin
Scientists Andrei Tropinov, Sergei Rizhov, Gennadi Benyok, Nicolai Tronov and Valery Lyalin died in a Russian plane crash. The five scientists were employed at the Hydropress factory, a member of Russia's state nuclear corporation and had assisted in the development of Iran's nuclear plant. They worked at the Bushehr nuclear power plant and helped to complete construction of it. Officially, Russian investigators say that human error and technical malfunction caused the deadly crash, which killed 45 and left 8 passengers surviving.

Rodger Lynn Dickey, 56, nuclear engineer
Nuclear engineer Rodger Lynn Dickey died from an apparent suicide Mar. 18, 2011 after he jumped from the Gorge Bridge. Dickey was a senior nuclear engineer with over 30 years of experience in support of the design, construction, start-up, and operation of commercial and government nuclear facilities. His expertise was in nuclear safety programmatic assessment, regulatory compliance, hazard assessment, safety analysis, and safety basis documentation. He completed project tasks in nuclear engineering design and application, nuclear waste management, project management,

and risk management. His technical support experience included nuclear facility licensing, radiation protection, health and safety program assessments, operational readiness assessments, and systems engineering.

Gregory Stone, 54, Coastal scientist
Gregory Stone died from an unknown illness Feb. 17, 2011. Stone, who was quoted extensively in many publications internationally after last year's BP oil leak, was the director of the renowned Wave-Current Information System. Stone quickly established himself as an internationally respected coastal scientist who produced cutting-edge research and attracted millions of dollars of research support to LSU.

As part of his research, he and the CSI Field Support Group developed a series of offshore instrumented stations to monitor wind, waves and currents that impact the Louisiana coast. The system is used by many fishermen and scientists to monitor wind, waves and currents off the Louisiana coast. Stone was a great researcher, teacher, mentor and family man.

Bradley C. Livezey, 56
Bradley C. Livezey died in a car crash Feb. 8, 2011. Livezey knew nearly everything about

the songs of birds, and was considered the top anatomist. Livezey, curator of The Carnegie Museum of Natural History, never gave up researching unsolved mysteries of the world's 20,000 or so avian species. Carnegie curator since 1993, Livezey oversaw a collection of nearly 195,000 specimens of birds, the country's ninth largest. Livezey died in a two-car crash on Route 910, authorities said. An autopsy revealed he died from injuries to the head and trunk, the Allegheny County Medical Examiner's Office said. Northern Regional Police are investigating.

Dr Massoud Ali Mohammadi, 50,

Dr Massoud Ali Mohammadi was assassinated Jan. 11 when a remote-control bomb inside a motorcycle near his car was detonated. This professor of nuclear physics at Tehran University was politically active, and his name was on a list of Tehran University staff who supported Mir Hossein Mousavi, according to Newsweek.

The London Times reports that Dr. Ali-Mohammadi told his students to speak out against the unjust elections. He stated "We have to stand up to this lot. Don't be afraid of a bullet. It only hurts at the beginning." Iran seems to be systematically assassinating high level professors and doctors who speak out against the regime of President Ahmadinejad. However, Iran proclaims that Israel and America used the "killing as a means of thwarting the country's nuclear program" per Newsweek.

John (Jack) P. Wheeler III, 66

Last seen Dec. 30, 2010, John (Jack) P. Wheeler III was found dead in a Delaware landfill. He had fought to get the Vietnam Memorial built and served in two Bush administrations. His death has been ruled a homicide by Newark, Del. police.

Wheeler graduated from West Point in 1966, and had a law degree from Yale and a business degree from Harvard. His military career included serving in the office of the Secretary of Defense and writing a manual on the effectiveness of biological and chemical weapons, which recommended that the United States not use biological weapons.

Mark A. Smith, 45, Alzheimer's disease researcher

Mark A. Smith died Nov. 15, 2010 after being hit by a car in Ohio. Smith was a pathology professor at Case Western Reserve University, and director of basic science research at the university's memory and cognition center. He also was executive director of the American Aging Association and co-editor-in-chief of the Journal of Alzheimer's Disease. He is listed as the No. 3 "most prolific" Alzheimer's disease researcher, with 405 papers written, by the international medical Journal.

Chitra Chauhan, 33, molecular biologist
Chitra Chauhan died Nov. 15, 2011, found dead in an apparent suicide by cyanide at a Temple Terrace hotel, police said. Chauhan left a suicide note saying she used cyanide. Hazmat team officials said the cyanide was found only in granular form, meaning it was not considered dangerous outside of the room it was found in.

Potassium Cyanide, the apparent cause of death, is a chemical commonly used by universities in teaching chemistry and conducting research, but it was not used in the research projects she was working on. Chauhan, a molecular biologist, was a post-doctoral researcher in the Global Health department in the College of Public Health. She earned her doctorate from the Institute of Genomics and Integrative Biology in New Delhi, India, in 2005, then studied mosquitoes and disease transmission at the University of Notre Dame.

Franco Cerrina, 62

On July 12, 2011, Franco Cerrina 12 was found dead in a lab at BU's Photonics Center. The cause of death is not yet known, but police have ruled out homicide. Cerrina joined the faculty of BU in 2008 after spending 24 years on the faculty at the University of Wisconsin-Madison. He co-founded five companies, including NimbleGen Systems, Genetic Assemblies (merged with Codon Devices in 2006), Codon Devices, Biolitho, and Gen9, according to Nanowerk News.

NimbleGen, a Madison, WI-based provider of DNA microarray technology, was sold to Basel, Switzerland-based Roche in 2007 for $272.5 million. Cerrina, chairman of the electrical and computer engineering department, came to BU two years ago from the University of Wisconsin at Madison as a leading scholar in optics, lithography, and nanotechnology, according to his biography on the university website. The scholar was responsible for establishing a new laboratory in the Photonics Center.

Vajinder Toor, 34
Vajinder Toor died April 26, 2011, when he was shot and killed outside his home in Branford, Conn. Toor worked at Kingsbrook Jewish Medical Center in New York before joining Yale.

Joseph Morrissey, 46

Joseph Morrissey died April 6, 2011 as a victim of a home invasion. Although the cause of death was first identified as a gun shot wound, the autopsy revealed that the professor died from a stab wound. Morrissey joined NSU in May 2009 as an associate professor and taught one elective class on immunopharmacology in the College of Pharmacy.

Maria Ragland Davis, 52, Biotechnologist

Maria Ragland Davis died February 13, 2011 at the hand of neurobiologist Amy Bishop. Her background was in chemical engineering and biochemistry, and she specialized in plant pathology and biotechnology applications. She had a doctorate in biochemistry and had worked as a postdoctoral research fellow at the Monsanto Company in St. Louis. She was hired at the University of Alabama after a seven-year stint as a senior scientist in the plant-science department at Research Genetics Inc. (later Invitrogen), also in Huntsville.

Gopi K. Podila, 54, Biologist

Gopi K. Podila died February 13, 2011 at the hand of neurobiologist Amy Bishop. The Indian American biologist, noted academician, and faculty member at the

University of Alabama in Huntsville listed his research interests as engineering tree biomass for bioenergy, functional genomics of plant-microbe interactions, plant molecular biology and biotechnology. In particular, Padila studied genes that regulate growth in fast growing trees, especially poplar and aspen. He has advocated prospective use of fast growing trees and grasses as an alternative to corn sources for producing ethanol.

Adriel D. Johnson Sr. , 52

Adriel D. Johnson Sr. died February 13, 2011 at the hand of neurobiologist Amy Bishop. His research involved aspects of gastrointestinal physiology specifically pancreatic function in vertebrates.

Amy Bishop, 45, Neurobiologist

Neurobiologist Amy Bishop murdered three fellow scientists February 13, 2011 after being denied tenure. Dead biology professors are: G. K. Podila, the department's chairman, a native of India; Maria Ragland Davis; and Adriel D. Johnson Sr.

Keith Fagnou, 38

Keith Fagnou died November 11, 2009 of H1N1. His research focused on improving the preparation of complex molecules for petrochemical, pharmaceutical or industrial uses. Keith's advanced and out–of-the-box thinking overturned prior ideas of what is possible in the chemistry field.

Stephen Lagakos, 63
Stephen Lagakos died October 12, 2009 in an auto collision. His wife, Regina, 61, and his mother, Helen, 94, were also killed in the crash, as was the driver of the other car, Stephen Krause, 52, of Keene, N.H.

Lagakos centered his efforts on several fronts in the fight against AIDS particularly how and when HIV-infected women transmitted the virus to their children. In addition, he developed sophisticated methods to improve the accuracy of estimated HIV incidence rates. He also contributed to broadening access to antiretroviral drugs to people in developing countries.

Malcolm Casadaban, 60, Molecular geneticist
Malcolm Casadaban died Sept. 13, 2009 of plague. Casadaban, a renowned molecular geneticist with a passion for new research, had been working to develop an even stronger vaccine for the plague. The medical center says the plague bacteria he worked with was a weakened strain that isn't known to cause illness in healthy adults. The strain was approved by the Centers for Disease

Control and Prevention for laboratory studies.

Wallace L. Pannier, 81, Germ warfare scientist
Wallace L. Pannier died Aug. 6, 2009 of respiratory failure and other natural causes. Pannier, a germ warfare scientist whose top-secret projects included a mock attack on the New York subway with powdered bacteria in 1966. Mr. Pannier worked at Fort Detrick, a US Army installation in Frederick that tested biological weapons during the Cold War and is now a center for biodefense research. He worked in the Special Operations Division, a secretive unit operating there from 1949 to 1969, according to family members and published reports. The unit developed and tested delivery systems for deadly agents such as anthrax and smallpox.

August "Gus" Watanabe, 67
August Watanabe died June 9, 2009, found dead outside a cabin in Brown County. Friends discovered the body, a .38-caliber handgun and a three-page note at the scene. They said he had been depressed following the death last month of his daughter Nan Reiko Watanabe Lewis. She died at age 44 while recovering from elective surgery. Watanabe was one of the five highest-paid officers of Indianapolis pharmaceutical

maker Eli Lilly and Co. when he retired in 2003.

Caroline Coffey, 28
Caroline Coffey died June 3, 2009 from massive cuts to her throat. Hikers found the body of the Cornell Univ. post-doctoral biomedicine researcher along a wooded trail in the park, just outside Ithaca, N.Y., where the Ivy League school is located. Her husband was hospitalized under guard after a police chase and their apartment set on fire.

Nasser Talebzadeh Ordoubadi, 53
Nasser Talebzadeh Ordoubadi died February 14, 2009 of "suspicious" causes. Dr. Noah (formerly Nasser Talebzadeh Ordoubadi) is described in his American biography as a pioneer of Mind-Body-Quantum medicine who lectured in five countries and ran a successful health care center General Medical Clinics Inc. in King County, Washington for 15 years after suffering a heart attack in 1989. Among his notable accomplishments was discovering an antitoxin treatment for bioweapons.

Bruce Edwards Ivins, 62
Bruce Edwards Ivins died July 29, 2008 of an overdose. He committed suicide prior to formal charges being filed by the Federal Bureau of Investigation for an alleged

criminal connection to the 2001 anthrax attacks. Ivins was likely solely responsible for the deaths of five persons, and the injury of dozens of others, resulting from the mailings of several anonymous letters to members of Congress and members of the media in September and October, 2001, which letters contained Bacillus anthracis, commonly referred to as anthrax. Ivins was a coinventor on two US patents for anthrax vaccine technology.

Laurent Bonomo, 23 and Gabriel Ferez, 23
Laurent Bonomo and Gabriel Ferez died July 3, 2008 after being bound, gagged, stabbed and set alight. Laurent, a student in the proteins that cause infectious disease, had been stabbed 196 times, with half of them being administered to his back after he was dead. Gabriel, who hoped to become an expert in ecofriendly fuels, suffered 47 separate injuries.

Yongsheng Li, 29
Yongsheng Li died as a result of unknown causes sometime after 4 p.m. on March 10, 2007 when he was last seen. He was found in a pond between the Women's Sports Complex and State Botanical Gardens on South Milledge Avenue Sunday and had been missing 16 days. Li was a doctoral student from China who studied receptor

cells in Regents Professor David Puett's biochemistry and molecular biology laboratory.

Dr. Mario Alberto Vargas Olvera, 52,
Biologist

Dr. Mario Alberto Vargas Olvera died Oct. 6, 2007 as a result of several blunt-force injuries to his head and neck. Ruled as murder. Found in his home. He was a nationally and internationally recognized biologist.

Yoram Kaufman, 57

Yoram Kaufman died May 31, 2006 (one day before his 58th birthday) when he was struck by an automobile while riding his bicycle near the Goddard center's campus in Greenbelt. Dr. Kaufman began working at the space flight center in 1979 and spent his entire career there as a research scientist. His primary fields were meteorology and climate change, with a specialty in analyzing aerosols — airborne solid and liquid particles in the atmosphere. In recent years, he was senior atmospheric scientist in the Earth-Sun Exploration Division and played a key role in the development of NASA's Terra satellite, which collects data about the atmosphere.

Lee Jong-woo, 61

Lee Jong-woo died May 22, 2006 after suffering a blood clot on the brain. Lee was spearheading the organization's fight against global threats from bird flu, AIDS and other infectious diseases. WHO director-general since 2003, Lee was his country's top international official. The affable South Korean, who liked to lighten his press conferences with jokes, was a keen sportsman with no history of ill-health, according to officials.

Leonid Strachunsky, Bio-weapons researcher
Leonid Strachunsky died June 8, 2005 after being hit on the head with a champagne bottle. Strachunsky specialized in creating microbes resistant to biological weapons. Strachunsky was found dead in his hotel room in Moscow, where hed come from Smolensk en route to the United States. Investigators are looking for a connection between the murder of this leading bio weapons researcher and the hepatitis outbreak in Tver, Russia.

Robert J. Lull, 66
Robert J. Lull died May 19, 2005 of multiple stab wounds. Despite his missing car and apparent credit card theft, homicide Inspector Holly Pera said investigators aren't convinced that robbery was the sole motive for Lull's killing. She said a robber

would typically have taken more valuables from Lull's home than what the killer left with. Lull had been chief of nuclear medicine at San Francisco General Hospital since 1990 and served as a radiology professor at UCSF. He was past president of the American College of Nuclear Physicians and the San Francisco Medical Society and served as editor of the medical society's journal, San Francisco Medicine, from 1997 to 1999. Lee Lull said her former husband was a proponent of nuclear power and loved to debate his political positions with others.

Todd Kauppila, 41
Todd Kauppila died May 8, 2005 of hemorrhagic pancreatitis at the Los Alamos hospital, according to the state medical examiner's office. Picture of him was not available to due secret nature of his work. His death came two days after Kauppila publicly rejoiced over news that the lab's director was leaving. Kauppila was fired by director Pete Nanos on Sept. 23, 2004 following a security scandal. Kauppila said he was fired because he did not immediately return from a family vacation during a lab investigation into two classified computer disks that were thought to be missing. The apparent security breach forced Nanos to shut down the lab for several weeks.

Kauppila claimed he was made a scapegoat over the disks, which investigators concluded never existed. The mistake was blamed on a clerical error. After he was fired, Kauppila accepted a job as a contractor at Bechtel Nevada Corp., a research company that works with Los Alamos and other national laboratories. He was also working on a new Scatter Reduction Grids in Megavolt Radiography focused on metal plates or crossed grids to act to stop the scattered radiation while allowing the unscattered or direct rays to pass through with other scientists: Scott Watson (LANL, DX-3), Chuck Lebeda (LANL, XTA), Alan Tubb (LANL, DX-8), and Mike Appleby (Tecomet Thermo Electron Corp.)

David Banks, 55, Scientist

David Banks died May 8, 2005. Banks, based in North Queensland, died in an airplane crash, along with 14 others. He was known as an Agro Genius inventing the mosquito trap used for cattle. Banks was the principal scientist with quarantine authority, Biosecurity Australia, and heavily involved in protecting Australians from unwanted diseases and pests. Most of Dr Banks' work involved preventing potentially devastating diseases making their way into Australia. He had been through Indonesia looking at the potential for foot and mouth disease to spread through the archipelago and into Australia. Other diseases he had fought to keep out of Australian livestock herds and fruit orchards include classical swine fever, Nipah virus and Japanese encephalitis.

Dr. Douglas James Passaro, 43

Dr. Douglas James Passaro died April 18, 2005 from unknown cause in Oak Park, Illinois. Dr. Passaro was a brilliant epidemiologist who wanted to unlock the secrets of a spiral-shaped bacteria that causes stomach disease. He was a professor who challenged his students with real-life exercises in bioterrorism. He was married to Dr. Sherry Nordstrom.

Geetha Angara, 43, Chemist

Geetha Angara died February 8, 2005. This formerly missing chemist was found in a Totowa, New Jersey water treatment plant's tank. Angara, 43, of Holmdel, was last seen on the night of Feb. 8 doing water quality tests at the Passaic Valley Water Commission plant in Totowa, where she worked for 12 years. Divers found her body in a 35-foot-deep sump opening at the bottom of one of the emptied tanks. Investigators are treating Angara's death as a possible homicide. Angara, a senior chemist with a doctorate from New York University, was married and mother of three.

Jeong H. Im, 72, Protein chemist
Jeong H. Im died January 7, 2005. Korean Jeong H. Im died of multiple stab wounds to the chest before firefighters found in his body in the trunk of a burning car on the third level of the Maryland Avenue Garage. A retired research assistant professor at the University of Missouri – Columbia and primarily a protein chemist, MUPD with the assistance of the Columbia Police Department and Columbia Fire Department are conducting a death investigation of the incident. A "person of interest" described as a male 6'–6'2" wearing some type of mask possible a painters mask or drywall type mask was seen in the area of the Maryland Avenue Garage. Dr. Im was primarily a protein chemist and he was a researcher in the field.

Darwin Kenneth Vest
Darwin Kenneth Vest, born April 22, 1951, was an internationally renowned entomologist, expert on hobo spiders and other poisonous spiders and snakes. Darwin disappeared in the early morning hours of June 3, 1999 while walking in downtown Idaho Falls, Idaho (USA). The family believes foul play was involved in his disappearance. A celebration of Darwin's life was held in Idaho Falls and Moscow on the

one-year anniversary of his disappearance. The services included displays of Darwin's work and thank you letters from school children and teachers. Memories of Darwin were shared by at least a dozen speakers from around the world and concluded with the placing of roses and a memorial wreath in the Snake River. A candlelight vigil was also held that evening on the banks of the Snake River.

Darwin was declared legally dead the first week of March 2004, and now the family is in the process of obtaining restraining orders against several companies who saw fit to use his name and photos without permission. His brother David is legal conservator of the estate and his sister Rebecca is handling issues related to Eagle Rock Research and ongoing research projects.Media help in locating Darwin is welcome. Continuing efforts to solve this mystery include recent DNA sampling. Stories about his disappearance continue to appear throughout the world. Issues surrounding missing adult investigations have received new attention following the tragedies of 911.

Tom Thorne, 64; Beth Williams, 53
Tom Thorne and Beth Williams died December 29, 2004. The husband-and-wife wildlife veterinarians were nationally

prominent experts on chronic wasting disease and brucellosis. The two wildlife scientists were killed in a snowy-weather crash on U.S. 287 in northern Colorado.

Taleb Ibrahim al-Daher, Nuclear scientist
Taleb Ibrahim al-Daher died December 21, 2004. The Iraqi nuclear scientist was shot dead north of Baghdad by unknown gunmen. He was on his way to work at Diyala University when armed men opened fire on his car as it was crossing a bridge in Baqouba, 57 km northeast of Baghdad. The vehicle swerved off the bridge and fell into the Khrisan river. Al-Daher, who was a professor at the local university, was removed from the submerged car and rushed to Baqouba hospital where he was pronounced dead.

John R. La Montagne, 61
John R. La Montagne died November 2, 2004 while in Mexico, no cause stated, later disclosed as pulmonary embolism. PhD, Head of US Infectious Diseases unit under Tommie Thompson. Was NIAID Deputy Director. Expert in AIDS Program work and Microbiology and Infectious Diseases.

Matthew Allison, 32
Matthew Allison died October 13, 2004, after the fatal explosion of a car parked at an

Osceola County, Fla., Wal-Mart store. It was no accident, Local 6 News has learned. Allison was found inside a burned car. Witnesses said the man left the store at about 11 p.m. and entered his Ford Taurus car when it exploded. Investigators said they found a Duraflame log and propane canisters on the front passenger's seat. Allison had a college degree in molecular biology and biotechnology.

Mohammed Toki Hussein al-Talakani, 40,
Nuclear scientist

Mohammed Toki Hussein al-Talakani died September 5, 2004. The Iraqi nuclear scientist was shot dead in Mahmudiya, south of Baghdad. He was a practicing nuclear physicist since 1984.

John Clark, 52, Professor

Professor John Clark died August 12, 2004. Found hanged in his holiday home, he was an expert in animal science and biotechnology where he developed techniques for the genetic modification of livestock; this work paved the way for the birth, in 1996, of Dolly the sheep, the first animal to have been cloned from an adult. Clark was Head of the science lab which created Dolly the sheep.

Prof Clark led the Roslin Institute in Midlothian, one of the world s leading animal biotechnology research centers. He played a crucial role in creating the transgenic sheep that earned the institute worldwide fame. He was put in charge of a project to produce human proteins (which could be used in the treatment of human diseases) in sheep's milk. Clark and his team focused their study on the production of the alpha-I-antitryps in protein, which is used for treatment of cystic fibrosis. Prof Clark also founded three spin-out firms from Roslin – PPL Therapeutics, Rosgen and Roslin BioMed.

Dr. John Badwey, 54, Biochemist

Dr. John Badwey died July 21, 2004. He was a scientist and accidental politician when he opposed disposal of sewage waste program of exposing humans to sludge. Badwey suddenly developed pneumonia-like symptoms and died within two weeks. He was a Biochemist at Harvard Medical School specializing in infectious diseases.

Dr. Bassem al-Mudares

Dr. Bassem al-Mudares died July 21, 2004. His mutilated body was found in the city of Samarra, Iraq*. He was a Phd. chemist and had been tortured before being killed. He was a drug company worker who had a chemistry doctorate.

Stephen Tabet, 42, Professor

Professor Stephen Tabet died on July 6, 2004 from an unknown illness. He was an associate professor and epidemiologist at the University of Washington. A world-renowned HIV doctor and researcher who worked with HIV patients in a vaccine clinical trial for the HIV Vaccine Trials Network

Dr. Larry Bustard, 53

Dr. Larry Bustard died July 2, 2004 from unknown causes. He was a Sandia scientist in the Department of Energy who helped develop a foam spray to clean up congressional buildings and media sites during the anthrax scare in 2001. He worked at Sandia National Laboratories in Albuquerque. As an expert in bioterrorism, his team came up with a new technology used against biological and chemical agents.

Edward Hoffman, 26

Edward Hoffman died July 1, 2004 from unknown causes. Hoffman was a professor and a scientist who also held leadership positions within the UCLA medical community. He worked to develop the first human PET scanner in 1973 at Washington University in St. Louis.

John Mullen, 67, Nuclear physicist

John Mullen died June 29, 2004, poisoned with a huge dose of arsenic. Mullen was a nuclear research scientist with McDonnell Douglas. Police investigating will not say how Mullen was exposed to the arsenic or where it came from. At the time of his death he was doing contract work for Boeing.

Dr. Paul Norman, 52

Dr. Paul Norman was killed on June 27, 2004 when the single-engine Cessna 206 he was piloting crashed in Devon. An expert in chemical and biological weapons, he traveled the world lecturing on defending against the scourge of weapons of mass destruction. He was married with a 14-year-old son and a 20-year-old daughter, and was the chief scientist for chemical and biological defense at the Ministry of Defense's laboratory at Porton Down, Wiltshire. The crash site was examined by officials from the Air Accidents Investigation Branch and the wreckage of the aircraft was removed from the site to the AAIB base at Farnborough.

Dr. Assefa Tulu, 45

Dr. Assefa Tulu died of a hemorrhagic stroke on June 24, 2004. Dr. Tulu joined the health department in 1997 and served for five years as the county's lone epidemiologist. He was charged with trackcing the health of the county, including the spread of diseases, such as syphilis, AIDS and measles. He also designed a system for detecting a bioterrorism attack involving viruses or bacterial agents. Tulu often coordinated efforts to address major health concerns in Dallas County, such as the West Nile virus outbreaks of the past few years, and worked with the media to inform the public. The Dallas County Epidemiologist was found face down, dead in his office.

Thomas Gold, 84
Thomas Gold died June 22, 2004 after a long term battle with heart failure. Austrian born scientist became famous over the years for a variety of bold theories that flout conventional wisdom and reported in his 1998 book, "The Deep Hot Biosphere," the idea challenges the accepted wisdom of how oil and natural gas are formed and, along the way, proposes a new theory of the beginnings of life on Earth and potentially on other planets.

Gold's theory of the deep hot biosphere holds important ramifications for the possibility of life on other planets, including seemingly inhospitable planets within our own solar system. He was Professor Emeritus of Astronomy at Cornell University and was the founder (and for 20 years director) of Cornell Center for Radiophysics and Space Research. He was also involved in air accident investigations.

Antonina Presnyakova, 46

Antonina Presnyakova died May 25, 2004. A Russian scientist at a former Soviet biological weapons laboratory in Siberia, Presnyakova died after an accident with a needle laced with ebola. Scientists and officials said the accident had raised concerns about safety and secrecy at the State Research Center of Virology and Biotechnology, known as Vector, which in Soviet times specialized in turning deadly viruses into biological weapons. Vector has been a leading recipient of aid in an American program.

Dr. Eugene Mallove, 56

Dr. Eugene Mallove died May 14, 2004. Autopsy confirmed Mallove died as a result of several blunt-force injuries to his head and neck, and his death was ruled as murder. Found at the end of his driveway. Mallove, an Alternative Energy Expert, was working on a viable energy alternative program and announcement.

The Norwich Free Academy graduate was beaten to death during an alleged robbery.

Mallove was well respected for his knowledge of cold fusion. He had just published an "open letter" outlining the results of and reasons for his last 15 years in the field of "new energy research." Dr. Mallove was convinced it was only a matter of months before the world would actually see a free energy device.

William T. McGuire, 39
William T. McGuire was found May 5, 2004, last seen late April 2004. His body was found in three suitcases floating in Chesapeake Bay. He was NJ University Professor and Senior programmer analyst and adjunct professor at the New Jersey Institute of Technology in Newark. He emerged as one of the world's leading microbiologists and an expert in developing and overseeing multiple levels of biocontainment facilities.

Ilsley Ingram, age 84
Ilsley Ingram died on April 12, 2004 from unknown causes. Ingram was Director of the Supraregional Haemophilia Reference Centre and the Supraregional Centre for the Diagnosis of Bleeding Disorders at the St. Thomas Hospital in London. Although his age is most likely the reason for his death, why wasn't this confirmed by the family in the news media?

Mohammed Munim al-Izmerly, Chemistry professor
Distinguished Iraqi chemistry professor Mohammed Munim al-Izmerly died in American custody from a sudden hit to the back of his head caused by blunt trauma. It was uncertain exactly how he died, but someone had hit him from behind, possibly with a bar or a pistol. His battered corpse turned up at Baghdad's morgue and the cause of death was initially recorded as "brainstem compression". It was discovered that US doctors had made a 20cm incision in his skull.

Vadake Srinivasanm, Microbiologist
Vadake Srinivasanm died March 13, 2004 when his car crashed into the guard rail in Baton Rouge, LA. Death was ruled a stroke. He was originally from India, was one of the most-accomplished and respected industrial biologists in academia, and held two doctorate degrees.

Dr. Michael Patrick Kiley, 62
Dr. Michael Patrick Kiley died January 24, 2004 of massive heart attack. A world-class expert in Ebola, Mad Cow disease, it is interesting to note, he had a good heart, but it "gave out". Dr. Shope and Dr. Kiley were working on the lab upgrade to BSL 4 at the UTMB Galvaston [101]

The scientists were assassinated to make way for many reasons from biological warfare, chem trails to the Alien introduction soon to come, bringing the Messiah, who will be Jewish, of course.

Currently, it is generally accepted by "Ufologists" that **"Aliens" are making use of an underwater base in the Caspian Sea, which Kazakhstan borders.**

Russia spacecraft are now the only means by which astronauts can travel to the International Space Station, making Baikonur, Kazakhstan, the sole launch site used for manned missions to the ISS.

Future War in space: Kamikazes, kidnapper satellites and lasers
By Jim Sciutto and Jennifer Rizzo, CNN
Updated 9:06 AM ET, Tue November 29, 2016

Russia launched an additional satellite named **Luch** with both maneuvering and spying capabilities.
 Luch parked itself next to three US commercial satellites and one European satellite. The Russians flew the satellite close enough to collect both civilian and, possibly, sensitive military information.

(my girlfriend's name was Lutchy in Dubai, 2007)

But Luch's capabilities don't end with the ability to spy. "If the operators of this spacecraft so chose, they could direct it to actually hit another spacecraft," said Graziani.

Like Kosmos, Luch's ability to maneuver has the potential to make it into a satellite killer.

It appears the bankers were assassinated to make way for the NWO's cryptocurrencies and GoldMoney financial revolution,'the greatest experiment in monetary policy in the history of the world'. Quoted Jacob Rothschild, August 2016

REGARDING USA Interest Rates, Expect them to increase 7 times throughout 2017-18.

I never invested in cryptocurrencies, ever . I did 'test the waters' , by opening an account with KRAKEN in 2015 but never bought anything. I just wanted to see what might happen and sure enough, approximately 6 months after I opened the account, I received an email from Kraken saying that if I ever invested in cryptos I would be targeted.

The article below comes from the GoldMoney website.

GOLDMONEY
By Alasdair Macleod, July 06, 2017

Over half the world's population, living in the Eurasian land mass, understands that gold is money. The leaders of the Asian nations also know that this is true as well. The leaders of the security and economic alliance of the Shanghai Cooperation Organization, which now incorporates most of these peoples, also know that to become independent of Western hegemony and to forge their own way, they must abandon Western financial systems and markets, replacing them with a new monetary order, serving their own needs. This is demonstrated in the establishment of parallel multinational financial institutions, duplicating and replacing dollar-centric development banks and settlement organizations.

The direction of travel for the SCO is to eliminate the use of the dollar for cross-border settlements between SCO member states: that much has been made clear. The replacement monetary arrangement must avoid the fundamental weaknesses of the dollar as a fiat currency, partly because these weaknesses will be exposed as the emergence of the SCO undermines the dollar, and partly because the principal drivers of SCO economic policy, China and Russia, have shown through their actions that they have a different vision of their destiny from imperial America.

A battle between currencies.
The pace has been accelerated by the election of President Trump. It is now becoming more important for China and Russia to confront this issue and take the initiative. The time when they could just rely on America to make the strategic mistakes is probably over, and more positive action is required.

The most effective way for them to win this currency war is to expose the inherent weaknesses of the dollar by resorting to a sound money arrangement, backed by gold. The objective is for China and Russia to banish all foreign control of money in their trade arrangements and spheres of economic influence, and to create ubiquity in money within the enlarged SCO (Shanghai Cooperation Organization).

This appears to have been in accordance with the long-term planning of China, which has accumulated a substantial undeclared stash of bullion since 1983, likely in excess of 20,000 tonnes, and encouraged her private citizens to accumulate up to 15,000 tonnes since 2002. Russia has also been accumulating gold aggressively.

China and Russia must make the yuan and rouble sound without being blamed for the consequential collapse of the dollar, and the other welfare-nation currencies. This can be achieved by limiting access to gold-backed yuan and roubles to residents of their own countries initially, before making them available more widely. It will make it less easy for the Americans to blame the demise of the fiat dollar on the domestic actions of the Chinese and Russian governments.

The almost certain outcome of the currency war, if China and Russia pursue the sound-money route will be to secure the trade dominance of the Shanghai Cooperation Organization, and the isolation of America as a power. The era of state money unbacked by gold, which has ended up impoverishing everyone other than lending bankers and their favoured customers, will finally come to an end.

Here is my experience with GoldMoney/BitGold:

I invested in a Gold account with GoldMoney/BitGold in the fall of 2015 and had money taken out of my account. I noticed it within 24 hours and asked GoldMoney/BitGold support, "Who took it?"

The thief would have had a BitGold account, because the money was transferred from my account into another GoldMoney/BitGold account, but they never got back to me with a reply. I contacted BitGold a few times but never ever got a reply. To top it off, GoldMoney charged me a $25.00 fee to reverse the theft.

FOOTNOTES:
[90] - summarized from http://jesuits.org/aboutus

[91] - summarized from http://jesuits.org/aboutus; bolding added for emphasis

[92] - https://en.wikipedia.org/wiki/Crypto-Judaism

[93] - https://en.wikipedia.org/wiki/Dönmeh

[94] - https://www.bible.com/bible/105/AMO.3.7.ncv

[95] - summarized from http://cosmicconvergence.org/?p=14660

[96] - summarized from https://en.wikipedia.org/wiki/History_of_money

[97] - summarized with details from http://www.shemitah-blood-moons.net/jubilee.html

[98] - summarized from https://tabublog.com/2015/01/05/the-united-states-is-not-what-you-think-it-is/

[99] - summarized with details from https://www.bibliotecapleyades.net/vatican/esp_vatican37.htm

[100] - summarized with details from http://www.usavsus.info/

[101] - summarized from http://www.radioliberty.com/stones.htm

[102] - summarized from https://hillarydaily.com/brandon/2017/03/21/the-dead-pools-125-scientists-75-high-level-bankers-and-within-24-hours-3-investigative-journalists-2/

[103] - from https://www.davidicke.com/article/418491/emmanuel-bonaparte-macron-declares-will-govern-like-roman-god

CHAPTER #14 – Fake News and the Feast of Trumpets

The following recent 4 write-ups are very interesting and horrifying …

President of France:

Emmanuel Bonaparte: Macron Declares He Will Govern Like a Roman God

by Jack Montgomery 4 Jul 2017

French president Emmanuel Macron has declared he will govern France like Jupiter, the Roman king of the gods, shortly after officials told the media his thought process was "too complex" for journalists to understand.

"And the king shall do according to his will; and he shall exalt himself, and magnify himself above every god, and shall speak marvellous things against the God of gods, and shall prosper till the indignation be accomplished: for that that is determined shall be done." **Daniel11:36 (KJV)**

EDITOR'S NOTE:*Perhaps jealous that Jared Kushner was getting all the attention in 2017's Race To The Antichrist sweepstakes, French president Emmanuel Macron has now declared that he will "rule France like a Roman god", and that his thought processes are "too complex" for journalists to understand. Narcissist much? Honestly, this is a "wow" moment to say the least. If this is how he starts his presidency, as a self-declared Roman god, where does he plan on taking it? Needless to say we will be watching...closely. Don't be jelly, Jared, but you got some serious competition.*

Summoning over 900 politicians from both houses of the French parliament to a rare Congress at the palace of Louis XIV – the 'Sun King' – in Versailles, he threatened to overrule lawmakers with a referendum if they try to frustrate the "reforms" he wishes to impose on the legislature. Such assemblies are usually reserved for times of national crisis.

Reuters reports him as saying he desires to reign as a "Jupiterian" president — "a remote, dignified figure, like the Roman god of gods, who weighs his rare pronouncements carefully".

In 2010, Macron left the Commission To Improve French Growth for a job at **ROTHSCHILD & CIE BANQUE** in Paris, *despite having no experience in acquisitions and mergers*. He became an overnight millionaire, and quit his job for Rothschild to seek political office. He only served 18 months in the Ministry of Economy, Industry and Digital Data before seeking the Presidency.

Let's think about this. He was given a multi-million dollar job in a bank owned by the Rothschild family despite having no experience in banking, then quit to seek a $70K a year political office, in a field that he also had no experience in, before running for President of France.

It gets better. His political party, "En Marche", is funded by BNP Paribas, a French bank *owned by the Rothschilds!*

Now Macron, who worked so long for Rothschild, he is now the most powerful man in France. [97]

French President Macron has spent $30,000 on makeup services in just 3 months

https://www.washingtonpost.com/news/worldviews/wp/2017/08/25/french-president-macron-has-spent-30000-on-makeup-services-in-just-3-months/?utm_term=.a3358ee1a174

I emailed my story to the Washington Post in May, 2017... the editor called me to say, "It's not for us". I am not sure why he would say this... too dangerous, possibly... but a series of chain reactions have evolved since then. Events that cause people to believe this is another "huge cover-up" again.

http://www.cnn.com/2017/06/29/politics/donald-trump-macron-france-visit/index.html

Trump's surprise Paris visit July 14th, 2017, marks shrewd political calculation

By Stephen Collinson, CNN
Updated 8:17 AM ET, Thu June 29, 2017

Suddenly after three and a half years,,, and knowing this book is being published very soon.

AUGUST 17th, 2017

'FRENCH', SATELITE IMAGES went mysteriously missing in 2014 ???

"IMAGINE THAT"

> Scientists narrow search area of Flight 370A new analysis of satellite photos taken two weeks after Flight MH370 mysteriously vanished may help scientists narrow the search area for the missing Malaysian Airlines aircraft to three regions in the southern Indian Ocean.
>
> The drift analysis by Australian science agency CSIRO released Wednesday is based on ,,,, " French " ,,,, satellite images taken on March 23, 2014, and captures 12 "probably man-made" floating objects. The agency, however, could not determine whether the objects are actually the debris from an aircraft.
>
> INDYGO
>
> MH370: NEW CRASH SITE IDENTIFIED FOR MISSING BOEING 777 PLANE, SAY SCIENTISTS
>
> Narrowing down: the white line in the centre of the map shows possible locations for the crash site of MH370, just outside the search area marked by the magenta line / CSIRO

Leading Australian scientists have calculated the crash site 'with unprecedented precision and certainty'

SIMON CALDER TRAVEL CORRESPONDENT
@SimonCalder

Seven " 7 " months to the day after the search for the doomed Boeing 777 was officially called off, leading Australian scientists have calculated "with unprecedented precision and certainty" that the plane crashed at a point 35.6 degrees south of the Equator and 92.8 degrees east of Greenwich.

If they find anything in the Indian Ocean relating to MH370, it was brought in from the Ukraine .

Recent MH370 ... 'HORRIFIC' ... NEWS...

JET MURDER MYSTERY MH370 conspiracy rages as diplomat investigating Malaysia Airlines disaster is shot dead

The whereabouts of the Boeing 777 has remained a mystery since vanishing in 2014
By Marnie O'Neill for news.com.au
1st September 2017, 9:20 am
Updated: 2nd September 2017, 6:17 pm

A DIPLOMAT investigating doomed flight flight MH370 has been gunned down, has fuelled new conspiracy theories about the missing Malaysian Airlines jet.
Honorary Consul of Malaysia Zahid Raza was shot dead in Madagascar's capital Antananarivo in an apparent assassination last week.

https://www.thesun.co.uk/news/4368766/mh370-latest-conspiracy-malaysia-airlines-zahid-raza-assissination/

After recent research, I will end my book with the following...

SEPT. 23rd, 2017... the exciting... "FEAST OF TRUMPETS"

The Feast of Trumpets, one of the Holy Days of the Bible, pictures future times of both sadness and gladness—essential steps leading to the establishment of the Kingdom of God on earth!

Most biblical "trumpets" were shofars, made from animal horn.

The use of trumpets and bugles to send signals has a long history. In Old Testament times, it's fascinating to see how ancient

Israel used trumpet calls for numerous orders and announcements.

Few people realize that one of the seven annual festivals commanded by God is called the Feast of Trumpets . But why? Notice God's command:

"And in the seventh month [corresponding to our September/October], on the first day of the month, you shall have a holy convocation [a commanded worship assembly]. You shall do no customary work. For you it is a day of blowing the trumpets " (Numbers 29:1; see also Leviticus 23:24; emphasis added throughout).

In the original Hebrew ,"blowing of trumpets" has been translated from the single word teruah , which signifies the making of a loud noise or clamor. It is sometimes translated "shout," as made by human voices (e.g., Joshua 6:10). It's also rendered "alarm" in association with the sound of the shofar or ram's horn (Jeremiah 4:19).

A form of the word also refers to sounding an alarm with metal trumpets or hatsotserot (Numbers 10:9—silver trumpets in this case). In Psalm 98, the word is rendered "shout joyfully," and applies to loud singing as well as blowing metal trumpets and the ram's horn in celebration (Psalms 98:4-6).

Numbers 10:1-10 relates the uses of the two silver trumpets of the tabernacle, including calls to assemblies, announcing special occasions and events such as holy days and sacrifices, and for alarms of war, as mentioned. Interestingly, the shofar was used for some of the same purposes. One distinction, however, was that only the priests were authorized to blow the silver trumpets.

Thus, making a loud noise, particularly through the ram's horn and other trumpets, can be celebratory as well as a dire warning—like a tornado siren. Both aspects are part of the important meaning of this Holy Day.

A mighty trumpet announces the second coming of Christ

The Feast of Trumpets holds special excitement because it initiates the autumn "FALL" festival season of four festivals. As with all the annual feasts, we need the New Testament to fully understand the meaning and symbolism.

Most interesting is what the Bible reveals about trumpet calls in connection with future prophesied events —events pointed to by the Feast of Trumpets!

Scripture tells us that an earth-shaking trumpet call will announce the most important and exciting event that will ever happen to humanity— the second coming of Jesus Christ ! This will be the great climax and turning point of all history!

Note how Jesus described His future return: "Then the sign of the Son of Man will appear in heaven, and then all the tribes of the earth will mourn, and they will see the Son of Man coming on the clouds of heaven with power and great glory. And He will send His angels with a great sound of a trumpet , and they will gather together His elect from the four winds, from one end of heaven to the other" (Matthew 24:30-31).

Another great event: the resurrection of the saints

Another major event that happens at Christ's return is the resurrection of God's faithful servants, the saints.

Both the Old Testament and the New Testament frequently use the word "saints" to refer to the faithful followers of God. In the New Testament, they are also called the "elect," those selected or chosen (as in Matthew 24:31).

The apostle Paul wrote: "For the Lord Himself will descend from heaven with a shout, with the voice of an archangel, and with the trumpet of God. And the dead in Christ [the saints who have died] will rise first. Then we [saints] who are alive and remain shall be caught up together with them in the clouds to meet the Lord in the air. And thus we shall always be with the Lord" (1 Thessalonians 4:16-17).

The resurrection of the saints to glorified spirit life to "reign with" Christ is called in Scripture "the first resurrection." A second resurrection will follow 1,000 years later for "the rest of the dead" (Revelation 20:5-6).

While many of the saints will be protected during the end-time Great Tribulation (see Revelation 12:12-17), this will be on earth, not in heaven. In fact, the reward of the saints is not that of going to heaven at death, as so many think. It will be eternal life in the Kingdom of God, which Christ will establish on the earth when He returns (Matthew 5:5; Matthew 6:10; Revelation 5:10).

Those who are a part of the first resurrection will rule with Jesus Christ here on earth.

Eternal life in the Kingdom of God will then be offered to all those who inhabit the earth.

A scroll sealed with seven seals

Many people have a very limited perspective of Jesus Christ. They think only of His first coming as the suffering Savior and as the Lamb of God. But He, along with the Father, is a God of justice and judgment as well as a God of mercy and forgiveness. When Jesus comes the second time, it will be as "the Lion of the tribe of Judah" to punish those who are in rebellion against God (Revelation 5:5). That will be essential to prepare the way for true peace on earth.

The end-time sequence of events is pictured as Christ unrolling a scroll by breaking open its seven seals one by one (Revelation 5). The sequence of the seals is the same sequence of events Jesus described in His prophecy about His return recorded in Matthew 24, Mark 13 and Luke 21. These are crises that will be growing in frequency and intensity leading up to that time.

The opening of the first four seals unveils what are commonly referred to as the "four horsemen of the Apocalypse ," representing false religion, war, famine and death by pestilence and various disasters (see

Revelation 6:1-8). The fifth seal represents the persecution of God's people and the Great Tribulation, when God will use gentile nations to punish the nations that are the modern descendants of ancient Israel (Revelation 6:9-11; Matthew 24:21; Jeremiah 30:7).

Then "immediately after the tribulation" will be heavenly signs with the opening of the sixth seal (Matthew 24:29-30; Revelation 6:12-16).

The seventh seal: the Day of the Lord

The heavenly signs of the sixth seal announce the Day of the Lord, with fearful people crying out: "For the great day of His wrath has come, and who is able to stand?" (Revelation 6:17). Likewise, the prophet Joel tells us that the heavenly signs will happen just "before the coming of the great and awesome day of the Lord" (Joel 2:31). So the period of the seventh seal that follows in Revelation is the Day of the Lord. (Except for a few inset chapters, the book of Revelation is organized quite sequentially.)

The Day of the Lord is the time of God's major intervention on the earth. This age is Satan's "day," when "the whole world lies under the sway of the wicked one" (1

John 5:19). The Day of the Lord begins when Christ begins to take back control and mete out calamitous judgment on the rebellious nations that defy God.

Joel says, "The day of the Lord is great and very terrible; who can endure it?" (Joel 2:11; see also Joel 1:15; Joel 2:1; Joel 3:14). The Day of the Lord is also called, as we saw in Revelation 6:17, "the great day of His wrath." Numerous other prophecies describe the fierce wrath of God against the forces of evil during the Day of the Lord.

The opening of the "seventh seal," which is the Day of the Lord, reveals "seven angels" with "seven trumpets" (Revelation 8:1-2). Each trumpet blast announces terrifying calamities that will afflict rebellious mankind. The blowing of these trumpets apparently takes place over the course of a year, since Isaiah 34:8 refers to this time as "the Day of the Lord's vengeance, the year of recompense for the cause of Zion." And one trumpet plague takes five months, as we'll see in a moment.

This year comes at the end of the time of terrible tribulation and concludes with the return of Jesus Christ and the resurrection. Given the seven warning trumpets over this period, it would seem that the Feast of Trumpets pictures all of it, not just Christ's return and the resurrection at the end—though these events at the end following the final trumpet are certainly the high point.

Be assured that while Jesus Christ is sending plagues and other punishments on the earth, He will be protecting His faithful followers (although He will allow some to be martyred). To them He promises, "Because you have kept My command to persevere, I also will keep you from the hour of trial which shall come upon the whole world, to test those who dwell on the earth" (Revelation 3:10; see also Revelation 7:3).

The blowing of the seven trumpets

After each of the first three trumpets, devastating destruction befalls the earth (Revelation 8:1-11). The fourth trumpet announces a time of great darkness (Revelation 8:12).

When the fifth angel sounds, a mighty army suddenly comes on the scene with great power, including power that will be used against its enemies "to torment them for five months" (Revelation 9:1-12).

When the sixth angel sounds, a giant army of 200 million comes from the east, resulting in the deaths of a third of mankind (Revelation 9:13-21). One would think that all the survivors would then have enough sense and fear of God to repent of their sins, but not so—"they did not repent" (Revelation 9:20-21).

When the seventh angel sounds, he is announcing events both wonderful and terrifying. The wonderful events are the coronation of Jesus Christ as King of Kings, His return to rule all nations and the resurrection of the saints—"at the last trumpet" (1 Corinthians 15:52). And the terrifying events are a series of seven last plagues, as we'll see.

Revelation 11:15-18 proclaims: "The seventh angel sounded his trumpet, and there were loud voices in heaven, which said: 'The kingdom of the world has become the kingdom of our Lord and of his Messiah [or Christ], and he will reign for ever and ever.'

"And the twenty-four elders, who were seated on their thrones before God, fell on their faces and worshiped God, saying: 'We give thanks to you, Lord God Almighty, the One who is and who was, because you have taken your great power and have begun to reign.

"'The nations were angry, and your wrath has come. The time has come for judging the dead, and for rewarding your servants the prophets and your people who revere your name, both small and great—and for destroying those who destroy the earth" (NIV).

The warning in the seventh trumpet

Note what follows in Revelation 15:1: "Then I saw another sign in heaven, great and marvelous: seven angels having the seven last plagues, for in them the wrath of God is complete."

Revelation 16 goes on to describe the seven last plagues. The first is a terrible affliction on people, the second is on the sea and its creatures, and the third is on all the rivers and springs of water. The fourth plague is on the sun, which creates scorching heat. The fifth plague is darkness and extremely painful sores.

Again, in spite of the terrible pain and suffering, the prophecy recounts in advance that these people "did not repent of their deeds" (Revelation 16:9-11). Yet even these stubborn people will have an opportunity for salvation. After dying and being resurrected a thousand years later, they will at last be receptive to Christ's teachings.

The sixth angel announces a vast army coming from the east led by Satan and his demons. They "go out to the kings of the earth and of the whole world, to gather them to the battle of that great day of God Almighty" (Revelation 16:12-14).

"And they gathered them together to the place called in Hebrew, Armageddon" (Revelation 16:16). Armageddon means Mount or Hill of Megiddo. This place northwest of Jerusalem has been a gathering place for armies numerous times in the past. Other scriptures show that the actual "battle of that great day of God Almighty" will be in and around Jerusalem.

The seventh angel announces incredible cataclysms! "And there were noises and thunderings and lightnings; and there was a great earthquake, such a mighty and great earthquake as had not occurred since men were on the earth … And great hail from heaven fell upon men, each hailstone about the weight of a talent. Men blasphemed God because of the plague of the hail, since that plague was exceedingly great" (Revelation 16:18-21).

Then comes the Commander and His heavenly cavalry for the final battle!

The triumphant return of Jesus Christ

Revelation 17 describes a powerful and evil worldwide system called "Babylon the great." Its armies and the armies of its enemies are about to fight each other when they instead turn to fight against the returning Jesus Christ. Revelation 17:14 says, "These will make war with the Lamb, and the Lamb will overcome them, for He is Lord of lords and King of kings; and those who are with Him are called, chosen, and faithful." Revelation 18 goes on to describe the fall of this system called Babylon.

Revelation 19 begins with scenes in heaven. Then Revelation 19:7-9 refer to "the marriage of the Lamb" to "His wife," the Church, and "the marriage supper."

Then we read of the awesome arrival and conquest by Jesus Christ and His armies! "Now I saw heaven opened, and behold, a white horse. And He who sat on him was called Faithful and True, and in righteousness He judges and makes war" (Revelation 19:11).

"And the armies in heaven, clothed in fine linen, white and clean, followed Him on white horses" (Revelation 19:14).

"And He has on His robe and on His thigh a name written: KING OF KINGS AND LORDS OF LORDS" (Revelation 19:16).

The remainder of the chapter tells how all who will have tried to make war against Him will be killed.

God reveals more about the great final battle in Zechariah 14. Here are portions of that chapter: "Behold, the day of the Lord is coming" (Zechariah 14:1). "For I will gather all the nations to battle against Jerusalem (Zechariah 14:2). "Then the Lord will go forth and fight against those nations" (Zechariah 14:3). "And in that day His feet will stand on the Mount of Olives, which faces Jerusalem on the east" (Zechariah 14:4). "Thus the Lord my God will come, and all the saints with You [some translations say "Him"]" (Zechariah 14:5).

The symbolism of the Feast of Trumpets

So what does the Feast of Trumpets picture? It portrays everything that happens from the angel blowing the first trumpet to Christ conquering His enemies at the time of His return. It warns of global catastrophes and war and yet, at the same time, celebrates the coming of Jesus Christ as King and the raising to life of His followers. This paves the way for peace on earth at last as Jesus sets up His Kingdom and begins to rule the world! The next three annual Feasts explain the rest of the story.

from https://www.ucg.org/the-good-news/the-exciting-feast-of-trumpets

SEPTEMBER 23, 2017 AND THE JEWS

BIBLE

Gen; 1:14 and God said, Let there be lights in the firmament of the Heaven to divide the day from night; and let them be for signs, and for seasons, and for days and years.

Acts; 17:26 and hath determined the times before appointed and the bounds of their habitation.

Hab; 2:3 For the vision is yet for an appointed time

Revelation 12:1,2,5 and there appeared a great wonder in Heaven, a woman clothed with the Sun, and the Moon under her feet, and upon her head a crown of Twelve Stars: and she, being with child cried, travailing in birth, and pained to be delivered...

and she brought forth a man-child, who was to rule all nations with a 'rod of iron' : and her child was called up unto GOD, and to his throne.

On September 23, 2017, a great wonder will happen in Heaven.

The woman (constellation VIRGO) will be clothed with:

- The SUN on her shoulder.
- The MOON will be under her feet.
- Upon her Head will be a CROWN of 12 STARS.

The constellation LEO (9 stars) and 3 wandering Stars (MERCURY (Messenger), MARS (War) & VENUS (Jesus)

This alignment hasn't happened in over 6,000 years.

The first alignment (around CREATION) included the wandering Star SATURN.

SATURN represented 'SATAN' and it no longer appears in the coming alignment.

JUPITER (the King Planet) is in the Womb area of VIRGO for 9 months.

(French president Emmanuel Macron has declared he will govern France like Jupiter)

On December 23, 2016, exactly 9 months before Sept. 23, 2017, President OBAMA chose not to stand with Israel in U.N. resolution 2334 for 'Peace & Safety'.

Thes; 5:3 for why they shall say, Peace & Safety; then sudden destruction cometh upon them, as Travail upon a woman with child; and they shall not escape.

There is an International Day of Peace on Sept. 21st, 2017.

JUPITER will exit the Womb area on:

Sept. 23, 2017, when the revelation 12 alignment is complete.

Isaiah; 66:9 shall I curse to bring forth, and shut the Womb?

GOD will not shut the Womb but instead return to dealing with Israel (JEWS)

Cor; 1:22 for the JEWS require a sign, and the GREEKS seek after WISDOM.

JESUS speaking to the PHARISEE's ;

Matt; 16:3   Ye, Hypocrites, ye can discern the signs of the times?

We are the JEWS ?

The JEWS are GOD's chosen people.

Deut; 7:6   the LORD thy GOD hath chosen them to be a special people unto himself.....

Deut; 14:2   for there art a Holy people unto the LORD thy GOD ,,, above all Nations that are upon the Earth.

JESUS was sent to the JEWS

Matt; 15:24   I am not sent but unto the lost sheep of the house of Israel.

THE JEWS HAVE REJECTED JESUS AS THEIR MESSIAH. They have been Blinded ...until the time of the end.

Rom; 11:25   Blindness in part is happened to Israel, until the fulness of the Gentiles be come in.

Rom; 11:8   GOD hath them a spirit of slumber, eyes that thy should not SEE, and ears that thy should not Hear.

Rom; 11:10   Let their eyes be darkened, and that they may not SEE ,,,,

Because of this, Gentiles are able to be saved to provoke the JEWS to jealousy.

Rem; 11:11   through their 'FALL' salvation is come unto the Gentiles, for to provoke them to jealousy.

In the book of Acts, GOD transitions from JEWS to Gentiles until the Tribulation.

Micah; 5:3   therefore will be give them up, until the time that she which travailed hath brought forth ,,,,,

Isaiah; 66:7,8   before she travailed, she brought forth; before her pain came, she was delivered of a man child. Who hath heard of such a thing?

Before the pain (Tribulation) a man child delivers 'BELIEVERS' then returns to dealing with the JEWS.

GOD revives the JEWS after removing the Gentiles (Believers)

Hosea; 6:12   after 2 days will he revive us; in the 3rd day he will raise us up

The JEWS have been scattered for the last 2000 yrs. (2 days),,,,

after the Believers are removed the JEWS will realize what they missed

Hosea; 6:13   then shall we know, if we follow onto know the LORD …..

In the Bible, GOD refers to one Day as equal to 1,000 years.

2 Peter; 3:8   be not ignorant of this one thing, that one day is with the LORD as a 1,000 yrs, and to a 1,000 years as one day.

Psalm; 90:4   for a thousand years in thy sight are but as yesterday when it has past, and as a watch in the night.

Most JEWS still do not recognize JESUS as the Messiah but will after the fullness of the Gentiles are come in.

The Gentiles (Believers) must be removed before GOD can address the JEWS again for the final week missing on their calendar.

This final week referred to a Jacob's trouble is the 70th week of Daniel.

Jacob is represented as Israel.

Gen; 32:28   Thy name shall be called no more Jacob, but Israel…..

Daniel was shown a timeline of 70 weeks for the JEWS

Dan; 9:24   seventy weeks are determined upon thy people and upon thy Holy city to finish the transgression, and to make as end of sins, and to make reconciliation for iniquity, and to bring in everlasting righteousness, and to seal up the vision and prophecy, and to anoint the most Holy.

Dan; 9:25   know therefore and understand …. unto the Messiah the Prince shall be 7 weeks, and threescore and two weeks

Dan; 9:26   and after threescore and two weeks shall Messiah be cut off …….

1 week = 7 yrs

70 x 7 = 490 yrs

Messiah was cut off (died on cross) at 483 yrs.

7 yrs. now remaining (Tribulation)

This last week of 7 years will be the Tribulation when GOD returns his attention to the JEWS.

Dan; 9:27   and he shall confirm the covenant with many for one week ….

The week is patterned after creation

All things created in 6 days and the 7th day for rest …..

I Bible Genealogies Adam to JESUS is about 4,000 years from JESUS until now is 2,000 yrs.

After the 7 year Tribulation JESUS will reign on Earth for 1,000 years

   6,000 yrs. (6 days)

- 1,000 yrs. (1 day)

7,000 yrs. (7 day Creation Model)

The Great American Eclipse

The Moon is 400 times smaller than the Sun, the Sun is 400 times farther away from the Moon. Because of this, Earth is the only place a total eclipse can be seen.

The numerical value for the last Hebrew letter TAV is 400 and means "sign/mark/signal"

The temperature of the Sun is 5778 degrees Kelvin.

September 23rd, 2017 will be the 1st Day of the JEWISH NEW YEAR 5778.

The path of totality is 70 miles wide. This total eclipse will cross 12 states in the US just one month before the Revelation sign that will have 12 stars upon her head.

JESUS was 33yrs. old when he died on the cross for us.

The eclipse will happen exactly 33 days before Sept. 23, 2017. It will start in Oregon the 33rd State. It will cross the US on the 33rd parallel. The last American eclipse was 99 years ago (33x3), the same age as Abraham when he had Isaac. The 1918 eclipse was during the flu pandemic that killed 33% of the world's population.

The eclipse will first cross Salem, Oregon. In the Bible, Salem is another name for Jerusalem.

Gen; 14:18 Melchizedek King of Salem,, the total number of Salems in the path is '7'

- Salem,Or.
- Salem,ID
- Salem,Wy.
- Salem,NE
- Salem,MO
- Salem,KY
- Salem,SC

The eclipse begins at 10:16 AM in the US. It will be dark at 7:16 PM in Jerusalem, the start of their last month of ELUL.

ELUL is another word for 'Harvest', Elul is the last month of the Hebrew year, 5777.

The eclipse will be in the constellation LEO by the king star REGULUS (part of the Revelation 12 sign). The eclipse will happen exactly 40 days before the 'JEWISH FEAST OF ATONEMENT' this year 40 days = a time for repentance.

Jonah; 3:4   yet 40 days, and Nineveh shall be overthrown.

There was also an eclipse recorded at that time in 763 BC known as the BUR-Sagale eclipse , a sign to Nineveh to repent.

In 2024 ..... another American Eclipse, it will happen 7 years after the 2017 eclipse and also will happen on NISAN, the KEWISH religious New Year!

Both eclipses make an ' X ' directly across Salem, Illinois. ' X ' is the symbol of the Hebrew letter TAV which also means sign or mark.

Signs of the SUN are for Gentiles.

Signs of the MOON are for JEWS.

4 Blood Moons have appeared consecutively around important dates on JEWISH FEASTS in the past 70 years.

4 blood Moons 1949-1950, 1967-1968, 2014-2015

Also in 2015 the 'Bethlehem Star' appeared, which seems to mark 2 years before significant events in Bible history.

The Bethlehem star appeared 2 yrs. before the birth of Abraham

It appeared 2 yrs. before the birth of JESUS

It appeared Sept. 2015 ... 2 yrs. before Sept. 2017.

This 'Bethlehem Star', created by "CERN" in Geneva Switzerland.

There are '7' main Jewish Feasts each year and the first 4 feasts have been fulfilled in chronological order with JESUS '1st coming'

" FEAST OF TRUMPETS " IS NEXT ....

It will be celebrated September 23, 2017. JEWS call this Feast, "the day no man knoweth the day or hour".

They BLOW the TRUMPET (Shofar) 100 times and the last 'BLOW' is the   "LAST TRUMP"

1 Cor; 15:51,52 .... "I show you a mystery;

We shall not sleep, but we shall all be changed. In a moment, in the twinkling of an eye, at the " LAST TRUMP " for the TRUMPET shall sound .... and we shall be changed.......

GOD marks every 50 years as a JUBILEE.

Lev; 25:10 ... and ye shall hallow the 50th year ...... it shall be a JUBILEE unto you ...

Gen; 6:3 ... and the Lord said, " My spirit shall not always strive with man, for that he also is flesh: yet his days shall be 120 years.

Over the past 120 years, these events happened for the JEWS ....

1897 - 1ST ZIONIST Conference in SWITZERLAND.

1917 - Balfour Dec. land back to Israel.

1947 - UN votes Israel as a Nation.

1967 - 6 Day War won Jerusalem back.

2017 - this year .....

The average generation in the Bible is 70 years

We are currently in JEWISH year ' 5777 '.

The Number "5" means Grace

Man has 5 fingers & 5 toes

Nebuchadnezzar's Dream has a statue with 5 Parts (all Empires) ...

The Tabernacle contained '5' curtains, '5' bars, '5' pillars, 5 sockets, an alter made of wood '5' cubits long and '5' cubits wide, height of the court was '5' cubits, and the Holy anointing oil was made with '5' parts.

The Bible is structured on " 7's "

The number '7' is the Foundation of GOD's word and means:

'COMPLETION OR PERFECTION'

GOD made ' 7 ' days in a week.

Ivan Panin's work display how the Bible is structured on ' 7 ' and could not be mathematically be duplicated and impossible to be made by just a man.

DONALD TRUMP was born June 14th, 1946 , exactly 700 Days before the establishment of Israel as a nation May14th, 1948.

It just so happens that on January 21st, 2017, the 1st Day of DONALD TRUMP's Presidency, he was 70 Yrs, 7 Months, 7 Days old.

Netanyahu's 7th Year, 7th Month, 7th Day in office as Prime Minister of Israel on US Election Day, Nov. 8th, 2016

"777"

Inaugurated in the JEWISH Year of 5777

TRUMP PENCE "Make America Great again"

The running Slogan when you say together quickly just happens to sound like:

"TRUMPETS"

Number ' 58 ' - words that add up to a Numerical Value of ' 58 ' ...GEMATRIA

GRACE - H2580
NOAH - H5146
SON - H1121
BELOVED - H1730
HOPE - H3176
GREAT - H1419
DAY - H3117

* TRUMP IS 58th President

* Inaugurated on 01/20/2017 which equals '58',when added 1+20+20+17 = '58'

* Vice President, MIKE PENCE is now '58' yrs. old.

• Israel Prime Minister Benjamin Netanyahu is the '58th' Shepherd of Israel.

• Book of ENOCH, Chapter 90;1-5 states 35 shepherds till 2nd Temple then 23 more shepherds which equal '58'

GOD said at the end of the 10th Jubilee, JESUS will return to deal with the Nation.

1967-2017 is the Jubilee September 23, 2017 is the end of the 10th JUBILEE.....

These Great Wonders are signs.......

1 Cor; 15:1-4 ...... by which also ye are saved ... how that Christ died for our sins ..... he was buried ..... and that he rose again the 3rd day.

Venus (the morning star) will be in conjunction with Regulus & at the Christ angle of 26.3 degrees.

On FEAST OF TRUMPETS, JUPITER is at the Christ Angle below the horizon in VIRGO.

The alignments will not occur again after 2017.

Rabbi Meir Halevi Horowitz Prophecy from the 18th century, interpreted a 'time' as 700 yrs

50 cycles of double Shemitah

50 x 14 = 700 years

Time,time and a half a time = 3.5 ,,,,,, 3.5 x 700 = 2450 yrs. from Babylonian exile in 434 BC.

He considered that the Hebrew year in which Messiah should arrive is " 5777 " ...

He said someone would conquer and rule Israel for 8 Jubilee's (8x50=400 yrs)

In 1517, the 'Turks' conquered Jerusalem and took over until 1917 (exactly 400 years)

He said the beginning of the 9th Jubilee, Israel will take over the land but no one would live there during the 9th Jubilee.

In 1917 'Turks' were defeated Balfour Dec. gave land back to JEWS.

He said on the 10th Jubilee that the JEWS will own the land forever.

1967 - 6 day war ,,, JEWS received their land back

Acts; 16:31 .... Believe in the LORD JESUS CHRIST and Thou Shalt Be Saved!

THE TIME TO BELIEVE IS , NOW !!!

https://www.youtube.com/watch?v=9-xMgOu7G0k
https://www.youtube.com/watch?v=qVlVol9khjE

Conclusion

I am Alpha and Omega, the beginning and the ending, saith the Lord, which is, and which was, and which is to come, the Almighty. Revelation 1:8

In the beginning was the Word, and the Word was with God, and the Word was God. John 1:1

The wall builder, the man named Trump has now taken the only possible running mate who would complete his name. The last trump has become Trumpence.

Finally, going back to Strong's Concordance once more, for a numerical reference I cannot ignore and the reason I wrote this book.

"5307" - DICTIONARY OF BIBLE THEMES – 5307 ENVOY

"An official representative sent on behalf of a king or government to other kings or nations. Believers are God's envoys to his world, bearing the good news of salvation on his behalf."

Incidentally, I've had a 5-foot steel statue of 'Hermes the messenger' in my home since 2000, and my nickname from my hockey days is 'Herby'. As details about some of the people I met in Thomas Lilly's circle of friends and beyond are becoming clearer.

I believe GOD chose me to be 'the messenger' and bring these facts to light.

CHAPTER #15 – Release the Kraken, Donald of Dubai, the Aga Khan, Canada, Sharia Law & The Thomas Fire

"Release the Kraken!" is a catchphrase and image macro series based on a memorable quote uttered by Zeus in the 1981 fantasy adventure film The Clash of the Titans as well as the 2010 3D remake. Despite the dramatic delivery of the line in the reboot, the quote was perceived as unintentionally funny and quickly became a target of image macro jokes on the web.

The first Urban Dictionary entry for the phrase "Release the Kraken" was submitted on March 31st, 2010, defined as "to pwn or to kick the ass of whomever you're releasing the kraken on." Throughout the first week of April 2010, the phrase was dubbed the latest meme by various tech and internet news outlets including Geekosystem, Vulture, Now Public, MTV and Mediate among others. In December, the phrase was listed in TIME Magazine's Top 10 Buzzwords of the Year.

"Release the Kraken"

Kraken, formed in April 2014 (just after MH370 disappeared), is a Bitcoin exchange located in San Francisco, USA and is now the regulator of Bitcoin and other cryptocurrencies.

To this day (May 27th, 2017 as I write this), whenever the Crypto Currencies make a huge correction, it is the Kraken being released automatically to either steal or buy up Bitcoins that are on sell orders, by the Bitcoin Mines answering difficult equations. This is a self perpetuating " beast " that will destroy people and the financial systems of countries, as foretold in the NWO 14-year plan (double SHEMITAH) I'd read as "Release the Kraken".

http://knowyourmeme.com/memes/release-the-kraken

Not only can they steal your Bitcoins, they are also the regulators!

Sure enough, the following happened to verify my statements on "Release the KRAKEN".

HOW ETHEREUM CRASHED FROM $319 TO 10 CENTS IN SECONDS

By Soren K.Group Jun. 23, 2017 - **NOTE: THE SAME DATE AS BREXIT , JUNE 23rd** Blockchain blockchain blockchain.

CNBC Reports

"The price of ethereum crashed as low as 10 cents from around $319 in about a second" on the GDAX cryptocurrency exchange on Wednesday, a move that is being blamed on a "multimillion dollar market sell" order.

Ethereum is an alternative digital currency to bitcoin and had been trading as high as $352 on Wednesday. It has since rebounded from its flash-crash lows to trade to about $325 on the GDAX exchange. According to industry and price tracking website Coinmarketcap, which takes into account the price on several exchanges, ethereum was trading around $338.

Adam White, the vice president of GDAX which is run by U.S. firm Coinbase, posted on the exchange's blog, outlining what took place at around 12:30 p.m. PT on Wednesday. According to White, the multimillion dollar market sell order resulted in a number of orders being filled from $317.81 to $224.48.

On Wednesday, the price of ether -- the cryptocurrency of the Ethereum blockchain -- on the GDAX exchange briefly crashed from $328 to $0.10. The story seems to be that there was a big market sell order that blew through a lot of the buy orders on the book, pushing the price down. This triggered forced selling by margin accounts, blowing through the rest of the buy orders until the price hit 10 cents. "We understand this event can be frustrating for our customers," said GDAX, but everything is fine: "Our matching engine operated as intended throughout this event and trading with advanced features like margin always carries inherent risk." FOOTNOTE: The above article explains, "Release the KRAKEN".

Jul 7, 2017 | Jamie Redman
Class Action Lawsuit Filed Against Cryptocurrency Exchange Kraken
Bitcoin.com Wallet

This week a class-action lawsuit has been filed against the San Francisco-based trading platform Kraken. A group of customers have revealed that their holdings of 3,414 ETH was liquidated during an Ethereum market flash crash. According to the plaintiffs the cryptocurrency exchange suffered from a denial-of-service (DDoS) attack at the time having many Kraken users unable to use the service.

Five Kraken Customers File Class Action Lawsuit Against the Exchange
Class Action Lawsuit Filed Against Cryptocurrency Exchange Kraken. Just recently Bitcoin.com reported on the GDAX exchange dealing with an ethereum flash crash that caused quite a bit of controversy. Following the crash, the Coinbase-owned GDAX exchange made amends with its customers by offering to absorb customer losses. However, less than two months ago on May 7th, there was another ethereum market flash crash that allegedly liquidated five customers ETH holdings at $96 USD per token. According to the five plaintiffs, Kraken should have halted trading while under attack. However, Kraken has stated if they had stopped market trading the "consequences for traders would have been even worse."

At the time Kraken responded to ethereum traders about the margin liquidation incident on the subreddit Ethtrader after the crash and DDoS.

"We have completed our investigation into the May 7th DDoS attack, and the cascading margin liquidations on the ETH/USD order book," explains the exchange. "Despite the coincidental overlap in timing of the events, we did not find any evidence of a coordinated attack or market manipulation."

'The DDoS Did Neither Cause nor Exacerbate Liquidations'
According to Kraken the DDoS did not cause or prolong the liquidations.

Once liquidations are triggered, they cannot be stopped. The best that can be hoped for is that liquidity is there to absorb the market orders. Kraken's market price protection system attempts to protect those being liquidated by pausing at times to allow liquidity to fill in but there is no guarantee that others are willing and able to provide that liquidity.

"Traders are encouraged to use advanced order types such as stop-loss to set their own exits," explains Kraken. "Unfortunately, we cannot compensate traders for the outcome of naturally occurring events in the market, nor losses due to unavoidable DDoS attacks."

Redress for 'Unlawful Conduct'
The class-action lawsuit seeks restitution for what the plaintiffs believe was "unlawful conduct" from the Payward Incorporated Kraken cryptocurrency exchange.

"For unconscionably freezing and liquidating the ether holdings of plaintiffs and the class in the midst of an event that exposed fatal flaws in Kraken's business operations," explains the lawsuit's argument. The paperwork from the Silver Law Group details that ethereum markets dropped over 70 percent from approximately 3:30 pm PST until approximately 4:30 pm PST. "[Ethereum's] value almost fully restored to its previous position after the one-hour business interruption," the plaintiff's case reads.

All-Time Highs and Flash Crash Parties Class Action Lawsuit Filed Against Cryptocurrency Exchange Kraken
On 21 June 2017 a multimillion dollar market sell was placed on the GDAX ETH-USD order book. Thousands of ethers were bought and sold well below the day's market average.

The story comes at a time where exchanges are seeing a massive surge of new users and heavy trading. Customers have complained about nearly every exchange having operational issues, and almost every exchange has warned their clients of these nuisances. During the first week of April, Poloniex traders complained about a Ripple market flash crash taking place with a similar outcome.

People have tried to speculate on who may be behind the quick crashes taking place on these altcoin markets, more specifically ethereum markets have flash crashed twice in less than two months with little evidence to be found. Moreover, although there have been losses some people have made a lot of money too. One trader scooped up 3809 ethers at $0.10 per ETH making a cool million in a matter of seconds. Others grabbed many ether tokens at various amounts under $40 as well. At the time multitudes of ethereum traders hoping to get lucky with another flash crash created hundreds of bids for ether tokens under $50.
104

Thomson Reuters Posted: Oct 24, 2017 2:13 PM ET Last Updated: Oct 24, 2017 4:18 PM

House Republicans to investigate Russia uranium deal tied to Canadian company, Frank Giustra, the Vancouver-based mining executive who donated $31 million to Clinton Foundation initiatives around the world and pledged millions more,

Clinton, Obama critics have for at least 2 years tried to tie uranium deal to Clinton Foundation
Republican leaders of two committees in the U.S. House of Representatives launched an investigation on Tuesday into the purchase by a Russian firm several years ago of a Canadian-based company that owned some 20 per cent of U.S. uranium supplies.

Republican lawmakers say they want to know whether the 2010 transaction involving Rosatom and Uranium One, which has headquarters in Toronto, was fully investigated by the FBI and other agencies before it was approved by a panel that oversees foreign investment in U.S. strategic assets.

"We're not going to jump to any conclusions at this time," said Devin Nunes, a Republican from California. "But one of the things that you know that we're concerned about is whether or not there was an FBI investigation. Was there a [Department of

Justice] investigation? And if so, why was Congress not informed of this matter?"

Some Republicans have claimed that Hillary Clinton's State Department approved the deal after her husband's charitable foundation received a $145-million US donation, but the State Department controls only one seat on the panel that approved the transaction and the New York Times reported two years ago that she did not participate in the decision. [105]

Canadian stock surges over 600% after switching from mining gold to bitcoin

Open this photo in gallery:REUTERS Vancouver-based Hive Blockchain Technologies Inc. is among the first publicly traded stocks to provide exposure to cryptomining.

BENOIT TESSIER/REUTERS
NATALIE OBIKO PEARSON AND BRANDON KOCHKODIN
BLOOMBERG NEWS

OCTOBER 12, 2017
Frank Giustra, the Canadian mining maverick who amassed a fortune building what would become one of the world's largest gold companies, is digging for another kind of gold: cryptocurrencies.

The company he's backed, Vancouver-based Hive Blockchain Technologies Inc., is among the first publicly traded stocks to provide exposure to cryptomining – the vast data crunching needed to verify the blockchain and the volatile currencies they produce, such as bitcoin and ether.

So far, his decision to dig for data servers has paid off. Hive's shares have soared about 633 per cent, giving it a market value of $553-million, since it took over the listing of Leeta Gold Corp. and began trading on Sept. 18. After only three days, the company raised $30-million in a share sale led by GMP Securities LP.

"We're quite lucky to be first out of the gate," said Hive chief executive officer Harry Pokrandt, a former Macquarie Group investment banker who bought his first bitcoin for $100 in a Vancouver coffee shop on his iPad. Speaking from a makeshift office adjoining Mr. Giustra's Fiore Group, which is listed as an adviser to Hive, he said, "We're a unique way to get into the space."

Mr. Giustra helped build the company that would become Goldcorp Inc. then founded film studio Lions Gate Entertainment Corp. He counts Bill Clinton and George Soros among his close pals. Those connections may position him to grasp a nascent corner of finance and navigate bitcoin's uncertain regulatory waters. Mr. Giustra didn't respond to a request for an interview.

Blockchain is the technology used to verify and record transactions on a public, online ledger. "Miners" use computers to solve complex math problems to verify transactions, earning a reward of a newly issued coin, such as bitcoin or ether. Hive paid Hong Kong-based Genesis Mining Ltd., builder of the world's largest ether mining facility, $9-million and gave it a 30-per-cent stake to acquire a new data centre in Reykjanes, Iceland.

There, Hive plans to mine different cryptocurrencies, depending on which ones offer the best margins and build an inventory of coins on the expectation they'll appreciate.

Hive said it plans to buy a second Genesis data centre next door for $5-million and has the option to buy more in Iceland and Sweden, cold countries which can keep power and cooling costs down.

Institutional investors have largely watched bitcoin's development from the sidelines, put off by the difficulty of buying digital coins, their volatility, and the criminal activity the market's anonymity can draw. Governments are struggling to regulate the industry, with China closing all cryptocurrency exchanges and at least 13 other countries tightening rules. Hive is listed on the TSX Venture Exchange, no stranger to volatile stocks. Hive jumped 28.4 per cent to $2.49 in Toronto.

Hive may make investing in the market easier, but "I suspect the vast majority of accounts aren't contemplating an investment in virtual currencies right now," said Jeff Klingelhofer, managing director of Santa Fe, New Mexico-based Thornburg Investment Management Inc.

Still, in an era of low yields, bitcoin is drawing many investors. The market value of the world's roughly 1,000 cryptocurrencies, led by bitcoin, surged more than eight fold this year to top $150-billion (U.S.). Bitcoin has returned 445 per cent and set a record above $5,000 on Thursday. Ether has gained an even more dramatic 3,600 per cent this year.

Cryptocurrency miners are renting entire Boeing 747s just to stay in the game [106]

FOOTNOTE: I believe HIVE works in conjunction with "the KRAKEN" switching it's mining to another crypto currency just before the Kraken is Released, creating high volatility .

'Donald of Dubai'

UAE billionaire trading off President Trump's name is raising fresh conflict-of-interest questions
Hussain Sajwani owns a real estate company whose Trump-branded properties are raising eyebrows among the US President's critics

Jon Gambrell Tuesday 15 August 2017 08:00 BST0 comments

Hussain Sajwani, has a 70 per cent stake in Damac Properties which this week started selling Trump Estate villas in Dubai.

During recent trips to Croatia and Malta, a Dubai-based billionaire and business partner of the Trump Organisation looked more like a head of state himself, mingling with government dignitaries, receiving a presidential reception and visiting the glittering Mediterranean sea.

Hussain Sajwani met with leaders in the two European nations and addressed local journalists, many of whom made reference to his ties to President Donald Trump or simply called him **"the Donald of Dubai"**.

Sajwani's trips to Europe – as well as a recent deal in Oman – show that Trump's business partner in Dubai wants to expand his development empire beyond the Middle East, and a tower which is under construction in London.

Enter Sajwani's Damac Properties. As of this week, it has started selling Trump-branded villas on the Trump golf club estate in Dubai.

"My dream is, as we have put our major, iconic tower in London, that we do repeat that in major gateway cities around the world," Sajwani said in a July online video. "Tokyo, Toronto, New York, Paris, I don't know. But that would be a dream – to grow Damac with its iconic brands around the world."

Sajwani's dream for a global expansion – as well his growing online presence among social media videos and posts – received a major boost with Trump taking the White House. It also raised the public profile of a billionaire whose fortune grew in part out of contracting work his companies did in supplying US forces during the 1991 Gulf War that expelled Iraqi forces from Kuwait.

Damac Properties declined a request to interview Sajwani made by Associated Press. Damac spokesman Niall McLoughlin said the company is "exploring opportunities in major gateway cities across Europe and the US, hence the numerous and ongoing meetings over the past many years" by Sajwani.

Trump's conflicts of interest make US seem like a **'kleptocracy' (noun, plural kleptocracies. 1. a government or state in which those in power exploit national resources and steal; rule by a thief or thieves.)**

Trump's conflict of interest problem isn't going away

Sajwani wholeheartedly embraced Trump, even as the US presidential candidate's campaign saw him call for a "complete shutdown" of Muslims coming to the US. Once reaching office, Trump's travel ban on six predominantly Muslim countries avoided naming the UAE, a major US ally that hosts some 5,000 American troops and is the US Navy's busiest foreign port of call.

In February, 2017, Trump's sons Eric and Donald Jr. opened the Trump International Golf Club in Dubai, the first of two to be built in the kingdom by Sajwani. Damac share prices have nearly doubled from 2.17 dirhams a share on the day of the US election in November, to a high of just under £1. That made Sajwani, who owns over 70 percent of Damac stock, even richer.

In Oman he signed a deal in June with the state-run Oman Tourism Development Co. for Damac to help redevelop Port Sultan Qaboos in Muscat, a project valued overall at $1bn (£773m).

Then in July, Sajwani visited Croatia and met with president Kolinda Grabar Kitarovic. Sajwani also visited tourist towns along the coast of the Adriatic Sea, according to a Damac statement at the time. The local branch of Colliers International, a commercial real estate firm based in Toronto, said it organised the three-day trip for Sajwani, trying to pitch him on developments on the Istria peninsula and Central and Southern Dalmatia.

Damac "continues to look at the investment opportunities" in Croatia, primarily along the Adriatic, said Vedrana Likan, the managing partner of Colliers' Croatian arm.

Sajwani then travelled to Malta, an archipelago nation off Italy in the Mediterranean Sea, and met with Prime Minister Joseph Muscat.

Both Croatia and Malta are members of the European Union, which Emirati citizens have been able to travel to without visas since 2015. That can drive business for any possible Damac project in either country, as well as create new European interest in Dubai, where the developer makes its real money, said Issam Kassabieh, an analyst with the UAE-based firm Menacorp Finance.

"It's a very effective method of branding," Kassabieh said. "Once foreign investors see the Damac name in Europe, they'll follow it all the way back to the source, which is Dubai, so they can capitalise on it here."

This week Damac Properties launched a new set of Trump-branded duplex villas, priced from £624,000, including three years' golf course membership. The company previously offered standalone villas at priced from around £1m up to just over £3m.

The Trump Organisation, now run by Trump's sons though the president hasn't divested from it, also tweeted that the new villas were for sale. The villas are "not a new project" and represented "our longstanding relationship with Damac Properties."

While Damac merely mentions Trump as representing "the most respected developments throughout the world," one Dubai newspaper more bluntly suggested buyers could "own a piece of the Trump name."

And while it remains unclear how Sajwani trades on his Trump ties in private meetings with foreign leaders, advertising and marketing by Damac prominently features Trump. That could lead to potential conflicts, said Norman Eisen, who served as President Barack Obama's lead ethics attorney and who now is a part of a watchdog group suing Trump for his alleged violations of a clause of the US Constitution that prohibits foreign gifts and payments.

If Sajwani "is featuring the Trump name in his marketing materials and if, as one can fairly assume, that's being furnished to government officials and others, then that would be a not-very-subtle attempt to trade on his business partner's presence in the White House," Eisen said.

NOTE: GoldMoney Stock XAU on TSX (Toronto Stock Exchange) as of August 3rd was at $2.35 then along came Hussain Sajwani, Trump's partner from Dubai to Toronto and guess what, within 45 days, GoldMoney XAU shot up to $6.25

What a great way to pay for their Toronto investment and it is ruled under SHARIA LAW!

For his New Year's party for 2017, US President Donald Trump announced that Hussain Sajwani, his new billionaire buddy and business partner from Dubai, would be a featured guest at the festivities at Trump's Mar-a-Lago estate and golf course in Palm Beach, Florida.

This is the same guy Thomas had mentioned many times, as he continued trying to convince Sajwani, the founder and Chairman of global property development company DAMAC Properties, to invest in the 55,500 tons of gold. And I'd met the man three times in Thomas' office back in 2007-08, including the first time Grace hooked him up to the EPFX Bio-feedback Medical Device in 2007. From there, I was his bio-feedback practitioner on his return visits, and he had another 1-hour session on the bio-feedback device with me in early 2008.

And yes, this is the same Hussain Sajwani who Thomas confirmed had committed to buy over $600 million dollars of the gold and back the entire Gold Heist-Assassination, when he spoke with me in June 2010. So, Trump's newfound affection for the Saudi billionaire was an attention-getter for me, to say the least. [107]

When Donald Trump made this announcement that Hussain Sajwani was his best friend and business partner and was attending his Mar-Lago New Years Eve Party ringing in 2017, I waited a couple of months before sending a message to Sajwani.

Around the end of March 2017, I googled DAMAC Properties and noticed that the web-site had an automated messaging service, so, I sent the message, " Please have Hussain Sajwani call Boyd Anderson immediately with my phone number". I received a reply , " What is this regarding"? I simply replied , "Dr. Thomas and Dr. Boyd" ... Hussain Sajwani would have remembered me as Dr. Boyd as this is how I was introduced to him back in 2007-08.

I never got another reply, but the very next day, Jared Kushner got into a big fight with Steve Bannon and the day after that

Kushner was on a plane to an island in the Indian Ocean to meet with the Crown Princes of Dubai and Abu Dhabi and about a week later Trump dropped the MOAB (Mother of all Bombs) on Afghanistan.

Saudi corruption case spells trouble for Trump
David Andelman
By David A. Andelman
Updated 3:50 PM ET, Sun November 5, 2017 [108]

GOLDMONEY XAU on TSX (Toronto Stock Exchange) - Follows SHARIA LAW

Sharia Law

Select Language▼
Shariah lawSharia law is the law of Islam. The Sharia (also spelled Shari'a or Shariah) law is cast from Muhammad's words, called "hadith," his actions, called "sunnah," and the Quran, which he dictated. Sharia law itself cannot be altered, but the interpretation of Sharia law, called "fiqh," by muftis (Islamic jurists) is given some latitude.

As a legal system, Sharia law is exceptionally broad. While other legal codes regulate public behavior, Sharia law regulates public behavior, private behavior, and even private beliefs. Compared to other legal codes, Sharia law also prioritizes punishment over rehabilitation, and the penalties under Sharia law favor corporal and capital punishments over incarceration. Of all legal systems in the world today, Sharia law is deemed the most intrusive and restrictive, especially against women (see below), and is making inroads into Western democracies (see Sharia law in America, Canada, Europe and UK).

According to Sharia law (see links for details):

• Theft is punishable by amputation of the hands (Quran 5:38 - includes graphic image).
• Criticizing or denying any part of the Quran is punishable by death.
• Criticizing Muhammad or denying that he is a prophet is punishable by death.
• Criticizing or denying Allah is punishable by death (see Allah moon god).
• A Muslim who becomes a non-Muslim is punishable by death (See Compulsion).
• A non-Muslim who leads a Muslim away from Islam is punishable by death.
• A non-Muslim man who marries a Muslim woman is punishable by death.
• A woman or girl who has been raped cannot testify in court against her rapist(s).

- Testimonies of 4 male witnesses are required to prove rape of a female (Quran 24:13).
- A woman or girl who alleges rape without producing 4 male witnesses is guilty of adultery.
- A woman or girl found guilty of adultery is punishable by death (see "Islamophobia").
- A male convicted of rape can have his conviction dismissed by marrying his victim.
- Muslim men have sexual rights to any woman/girl not wearing the Hijab (see Taharrush).
- A woman can have 1 husband, who can have up to 4 wives; Muhammad can have more.
- A man can marry an infant girl and consummate the marriage when she is 9 years old.
- Girls' clitoris should be cut (Muhammad's words, Book 41, Kitab Al-Adab, Hadith 5251).
- A man can beat his wife for insubordination (see Quran 4:34 and Religion of Peace).
- A man can unilaterally divorce his wife; a wife needs her husband's consent to divorce.
- A divorced wife loses custody of all children over 6 years of age or when they exceed it.
- A woman's testimony in court, allowed in property cases, carries ½ the weight of a man's.

- A female heir inherits half of what a male heir inherits (see Mathematics in Quran).
- A woman cannot drive a car, as it leads to fitnah (upheaval).
- A woman cannot speak alone to a man who is not her husband or relative.
- Meat to eat must come from animals that have been sacrificed to Allah - i.e., be "Halal."
- Muslims are to subjugate the world under Islam (see Quran 9:29 and Palestine Issue).
- Muslims should engage in Taqiyya and lie to non-Muslims to advance Islam.
- The list goes on.

Aga Khan (Kazar) AND CANADA

From Wikipedia, the free encyclopedia
Prince Shah Karim Al Hussaini, Aga Khan IV, KBE, CC is the 49th and current Imam of Nizari Ismailism, a denomination of Isma'ilism within Shia Islam consisting of an estimated 25 million adherents. Wikipedia
Born: December 13, 1936 (age 80), Geneva, Switzerland

Aga Khan (Persian: آقاخان; also transliterated as Aqa Khan and Agha Khan is a name used by the Imam of the Nizari Ismailis. The current user of the name is the

49th Imam (1957–present), Prince Shah Karim Al Husseini Aga Khan IV (b. 1936).

The title is made up of the titles agha and khan. The **Turkish** "agha" is "aqa" (Āqā) in **Persian**. The word "agha" comes from the **Old Turkic and Mongolian** "aqa", meaning "elder brother", and "khan" means king, ruler in Turkic and Mongolian languages.

According to Farhad Daftary, Aga Khan is an honorific title bestowed on Hasan Ali Shah (1800–1881), the 46th Imam of Nizari Ismailis (1817–1881), by Persian king Fath-Ali Shah Qajar. However, Daftary contradicts what the Aga Khan III noted in a famous legal proceeding in India: that Aga Khan is not a title but instead a sort of alias or "pet name" that was given to the Aga Khan I when he was a young man.

During the latter stages of the First Anglo-Afghan War (1841-1842), Hasan Ali Shah and his cavalry officers provided assistance to General Nott in Kandahar Province and to General England in his advance from Sindh to join Nott. He was awarded the status of "Prince" by the British government's representatives in India and became the only religious or community leader in British India granted a personal gun salute; When Hasan Ali Shah, the first Aga Khan, came to

Sindh, which is now in Pakistan, from Afghanistan, he and his army were welcomed by Mir Nasir Khan of Baluchistan, Pakistan. In 1866, the Aga Khan won a court victory in the High Court of Bombay in what popularly became known as the Aga Khan Case, securing his recognition by the British government as the head of the Khoja community.

By ALEX BALLINGALLOttawa Bureau
Tues., March 21, 2017
OTTAWA—Prime Minister Justin Trudeau's controversial Christmas holiday to the Aga Khan's private island cost Canadian taxpayers at least $127,000, newly released documents show.

Most of the bill is related to security for the prime minister and his family. The **RCMP** detail that travelled with the Trudeaus cost at least $71,988.87 — including more than $18,000 in overtime wages and $53,000 in per diems for the **RCMP** members — according to the documents released to Parliament on Tuesday.

There those RCMP (Royal Canadian Mounted Police) again.....???

Further costs included $32,000 for the use of the government's CC-144 Challenger jet, and

roughly $15,000 for the transportation, accommodation and per diems of staff from Global Affairs Canada.
Outside the House of Commons Tuesday, Conservative MP Gérard Deltell told reporters that he found the cost of the trip to be "extremely" high.

You might be interested in
Air Canada spokesperson says the new measures are in effect for the airline but he wouldn't say what they consist of because security is handled by U.S. Customs and Border Protection.

Canadians flying into U.S. to face new security screenings, but airlines give few details

Abdullah Almalki, Muayyed Nureddin and Ahmad El-Maati the 3 Canadians tortured in Syria received $31-million settlement from Ottawa

Bardish Chagger, the Government Leader in the House of Commons, responded that it's normal for police to travel with the prime minister for security.

"**RCMP** have always accompanied prime ministers whether on personal or business travel," she said.

as mentioned earlier in my book:
Then, as announced at RCMP headquarters in Regina, Saskatchewan in October 2016, Canada's Royal Canadian Mounted Police offered an apology and a $100 million dollar pay off as compensation for harassment and sexual abuse against female members. What a great way to keep it in the family! [109]

In the face of media pressure, it was also later revealed that Trudeau travelled to the island with Liberal party president Anna Gainey and her husband, a former campaign operative and head of an Ottawa think tank. Newfoundland MP Seamus O'Regan and his husband were also on the trip.

Trudeau also admitted that he took the Aga Khan's helicopter to-and-from the Bahamian capital to Bell Island, prompting accusations that he broke Parliamentary ethics rules by accepting travel on a private aircraft.

The prime minister has repeatedly justified the trip as a family vacation to visit a longtime friend. But the vacation has come under close scrutiny because of the Aga Khan's foundation in Canada, which has landed more than $300 million in government aid contracts since 2004 and actively lobbies public officers in Ottawa.

The Elite are trying to force the public into investing with GoldMoney... because GoldMoney has the real stuff, 99.99% purity...

Meanwhile, they have the Banks, Canadian Mint and who knows, selling Fake Gold...

Fake Gold

Royal Canadian Mint-stamped gold wafer appears to be fake
Mint investigating after piece purchased by Ottawa jeweller Oct. 18 at Royal Bank of Canada branch
By Stu Mills, CBC News Posted: Oct 30, 2017 5:00 AM ET Last Updated: Oct 30, 2017 8:05 AM ET

Goldsmith Dennis Barnard subjected the bar to an acid test after he found he wasn't strong enough to roll the metal flat in his jewellers' mill.

NOTE: Carl A. Anderson on the list, (my father's name was Carl Anderson)
Thomas must have thought I was one of them.

Also on the list is Bronfman, Charles Rosner, the father of Steven Bronfman (Paradice Papers)

THE BRITISH MONARCHY AND THE COMMITTEE OF 300 (AS OF SEPTEMBER 2016)
CURRENT MONARCH AND SUPREME LEADER OF THE NWO:
Queen Elizabeth II
Abdullah II of Jordan
Kerry, John Forbes
Abramovich, Roman Arkadyevich
King, Mervyn
Ackermann, Josef
Kinnock, Glenys
Adeane, Edward
Kissinger, Henry
Agius, Marcus Ambrose Paul
Knight, Malcolm
Ahtisaari, Martti Oiva Kalevi
Koon, William H. II
Akerson, Daniel
Krugman, Paul
Albert II of Belgium
Kufuor, John
Alexander – Crown Prince of Yugoslavia
Lajolo, Giovanni
Alexandra (Princess) – The Honourable Lady Ogilvy
Lake, Anthony
Alphonse, Louis – Duke of Anjou

Lambert, Richard
Amato, Giuliano
Lamy, Pascal
Anderson, Carl A.
Landau, Jean-Pierre
Andreotti, Giulio
Laurence, Timothy James Hamilton
Andrew (Prince) – Duke of York
Leigh-Pemberton, James
Anne – Princess Royal
Leka, Crown Prince of Albania
Anstee, Nick
Leonard, Mark
Ash, Timothy Garton
Levene, Peter – Baron Levene of Portsoken
Astor, William Waldorf – 4th Viscount Astor
Leviev, Lev
August, Ernst – Prince of Hanover
Levitt, Arthur
Aven, Pyotr
Levy, Michael – Baron Levy
Balkenende, Jan Peter
Lieberman, Joe
Ballmer, Steve
Livingston, Ian
Balls, Ed
Loong, Lee Hsien
Barroso, José Manuel
Lorenz (Prince) of Belgium, Archduke of Austria-Este
Beatrix (Queen)
Louis-Dreyfus, Gérard

Belka, Marek
Mabel (Princess) of Orange-Nassau
Bergsten, C. Fred
Mandelson, Peter Benjamin
Berlusconi, Silvio
Manning, Sir David Geoffrey
Bernake, Ben
Margherita – Archduchess of Austria-Este
Bernhard (Prince) of Lippe-Biesterfeld
Margrethe II Denmark
Bernstein, Nils
Martínez, Guillermo Ortiz
Berwick, Donald
Mashkevitch, Alexander
Bildt, Carl
Massimo, Stefano (Prince) – Prince of Roccasecca dei Volsci
Bischoff, Sir Winfried Franz Wilhen "Win"
McDonough, William Joseph
Blair, Tony
McLarty, Mack
Blankfein, Lloyd
Mersch, Yves
Blavatnik, Leonard
Michael (Prince) of Kent
Bloomberg, Michael
Michael of Romania
Bolkestein, Frits
Miliband, David
Bolkiah, Hassanal
Miliband, Ed
Bonello, Michael C

Mittal, Lakshmi
Bonino, Emma
Moreno, Glen
Boren, David L.
Moritz – Prince and Landgrave of Hesse-Kassel
Borwin – Duke of Mecklenburg
Murdoch, Rupert
Bronfman, Charles Rosner
Napoléon, Charles
Bronfman, Edgar Jr.
Nasser, Jacques
Bruton, John
Niblett, Robin
Brzezinski, Zbigniew
Nichols, Vincent
Budenberg, Robin
Nicolás, Adolfo
Buffet, Warren
Noyer, Christian
Bush, George HW
Ofer, Sammy
Cameron, David William Donald
Ogilvy, David – 13th Earl of Airlie
Camilla – Duchess of Cornwall
Ollila, Jorma Jaakko
Cardoso, Fernando Henrique
Oppenheimer, Nicky
Carington, Peter – 6th Baron Carrington
Osborne, George
Carlos – Duke of Parma
Oudea, Frederic

Carlos, Juan – King of Spain
Parker, Sir John
Carney, Mark J.
Patten, Chris
Carroll, Cynthia
Pébereau, Michel
Caruana, Jaime
Penny, Gareth
Castell, Sir William
Peres, Shimon
Chan, Anson
Philip (Prince) – Duke of Edinburgh
Chan, Margaret
Pio, Dom Duarte – Duke of Braganza
Chan, Norman
Pöhl, Karl Otto
Charles – Prince of Wales
Powell, Colin
Chartres, Richard
Prokhorov, Mikhail
Chiaie, Stefano Delle
Quaden, Guy Baron
Chipman, Dr John
Rasmussen, Anders Fogh
Chodiev, Patokh
Ratzinger, Joseph Alois (Pope Benedict XVI)
Christoph, Prince of Schleswig-Holstein
Reuben, David
Cicchitto, Fabrizio
Reuben, Simon
Clark, Wesley Kanne Sr. (General)
Rhodes, William R. "Bill"

Clarke, Kenneth
Rice, Susan
Clegg, Nick
Richard (Prince) – Duke of Gloucester
Clinton, Bill
Rifkind, Sir Malcolm Leslie
Cohen, Abby Joseph
Ritblat, Sir John
Cohen, Ronald
Roach, Stephen S.
Cohn, Gary D.
Robinson, Mary
Colonna, Marcantonio (di Paliano) – Prince and Duke of Paliano
Rockefeller, David Jr.
Constantijn (Prince) of the Netherlands
Rockefeller, David Sr.
Constantine II Greece
Rockefeller, Nicholas
Cooksey, David
Rodríguez, Javier Echevarría
Cowen, Brian
Rogoff, Kenneth Saul "Ken"
Craven, Sir John
Roth, Jean-Pierre
Crockett, Andrew
Rothschild, Jacob – 4th Baron Rothschild
Dadush, Uri
Rubenstein, David
D'Aloisio, Tony
Rubin, Robert
Darling, Alistair

Ruspoli, Francesco – 10th Prince of Cerveteri
Davies, Sir Howard
Safra, Joseph
Davignon, Étienne
Safra, Moises
Davis, David
Sands, Peter A.
De Rothschild, Benjamin
Sarkozy, Nicolas
De Rothschild, David René James
Sassoon, Isaac S.D.
De Rothschild, Evelyn Robert
Sassoon, James Meyer – Baron Sassoon
De Rothschild, Leopold David
Sawers, Sir Robert John
Deiss, Joseph
Scardino, Marjorie
Deripaska, Oleg
Schwab, Klaus
Dobson, Michael
Schwarzenberg, Karel
Draghi, Mario
Schwarzman, Stephen A.
Du Plessis, Jan
Shapiro, Sidney
Dudley, William C.
Sheinwald, Nigel
Duisenberg, Wim
Sigismund (Archduke) – Grand Duke of Tuscany
Edward (Prince) – Duke of Kent
Simeon of Saxe-Coburg and Gotha

Edward (The Prince) – Earl of Wessex
Snowe, Olympia
Elkann, John
Sofia (Queen) of Spain
Emanuele, Vittorio – Prince of Naples, Crown Prince of Italy
Soros, George
Fabrizio (Prince) – Massimo-Brancaccio
Specter, Arlen
Feldstein, Martin Stuart "Marty"
Stern, Ernest
Festing, Matthew
Stevenson, Dennis – Baron Stevenson of Coddenham
Fillon, François
Steyer, Tom
Fischer, Heinz
Stiglitz, Joseph E.
Fischer, Joseph Martin
Strauss-Kahn, Dominique
Fischer, Stanley
Straw, Jack
FitzGerald, Niall
Sutherland, Peter
Franz, Duke of Bavaria
Tanner, Mary
Fridman, Mikhail
Tedeschi, Ettore Gotti
Friedrich, Georg – Prince of Prussia
Thompson, Mark
Friso (Prince) of Orange-Nassau
Thomson, Dr. James A.

Gates, Bill
Tietmeyer, Hans
Geidt, Christopher
Trichet, Jean-Claude
Geithner, Timothy
Tucker, Paul
Gibson-Smith, Dr Chris
Van Rompuy, Herman
Gorbachev, Mikhail
Vélez, Álvaro Uribe
Gore, Al
Verplaetse, Alfons Vicomte
Gotlieb, Allan
Villiger, Kaspar
Green, Stephen
Vladimirovna, Maria – Grand Duchess of Russia
Greenspan, Alan
Volcker, Paul
Grosvenor, Gerald – 6th Duke of Westminster
Von Habsburg, Otto
Gurría, José Ángel
Waddaulah, Hassanal Bolkiah Mu'izzaddin
Gustaf, Carl XVI of Sweden
Walker, Sir David Alan
Hague, William
Wallenberg, Jacob
Hampton, Sir Philip Roy
Walsh, John
Hans-Adam II – Prince of Liechtenstein
Warburg, Max

Harald V Norway
Weber, Axel Alfred
Harper, Stephen
Weill, Michael David
Heisbourg, François
Wellink, Nout
Henri – Grand Duke of Luxembourg
Whitman, Marina von Neumann
Hildebrand, Philipp
Willem-Alexander – Prince of Orange
Hills, Carla Anderson
William (Prince) of Wales
Holbrooke, Richard
Williams, Dr Rowan
Honohan, Patrick
Williams, Shirley – Baroness Williams of Crosby
Howard, Alan
Wilson, David – Baron Wilson of Tillyorn
Ibragimov, Alijan
Wolfensohn, James David
Ingves, Stefan Nils Magnus
Wolin, Neal S.
Isaacson, Walter
Woolf, Harry – Baron Woolf
Jacobs, Kenneth M.
Woolsey, R. James Jr.
Julius, DeAnne
Worcester, Sir Robert Milton
Juncker, Jean-Claude
Wu, Sarah
Kenen, Peter

Zoellick, Robert Bruce

https://www.youtube.com/watch?v=Ri5Rtxl0EHs

Country Population in :

        2025   vs   TODAY

1 China -1,358,640,000 ,,,,,,,,,,,, 1,370,000,000

2 India - 1,341,720,000 ,,,,,,,,,,,,,1,270,000,000

3 Russia -142,167,300 ,,,,,,,,,,,,,142,350,000

4 Japan - 109,299,040 ,,,,,,,,,,,,, 126,700,000

5 Brazil - 210,686,060,,,,,,,,,,,,,,, 205,820,000

6 Indonesia - 267,684,400,,,,,,,,, 258,320,000

7 Italy - 45,346,640 ,,,,,,,,,,,,,,,,,,,,,62,000,000

8 Mexico - 124,108,280 ,,,,,,,,,,,,,, 123,170,000

9 France - 42,044,920 ,,,,,,,,,,,,,,,,,, 66,840,000

10 Canada - 26,479,240 ,,,,,,,,,,,,,,,,35,360,000

11 U.S.A - 54,326,300 ,,,,,,,,,,,,,,,,,,, 323,990,000

From Deagal country forecast
http://www.deagel.com/country/forecast.aspx

The key element to understand the process that the USA will enter in the upcoming decade is migration. In the past, specially in the 20th century, the key factor that allowed the USA to rise to its colossus status was immigration with the benefits of a demographic expansion supporting the credit expansion and the brain drain from the rest of the world benefiting the States. The collapse of the Western financial system will wipe out the standard of living of its population while ending ponzi schemes such as the stock exchange and the pension funds. The population will be hit so badly by a full array of bubbles and ponzi schemes that the migration engine will start to work in reverse accelerating itself due to ripple effects thus leading to the demise of the States. This unseen situation for the States will develop itself in a cascade pattern with unprecedented and devastating effects for the economy. Jobs offshoring will surely end with many American Corporations relocating overseas thus becoming foreign Corporations!!!! We see a significant part of the American population migrating to Latin America and Asia while migration to Europe - suffering a similar illness - won't be relevant. Nevertheless the death toll will be horrible. Take into account that the Soviet Union's population was poorer than the Americans nowadays or even then. The ex-

Soviets suffered during the following struggle in the 1990s with a significant death toll and the loss of national pride. Might we say "Twice the pride, double the fall"? Nope. The American standard of living is one of the highest, far more than double of the Soviets while having added a services economy that will be gone along with the financial system. When pensioners see their retirement disappear in front of their eyes and there are no servicing jobs you can imagine what is going to happen next. At least younger people can migrate. Never in human history were so many elders among the population. In past centuries people were lucky to get to their 30s or 40s. The American downfall is set to be far worse than the Soviet Union's one. A confluence of crisis with a devastating result.

Jason Goodman with Quinn Michaels:
https://www.youtube.com/watch?v=YSn7I...

UW dropout, hailed as internet rock star

NEWS Oct 15, 2017 by Jeff Outhit Waterloo Region Record
Buterin
Ethereum inventor Vitalik Buterin speaks onstage in San Francisco last month. - Steve Jennings,Getty Images

WATERLOO — A skinny 23-year-old who dropped out of the University of Waterloo is at the heart of what could be the next big thing online.

Vitalik Buterin, a Russian-born Canadian, basked in a standing ovation Saturday from computer coders and futurists who came to Waterloo to help change how the internet works.

In 2013, Buterin invented Ethereum, an open software platform to help people reach agreements by cutting out middle parties such as banks.

His new technology has seen setbacks and successes.

And some 400 computer coders came to Waterloo this past weekend to spend 36 hours creating possible software applications that use it. Buterin helped judge the best ideas.

The mostly-male crowd met Buterin with a fan-boy vibe when he participated in a panel discussion. Handlers gave him rock-star treatment, keeping him away from the media.

Buterin quit UW in 2013 after one year. He wore a T-shirt that said Hard Fork Café, an inside joke riffing on a computing term, and was introduced as someone "literally ahead of the technology" who beat out Facebook's Mark Zuckerberg for a global technology prize in 2014.

Ethereum aims to exploit what some predict is the next version of the internet, in which millions of computers work collectively to continuously update ledgers that everyone can inspect but no single user controls.

Futurists argue that decentralizing the internet in this way makes transactions tamper-proof, without a central point for hackers to target, free from censorship or interference. The technical term for this is a blockchain.

SUMMARY:
Now this is quite a story , when one considers that I read about ETHEREUM back in 2008 in the NWO (New World Order) 14 year plan that Thomas handed me.

To prove that I am telling the TRUTH, I will make the announcement that ETC CLASSIC (ETHEREUM CLASSIC) will become the new 'HERO' of the crypto-currencies by becoming the 3rd party GOVERNANCE for Ethereum.

There is a FLAW in the BLOCKCHAIN Technology... the SWISS Jews have access to the Blockchain ledger...

The Thomas Fire

Hundreds of homes in Montecito threatened as winds push Thomas fire toward coast; new evacuations

One of the largest wildfires in California history broke out on December 4th — and it's still raging. The Thomas Fire has been burning Ventura and Santa Barbara counties for 12 days now, and one firefighter has been killed battling it. But how did the Thomas Fire get its name?

The Thomas Fire started in Santa Paula, Ventura County on December 4th. The blaze ignited near Thomas Aquinas College, a small, Catholic-affiliated liberal arts college. The fire was named after its proximity to the school. Like the Thomas Fire, most wildfires are often named after nearby landmarks. The group that first begins fighting the fire gets to pick what to call it, but fire dispatchers can decide if the name is too similar to other fires.

Thankfully, the Thomas Fire's namesake is safe. The college was evacuated after the fire began, and classes were canceled the week of December 5th. But the campus survived the blaze, and although the campus will remain closed until January, students were able to return to collect their belongings as of December 12th. [110]

https://www.youtube.com/watch?v=evWBgNdWNDk

The Future is not Blockchain. It's Hashgraph.

David Icke - "The Fall of Man"

https://www.youtube.com/watch?v=VJorKZEbQsA

FOOTNOTES:

[104] - *https://www.cnbc.com/2017/06/22/ethereum-price-crash-10-cents-gdax-exchange-after-multimillion-dollar-trade.html*
[105] - *http://uk.businessinsider.com/cryptocurrency-miners-rent-boeing-747s-2017-7*
[106] - http://www.businessinsider.com/cryptocurrency-miners-rent-boeing-747s-2017-7
[107] - http://www.cnn.com/2017/01/02/politics/donald-trump-new-years-eve-speech/index.html

[108] - http://www.cnn.com/2017/11/05/opinions/saudi-prince-corruption-opinion-andelman/index.html
[109] - http://www.cbc.ca/news/politics/rcmp-paulson-compensation-harassment-1.3793785
[110] - http://www.latimes.com/local/lanow/la-me-thomas-fire-ledeall-20171216-story.html

ABOUT THE AUTHOR

Boyd Anderson is a free-spirited former pro-hockey player with a positive attitude, who set 3 hockey records one night in 1972, the most impressive being, the fastest 5 goals in a game, 5 goals in 3:07
(3 minutes & 7 seconds).

Boyd was never a member of any secret society.

He became a salesman and through hard work and "Fate" connected the dots, putting the pieces of the puzzle together with respect to what really happened to MH370, MH17, 55,500 tons of Gold... and more.

CPSIA information can be obtained
at www.ICGtesting.com
Printed in the USA
LVHW011106060621
689475LV00013B/614